IRISH ARCHITECTURAL AND DECORATIVE STUDIES
Volume I, 1998

IRISH ARCHITECTURAL AND DECORATIVE STUDIES

THE JOURNAL OF THE IRISH GEORGIAN SOCIETY – VOLUME I, 1998

IRISH ARCHITECTURAL AND
DECORATIVE STUDIES
The Journal of the Irish Georgian Society
Volume I, 1998

Published by the Irish Georgian Society
© Irish Georgian Society and the authors,
    1998. All rights reserved.

ISBN 0946846 162

Edited by Dr Seán O'Reilly

Design   John O'Regan
Production   Nicola Dearey
Printing   Betaprint, Dublin
Distribution   Gandon, Kinsale

Produced for the Irish Georgian Society by
Gandon Editions, Oysterhaven, Kinsale

The Irish Georgian Society gratefully
acknowledges the grant-aiding
of this publication by
THE IRELAND FUNDS
and the support of
MARC FITCH FUND
ESME MITCHELL TRUST
SCHOOL OF IRISH STUDIES
    FOUNDATION

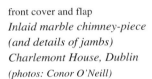

The Irish Georgian Society aims to encourage
an interest in and the preservation of
distinguished examples of architecture and
the allied arts in Ireland.

Further information – and membership
application details – may be obtained from:
IRISH GEORGIAN SOCIETY
74 Merrion Square, Dublin 2
tel: +353 (0)1-6767053 / fax: 6620290
e-mail: igs@iol.ie

IRISH ARCHITECTURAL AND DECORATIVE STUDIES

THE JOURNAL OF THE IRISH GEORGIAN SOCIETY – VOLUME I, 1998
EDITOR: SEÁN O'REILLY

———

Introduction:
the Bulletin and the Journal

DESMOND GUINNESS

IN 1957 MARIGA AND I WERE RENTING CARTON, THE GREAT HOUSE NEAR Maynooth, Co Kildare, designed by Richard Castle in 1739 for the Earls of Kildare, later the Dukes of Leinster, which had been sold to Lord Brocket in 1949. We had been looking for a farm to buy, specifically one with a beautiful house. Kilshannig, Bellamont Forest and Rathbeale Hall were all for sale, as were numerous other architectural masterpieces, but living at Carton, surrounded by a thousand acres of beauty, was such a pleasure that, until we had to, we were in no hurry to move. During our stay there, in 1956 and 1957, we had no responsibilities as to the farm, the house or the garden. We were therefore free to explore Dublin, as well as the rest of the country, and our mutual interest in and concern for Ireland's architectural heritage had time to develop.

The white and gold organ in the saloon at Carton had been installed in 1857, and the Music Association of Ireland arranged a concert to celebrate its one hundredth anniversary while we were living there. It struck me that the programme was very elegantly printed, in a beautiful typeface, using red and black on a handmade cream paper. We were told that the Dolmen Press had printed it, and, when in 1958 we started to plan the *Quarterly Bulletin*, we went to Liam Miller, who owned the Press, and he agreed to undertake the printing for us. More than that, he laid out the title page, helped to word the membership form, and generally encouraged us in this leap into the dark.

Maurice Craig, an old friend, then working in London, wrote 'A note on courthouses' for the first quarterly issue, dated January-March 1958. Thomas Ulick Sadleir's widow produced a piece by him on 'Industry at Celbridge', which, as Sadleir had been a mainstay of the original Georgian Society, forged a significant link with the past. The fledgling Irish Georgian Society was officially founded on 25 February 1958, fifty years to the day after the founding of the Georgian Society in 1908. The original society was to last five years and publish five photographic volumes as a record of buildings and interiors 'doomed to decay and disappearance'. It was not a preservation group in that it did not engage in planning battles or undertake restoration work as does its successor. When the five years had run their course, the Society came to an end.

The Dolmen Press used to set each letter in the old way of printing, and illustrations had to be clustered together on art paper instead of going with the text. Accordingly, from 1963 the Dolmen Press was deserted temporarily for a printer with off-set litho, allowing the illustrations to interleave more freely with the text. The first article to benefit from this was that on the 'Irish career of Gilbert Stuart', by Charles Merrill Mount. An engraving of the Conolly Folly, taken from a vignette on Noble and Keenan's map of Co Kildare, published in 1752, was on the cover of the first issue, and the cover designs changed from year to year. The folly was soon to become the Society's first job of restoration and repair (1960), and has served as our distinctive emblem ever since.

The *Bulletin* has provided an invaluable platform for the rediscovery of the rich history of Ireland's architectural and artistic heritage. Many architects who have worked in Ireland have come from other countries, and some even left their mark here without setting foot. The Irish careers of William Robinson, Richard Castle, John Nash, Sir William Chambers, Sir John Soane, and Decimus Burton have all found a place in the *Bulletin* over the years, as well as artists such as the painter Francis Wheatley. A complete list of contents of the *Bulletin* is appended to its last issue.

The present volume, *Irish Architectural and Decorative Studies – The Journal of the Irish Georgian Society*, celebrates our fortieth anniversary. It is the first volume of the revised and updated academic publication of the Society and recognises our present wider remit. As we are no longer concerned solely with Georgian architecture, this new manifestation of the *Bulletin* acknowledges the importance of the entire spectrum of Ireland's post-medieval architecture and its special need for protection, interpretation, understanding and appreciation. We hope that you will enjoy our new *Journal* as much as the *Bulletin*.

The Society owes a debt of gratitude to the many people involved in the development of the new *Journal*, not least the authors who have contributed so much through their researches. In addition, the Irish Georgian Society would like to thank the following bodies for their generous support of this publication: The Ireland Funds, Marc Fitch Fund, Esme Mitchell Trust, and the School of Irish Studies Foundation.

DESMOND GUINNESS
co-founder of The Irish Georgian Society

This Church is of my Invention for Leeds in Yorkshire.

1 – William Halfpenny, design for a church in Leeds, Yorkshire (1723?, unexecuted)
engraving in The Art of Sound Building *(London, 1725)*

William Halfpenny's designs for an 'Early Christian' cathedral at Waterford

TERRY FRIEDMAN

OUND IN A MANUSCRIPT ALBUM DECEPTIVELY ENTITLED *Miscellaneous Antique Prints 1737*, in the Royal Institute of British Architects Drawings Collection, is a precious set of nine presentation drawings associated with an ambitious project for a new Protestant cathedral at Waterford City in 1739.[1] They represent an approach to cathedral design in the eighteenth century, in itself a rare occurrence, dominated by the classical language of architecture which would have made such a building, had it been realised, unique in Britain in its day, and of an austerity uncommon even by Protestant standards. Moreover, a majority of the drawings incorporate the unprecedented and astonishing feature of a separate baptismal building attached to the west end of the nave. They were drawn by William Halfpenny (?-1755), an interesting minor figure in the mid-Georgian building world, whose career as a practising architect is shrouded in mystery and who seems to have enjoyed only tenuous connections with Ireland. Nor is anything recorded about the circumstances surrounding the new cathedral commission itself, so that any reconstruction of the event must be a matter of some speculation. In this article I suggest that these designs went beyond both Halfpenny's own architectural experience and the parochial visions of much contemporary British ecclesiastical architecture; that they represent ideas based on the liturgy and layout of the early Christian church on the Continent, and so help place Irish church building of the early Georgian period in the wider arena of western architecture and the revival of Antiquity (in the way that Irish domestic building at the same time was stimulated by Richard Castle, an other interloper); and that this unconventional, cosmopolitan experiment was promoted by an Irish clerical triumvirate in a unique position to recall the distant past in such an extraordinary way.[2] This complex story, as I imagine it might have unfolded, therefore, is best begun at the beginning.

Of Halfpenny's birth date and place, and his private life, we know nothing. He sometimes used the alias Michael Hoare. By 1725 he was describing himself as an 'Architect and Carpenter'.[3] He is recorded working in Leeds, London, Bristol, and on two occasions in Ireland, but during a long career apparently succeeded in erecting few buildings. Perhaps his finest extant work is Cooper's Hall (1743-44) in Bristol.[4] A small body of carefully rendered architectural drawings also survive, among which those for Waterford are arguably the most important. Halfpenny was also an accomplished topographical artist, as is revealed in a perspective view, dated 1742, of Redland Chapel, Bristol (1740-43), on which he completed the construction after the death in 1740 of its architect, John Strahan.[5] However, Halfpenny's reputation during and after his lifetime rested on the eighteen architectural manuals published between 1724 and 1757, sometimes in collaboration with Timothy Lightoler, Robert Morris and a relative named John Halfpenny.[6] These deal in buildings in a variety of fashionable and often bizarre styles,

> With angles, curves, and zigzag lines,
> From *Half-penny's* exact designs[7]

They are almost entirely domestic in type. Churches appear to have played a very minor role in his career, yet it is significant that the first thing we know about him is in connection with church work.

On 8 May 1723, Halfpenny received £1 11s 6d as payment for drawings for a proposed new church at Leeds in Yorkshire; though rejected, he published a perspective of the design two years later (Plate 1).[8] This was one of the earliest reflections in northern England of current metropolitan thinking on advanced classical church design, in particular the treatment of the rectangular body as a modified Antique temple. Modern churches adopting ancient forms (of which James Gibbs's St Martin-in-the-Fields in London (1720-26) was then the outstanding example),[9] and also the conversion of pagan temples to Christian worship, were enormously attractive ideas among architects and churchmen alike. These ideas were given historical authority by modern commentators on the early Church, who believed that such transformed buildings 'became another thing from what they were in former ages, that is, more noble and stately edifices, more rich and beautiful'.[10] An equivalent architectural authority had long been established in the beautiful example of the Temple of Fortuna Virilis at Rome (second century BC), which became the church of St Mary the Egyptian in the ninth century, and was well represented in Andrea Palladio's *I Quattro Libri* (Venice 1570) and in its most recent English edition published in 1715-20.[11] Robert Morris, Halfpenny's sometime collaborator, advanced the notion that buildings alone contain the 'sacred Deity' and that

> It is this which has set Men at work on Temples and publick Places of
> Worship, not only that they might, by the Magnificence of the Building,
> invite the Deity to reside within it [but because it] opens the Mind to vast
> Conceptions, and fits it to converse with the Divine of the Place; for every

thing that is majestick, imprints an Awfulness and Reverence on the Mind of the Beholder, and strikes it with the natural Greatness of the Soul.

Palladio is praised for his

indefatigable Care and Industry [in collecting] the never-dying Remains of [Antiquity's] endless Glories ... How great is his Manner, how elevated his Ideas, and how bold in the Execution, is best discovered in those noble Productions he left as Examples for our Imitation... In them we see the lively Images of Antiquity rising from Heaps of Ruins, where all the Lustre of Beauty and Art conspire to raise our Sentiments and Ideas to that height, that we may easily perceive the immense difference between those ancient beautiful Productions, and the lame and disorder'd Performances of our Moderns.[12]

Equivalent critical comparisons were made by the architectural writer, James Ralph, who measured Nicholas Hawksmoor's churches, which 'are not to be looked at without displeasure. They are mere Gothique heaps of stone, without form or order, and meet with contempt from the best and worst tastes alike', against Inigo Jones's Tuscan temple-form church of St Paul, Covent Garden, which 'is, without a rival, one of the most perfect pieces of architecture that the art of man can produce'.[13] Halfpenny cites St Paul's in his first publication, *Practical Architecture* (London 1724) as a demonstration of the correct use of the classical order, and his own subsequent architectural programme relied heavily on Palladio and the English Palladians.[14]

This, then, is the general architectural background of the Waterford Cathedral commission. The specific sources of Halfpenny's designs are a veritable minefield since it is unlikely that he travelled abroad and no record exists of his library or the architectural and travel books he may have consulted, though as an architectural writer some such items were undoubtedly available to him. However, there can be little doubt that he was guided in his selection of models by Thomas Milles (1671-1740), the Bishop of Waterford and Lismore, and his two Grand Touring nephews – Jeremiah Milles (1714-84), the precentor of Waterford between 1737 and 1744 (later Dean of Exeter and President of the Society of Antiquaries of London), and Richard Pococke (1704-65), the vice-general of the Waterford and Lismore diocese between 1734 and 1744 (later Bishop of Ossory and Meath).[15] Though little is known about the bishop's architectural interests – he was a subscriber to Gibbs's *A Book of Architecture* (London 1728) – it is significant that he had been Regius professor of Greek at Oxford in 1705-6 and published an edition of the works of the early Christian St Cyril of Jerusalem, *S. Patris nostri Cyrilli* (London 1703).

More enlightening for us are the observations made by Jeremiah Milles during an English building tour in 1735. He was particularly curious about the condition and treatment of old cathedrals and churches. At Cambridge he found the Gothic St Mary-the-Great 'a very handsome church on ye outside, but ... very slovenly within', and condemned the practice where the congregation stood in the nave 'promiscuously'. The majestic chapel at King's was 'one of ye finest Gothic buildings in ye world ... ye inside exceeds ye outside', and only the 'meanness' of the altarpiece, 'a little wooden screne with two or three strips of silk put upon it ... takes of very much from ye beauty'. Norwich Cathedral was 'a stately, & very Beautiful Gothic building on ye outside [but] ye inside ... is dark, & not at all answerable'. At Peterborough the choir 'is now repairing, & new seating; and a new organ putting up; so yt. it will be very beautiful when it is finished'.[16] Another visitor to Peterborough in 1735 reported in more detail that the authorities 'are laying out large Sums in repairing and adorning... The Throne, Stalls and Pews are just made new, of deal painted, they are very plain and decent', and that the choir 'is really very elegant, more than can truly be said of any other part of the Church',[17] while a contemporary poem entitled 'On the Dean and Chapter beautifying the Inside of the Cathedral Church of Peterborough' stressed that it was

> Embellished outwardly with stately shew,
> But left to be adorned within by you.[18]

Bishop Milles may have entertained a similar rehabilitation of the medieval fabric at Waterford. Since the Reformation, ecclesiastical buildings throughout Ireland had suffered terrible iconoclasm and destruction; by the mid-eighteenth century twenty-two of the thirty-one churches in the Protestant diocese of Waterford still remained ruinous.[19] Irish churchmen bitten by building fever would have found, like Eusebius, the fourth-century bishop of Caesarea and author of the celebrated *History of the Church*, an 'inexpressible joy and a kind of celestial gladness' in proclaiming those churches which had been restored from the ruins wrought by the 'Irreligion of the Tyrants', and perhaps even associated themselves with Eusebius's famous panegyrical oration on Paulinus, Bishop of Tyre, who, having restored his cathedral to 'the stateliest Fabrick amongst all the Churches within the Country of Phoenicia', was called 'a new Besellel, the Architect of the holy Tabernacle; or another Solomon, King of a new, and far more excellent Jerusalem ... in regard You have added a far greater splendour to the Temple of God, than it had before'.[20]

Among the drawings in the RIBA album is 'A General Plan of Christ Church Waterford', signed 'Wm. Halfpenny 1739',[21] and an identical engraving inscribed 'The Ichnography of the Cathedral Church of the Holy and undivided Trinity in Waterford', while three related perspective drawings, signed 'William Halfpenny 1739' and dedicated to Bishop Milles, are in the National Library of Ireland,

Dublin.[22] They appear to be a record of the medieval building made in anticipation of a major restoration. But within the year, Milles had decided to build anew.

Why and how Halfpenny was chosen for this important enterprise remains a mystery. Bristol, where he had settled probably already by 1731, and Waterford were mutual trading ports across St George's Channel,[23] and news of his activities, particularly in connection with the proposed Bristol Exchange and Market, the most prestigious public building in the town, may have reached Bishop Milles's ears.[24] But Halfpenny was already known in Ireland. In 1732 he had designed a Horse Barrack for the 1st Viscount Hillsborough at Hillsborough, Co Down,[25] and a small group of prospects of Irish cathedrals in the RIBA album, similar to those for Waterford, mentioned above, bear the initials W.H. and dates of 1738 and 1739.[26] The album also contains six drawings for stately Palladian town mansions, each with a plan and elevation presented, like the Waterford Cathedral drawings, in pattern book fashion, complete with ruled scales; one is annotated 'This Building may be Executed for 850 pounds', another 'This Design may be Executed for 1400 pounds' and signed 'Wm. Halfpenny delin 1739'. These are most likely proposals for a new bishop's palace to be built next to the cathedral.[27] So, Halfpenny was involved in several different but connected ecclesiastical enterprises, any one of which might have brought him to the city in the last years of the 1730s.

Of the nine sheets in the album devoted to designs for new churches, seven (ff. 1-3, 6-8 and 14) form a homogeneous group of alternative schemes which are probably correctly associated with the proposed cathedral. They are for structures measuring overall from 84 by 140 feet (ff. 1-2) to 75 by 176 feet (f 8) to 105 by 166 feet (f 7), comparable in size to the royal parish church of St Martin-in-the-Fields (80 by 170 feet). In all but Plate 7, the vestries are semi-detached blocks placed outside the nave walls in order to maximise the congregational seating space, which is accommodated in from twenty-four to thirty-three double rows of box pews. In Plates 9-11 these are arranged in the form of a Greek cross, with the central area rising into a flattened or saucer dome.[28] These pew-packed spaces bring to mind Joseph Bingham's description of early Christian churches as 'the peoples' oratory, because the people chiefly filled this place, having their different stations or apartments in it, according to the difference of age, or sex, or quality, or state and condition'.[29] Several of the designs (Plates 6, 8, 10) feature prominent enclosures towards or in the north-east corners of the nave, which I take to designate the bishop's throne. Finally, all the drawings in this group have separate baptismal buildings, the salient idea of the episcopal project. Since at some later date these drawings were evidently rearranged and bound arbitrarily, for purposes of the present discussion a more appropriate sequence has been adopted: folio 14 (which is the simplest of the designs and the only sheet bearing the architect's signature and 1739 date), followed by folios 3, 8, 1-2, 7 and 6. Two other drawings (ff. 4-5) previously associated with the cathedral I am inclined to consider as schemes apart. The letter designations on the plan in Plate 3 relate to an accompanying key which cannot now be traced, and suggests that the set is incomplete. All but one of the drawings (f 1, a less detailed copy of the plan in f 2) are reproduced in this article, most for the first time.[30]

There are good reasons to treat folios 4 and 5 independently (Plates 2, 3). They are for smaller, modest buildings, measuring 114 by 63 feet and 80 by 34 feet, respectively, and containing no more than thirteen rows of pews, hardly of cathedral stature. Instead of the prerequisite baptismal building they have a tower at the west end. The short octagonal steeple rising from a slender porch in Plate 2 particularly has the look of a parochial church.[31] Perhaps they relate to another of Thomas Milles's building enterprises. Charles Smith, writing between 1744 and 1746, records that St Olave, Waterford, consecrated on 29 July 1734, was rebuilt by the bishop so that the inhabitants 'might have a convenient and decent place to offer up their morning and evening devotions to God', and described it as

> quite plain on the outside, except a handsome Door Case, over which is a Pediment. The inside is very neat, the Floor ... paved with black and white Marble; that of the Chancel is handsomely inlaid with Wood in several geo-metrical Figures. The Altar-Piece consists of four fluted Pillars of the *Corinthian Order*, two on each side of the East Window; over which is an handsome carved Freeze and Cornice. The Bishop's Throne and Pulpit are of Oak, and the Carving of both well executed. The Seats are so disposed, as that the whole Congregation can only face the East ... The Seats of the Windows are of black Marble, as are also the Steps leading to the Chancel.[32]

Richard Pococke reported that Milles also rebuilt nearby St Patrick's.[33] Smith described it as

> a plain building ... The inside is well pewed, and the seats disposed in the same manner as at St. *Olave*'s ... The floor is layed with marble. There is a handsome Altar-Piece, on which is a painted Glory by *Vander-Egan*'s well performed.[34]

Furthermore, Youghal church, Co Cork, was 'roofed & covered by Bishop Milles, but all the Protestant inhabitants leaving the Parish it was not finished'.[35]

In Plate 2 the windows enriched with shouldered architraves and scrolled frames (motifs also found in Plates 10, 11) recall the treatment of the chancel win-dow of St Mary's, Dublin (1701-3, designed by Sir William Robinson); another work by the same architect, the Royal Hospital at Kilmainham (1680-87), may have been the model for the Y-traceried windows in several of the Waterford cathedral

2 – William Halfpenny, design for a church (1739?, unexecuted)
(The British Architectural Library, RIBA, London, Shelf B3, f 5)

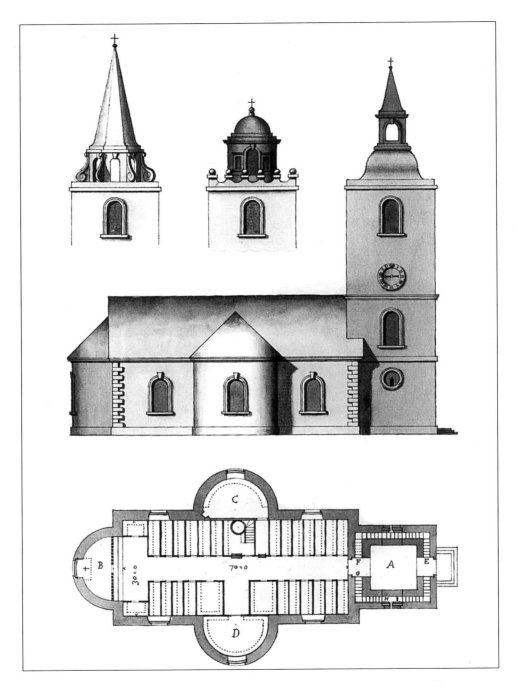

3 – William Halfpenny, design for a church (1739?, unexecuted)
(The British Architectural Library, RIBA, London, f 4)

designs. These features hint at the possibility that Halfpenny self-consciously introduced such anachronisms in order to give a familiar Irishness to his designs.[36]

Plate 3 is a more heroic classical concept. Of the three alternative designs for the steeple, one has a miniature Venetian window fortified by Venetian ball-crenellation, motifs recently popularised by Lord Burlington at his Villa at Chiswick (*c* 1725-29),[37] and another is crowned by an octagonal, scroll-bracketed spire based on a detail of an engraving published in William Kent's *The Designs of Inigo Jones* (London, 1727) of the west front (1633-42) of the pre-fire St Paul's Cathedral (Plate 4). Halfpenny's window surrounds also probably derive from this print. His commitment here to a Palladian vocabulary is powerfully expressed in the trilobed plan, where the semicircular shape of the chancel (marked B) is repeated as projecting vestry-rooms (C and D) in the middle of the side elevations, an arrangement reminiscent of Palladio's S Giorgio Maggiore in Venice (begun 1566), the only one of his churches to appear in Kent's publication (Plate 5). The derivative nature of Halfpenny's scheme should not, however, mitigate its originality. Though the advertisement in the *Designs* praised St Giorgio as 'so deservedly admired by all good Architects', it found few Protestant advocates, and Halfpenny appears to have been the only Briton to have used it in this particular way. Yet it hardly seems coincidental that Palladio's own description of St Giorgio as a 'laudable' example of 'strength and perpetuity', qualities sought in church buildings 'since they are dedicated to the omnipotent and supreme God', should be quoted in Isaac Ware's *The Four Books of Andrea Palladio's Architecture*, which appeared fortuitously in 1738.[38] Halfpenny translated this into an austere geometry in which not only ornament but the classical order played no part. While this treatment may have been dictated by financial constraints, it was, too, an ideal of the Anglo-Palladian church: recall Ralph's evocation a few years earlier of Jones's St Paul, Covent Garden where 'nothing can possibly be imagined more simple'.[39] The Waterford churchmen, perhaps alert to the close proximity of Lord Burlington's estate at Lismore, within sight of its cathedral,[40] were also admirers of this advanced architecture. For example, in 1734 Jeremiah Milles wrote to his uncle from northern Italy about the 'great number of very agreeable country houses ... most of which are in Palladio's taste, & some I believe built by him', particularly along the Brenta, where he saw 'a great number of very beautiful country houses of Palladio's architecture'.[41] In the following year, back in England, Jeremiah described the newly built Palladian-style parish church of Blandford Forum in Dorset as being in a 'very genteel taste ... there are few in England exceed it'.[42] Not surprisingly, Palladian features crop-up in some of the Waterford Cathedral drawings: the Diocletian windows in the pediments and bell turret of Plate 11, and the blocked-architrave (or Gibbs-surround) windows and doors of Plate 9. The latter features prominently in Gibbs's *A Book of Architecture*

4 – Inigo Jones, St Paul's Cathedral, London (1633-42), west front
(in William Kent, The Designs of Inigo Jones *(London, 1727), ii, pl. 55)*

5 – Andrea Palladio, S Giorgio Maggiore, Venice (begun 1566), plan
(in William Kent, The Designs of Inigo Jones *(London, 1727), ii, pl. 57)*

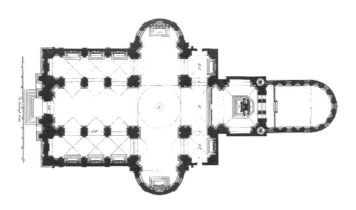

(1728), a copy of which Bishop Milles owned, but it is interesting that Halfpenny had already in 1724 identified the motif as 'A Rustic Door from Palladio, much used by the Modern Architects'.[43] Generally, however, the plain and at times primitive appearance of the Waterford designs is due to other and more unexpected but equally potent classicising traditions of the past, represented above all by the religious architecture of early Christianity.

Jeremiah Milles and Richard Pococke, his travelling companion in Italy in 1734, visited a remarkably well preserved group of fourth and fifth centuries ecclesiastical buildings in Ravenna, which had been the western capitol of the early Christian emperors. There they saw the tomb of Galla Placidia (c 425) and two rectangular churches with simple, apsidal-shaped chancels: S Apollinare Nuova (c 490), Theodoric's palace church, 'remarkable for ye Mosaich all along each side of [the] nave above ye pillars', and S Apollinare at Classe (532-49), where the nave 'is supported by 24 Composite marble pillars, with Gothick Capitals'.[44] By the 1730s, a rich and varied literature existed in the English language devoted to these 'first churches', as they were called by Joseph Bingham in *Origines Ecclesiasticae: or, the Antiquities of the Christian Church* (London, 1711).[45] They were 'simple and plain' buildings, according to Bingham, and he quoted the passage concerning Isidore of Pelusium's desire

> to have lived in those days, when there were no such beautiful temples, but yet the Church was crowded with divine and heavenly graces, than in these days, when temples are adorned with all kinds of marbles, but the Church is deprived of all those spiritual gifts.[46]

Architectural austerity was seen as an essential condition for observing 'the simplicity of the primitive Christian-worship'.[47] In Hawksmoor's unrealised design for a 'Basilica after the Primitive Christians', proposed in 1711-12 for Bethnal Green in London, which he described as in the 'Manner of Building the Church – as it was in ye fourth Century in ye purest times of Christianity', the 'place for the font for ye Converts' (the baptistery) is located in a square 'Porch' attached to the west end of the nave.[48] This corresponds to its location in the western narthex of churches built in the 'sixth ages' of Christendom, as described by Bingham.[49] This is the formula Halfpenny followed in what I take to be his inaugural Waterford cathedral offering (Plate 6). The subsequent drawings (Plates 7-11), however, favoured the more powerful geometry of a monumental octagon in which rays of light from a cupola crowning the steeply-pitched roof would funnel dramatically on to a centralised font (Plate 11).[50] Halfpenny introduced a similar shape as the centrepiece in one of his designs for Bishop Milles's palace at Waterford, suggesting that the two adjacent buildings were to be thought of as an ensemble.[51]

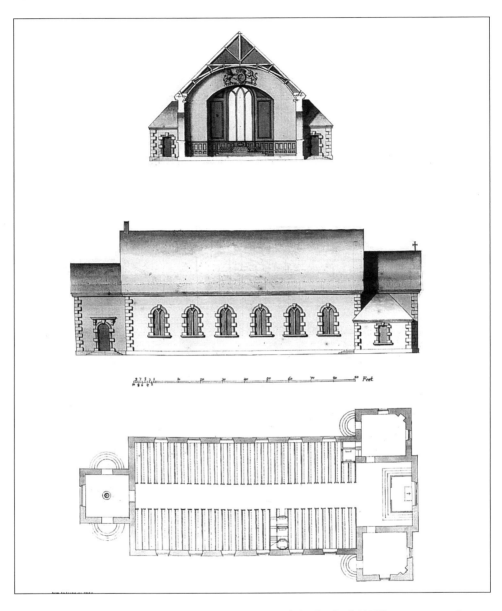

6 – William Halfpenny, design for Waterford Cathedral (1739, unexecuted)
(The British Architectural Library, RIBA, London, f 14)

opposite
7-8 – William Halfpenny, designs for Waterford Cathedral (1739?, unexecuted)
(The British Architectural Library, RIBA, London, f 3 (top), f 8 (bottom))

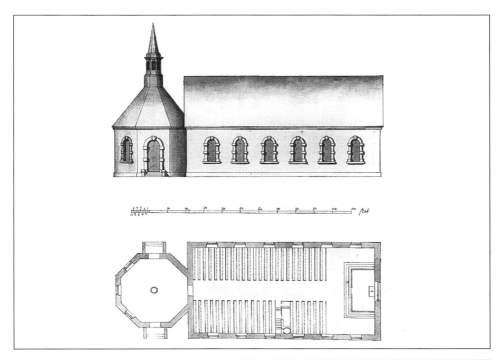

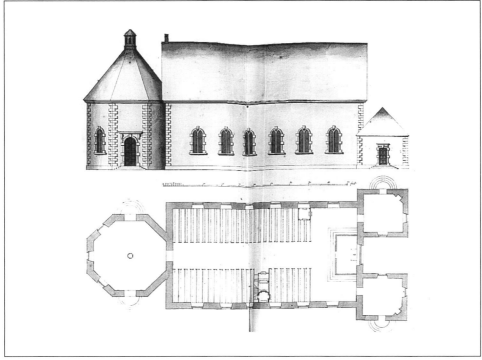

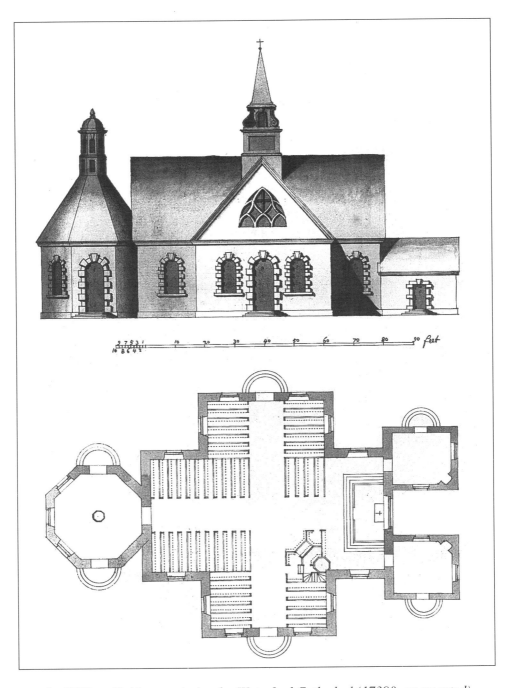

9 – William Halfpenny, design for Waterford Cathedral (1739?, unexecuted)
(The British Architectural Library, RIBA, London, f 2)

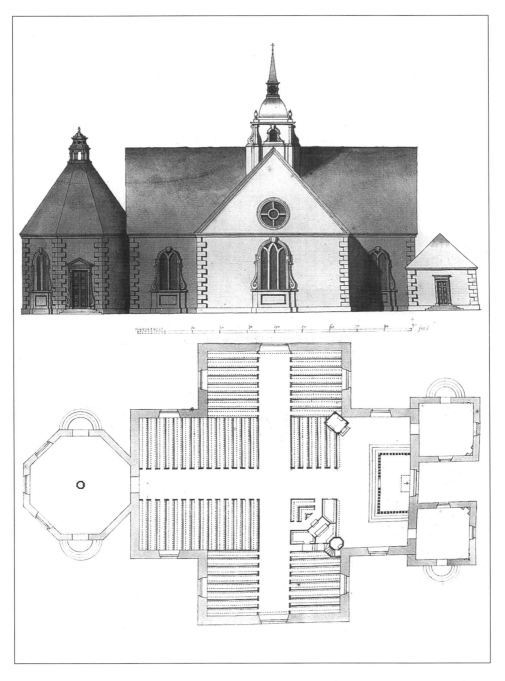

10 – William Halfpenny, design for Waterford Cathedral (1739?, unexecuted)
(The British Architectural Library, RIBA, London, f 7)

11 – William Halfpenny, design for Waterford Cathedral (1739?, unexecuted)
(The British Architectural Library, RIBA, London, f 6)

This was an unprecedented use in Georgian church architecture of octagonal baptisteries. However, the form is commonly found in much earlier churches on the Continent, and examples had been noted by British travellers, particularly architects. James Gibbs, who was training in Rome between 1703 and 1709, wrote of S Giovanni in Laterano's Constantinian baptistery (c 315 and c 432-40, restored in the seventeenth century) that it was 'a most elegant peece of building, and much admired by all who see it ... Paladio has given a draught of it'.[52] John Talman made a number of detailed drawings of the Baptistery of the Orthodox at Ravenna (c 400-500) between 1713 and 1716.[53] Milles and Pococke must also have seen this building in 1734, though it is not mentioned in the correspondence. However, on that occasion they did visit S Vitale (546-48), which Milles considered 'by much ye most beautiful [church] in ye city. It is an Octagon', and the Mausoleum of Theodoric (c 526), 'an octagon figure without, & round within'; interestingly, Milles imposed a Christian connotation on the building by identifying the pierced spurs round the perimeter of the dome as '12 Pedestals on which stood ye statues of 12 Apostles'.[54] Undoubtedly the two travellers saw the famous Romanesque octagonal baptistery of S Giovanni during their stay in Florence in December-January 1733-34 (Plate 12); Pococke noted it on his second visit to the city in 1737.[55] The similarities to Halfpenny's treatment of the roof and cupola at Waterford may not be coincidental. However, in this and other Italian examples the octagonal structure is located at the west end of the church yet detached from it, or when attached is done so to the east end of the chancel. An arrangement specifically comparable to Halfpenny's designs seems only to have been found in the early eighteenth century beyond Italy and out of reach to most British travellers. This is where Richard Pococke made a crucial contribution.

After his Italian tour of 1733-34, he returned with his cousin to England. In May of 1736 he set off alone on a journey through Germany, Austria and Italy. Then, in September 1737, he crossed the Mediterranean to Alexandria, and during the next three years explored the ancient, early Christian and Islamic architecture of Egypt, Sinai, Palestine, Syria, Mesopotamia, Cyprus, Crete, Asia Minor and Greece, finally returning to England in 1741. This extraordinary expedition is recorded in *A Description of the East, and Some other Countries* in two magnificently illustrated volumes published in London in 1743 and 1745.[56] Among the many buildings which especially interested Pococke, and which he illustrated in a plan and elevation 'took ... by the eye', was the Dome of the Rock (begun 688) at Jerusalem (Plate 13), about which he wrote:

> the Christians built a church on this spot, which the Saracens, under Omar, converted into a mosque; and when Jerusalem was taken in the holy wars, it

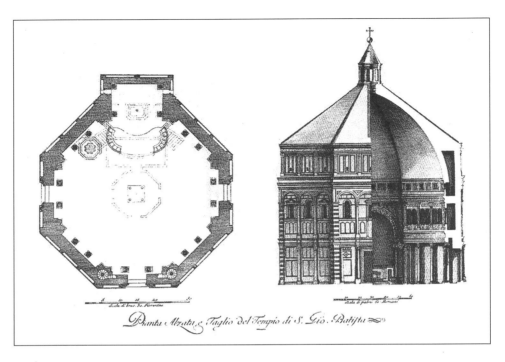

Pianta Alzata, e Taglio del Tempio di S. Gio. Batista

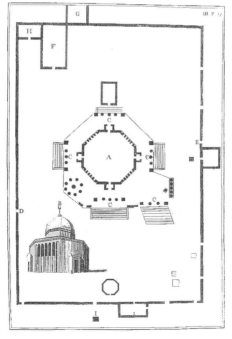

A PLAN and VIEW of the MOSQUE of SOLOMONS TEMPLE

*12 – Baptistery, Florence
(11-12th centuries)
(engraving in G.B.C. Nelli,* Studio di
Architettura Civile *(Florence, 1755),
2nd ed., iv, pl. xvii)*

*13 – Dome of the Rock, Jerusalem
(begun 688)
(in R. Pococke,* A Description of the East,
London *(1745) ii, part i, pl. iii.)*

opposite
*14 – Cathedral, Parenzo
(modern Porec), Istria (c 550), plan
(based on R. Krautheimer,* Early Christian and
Byzantine Architecture *(1965) fig. 242)*

was again made a place of Christian worship. At present there is a beautiful octagon mosque in the middle of the court, covered with a dome [which] has a beautiful appearance.[57]

He also published a plan of the Church of the Nativity at Bethlehem (between 503-604), whose trilobed arrangement is a reminder of one of Halfpenny's church designs (Plate 3),[58] and mentioned several other early Christian churches with simple, apsidal east ends, as in Plates 2 and 3.[59] At the Great Mosque of Damascus, 'one of the finest things that the zeal of the first Christians produced', which was remodelled by Islam in 706-15, he shows 'an octagonal baptistery built on eight pillars' standing in the main courtyard. At Kalat Siman in Syria, the Martyrium of St Simon Stylites (c 480-90) was 'very magnificent, and ... built in [the] form of a Greek cross; under the middle of an octagonal dome'.[60] Such was Pococke's fascination with these early church forms.

Most importantly, arriving at Trieste in August 1737, Pococke travelled along the Istrian coast to Parenzo (ancient Parentium, modern Porec). The *Description* mentions the foundations of the 'famous ... temple of Neptune' but the cathedral (c 550) only in passing.[61] Additional information comes from a letter to his mother in England, dated 25 August:

> The Arch Presbyter of ye Cathedral came to us, & told us hed show us some antiquities, he had us to his house, showed a MSS Accot he had writ of ye City ... went to ye Cathedral built by ye Emperor Otho 1st out of ye ruins of a temple to Neptune, & is a very curious church ... for Gothic antiquities.[62]

A more germane reference appears in Pococke's personal travel diary: 'The Cathedral a very antient building ... Before the entrance is a Hexagon Baptistery now uncovered, and not made use of, but there are some antient pillars in it'.[63] In fact, an octagonal shaped baptistery (not an hexagonal one, as mistakenly described by Pococke) is attached to the west end of the atrium of a rectangular church with pedimented ends and a semicircular chancel, an original arrangement preserved intact even to this day (Plate 14).[64]

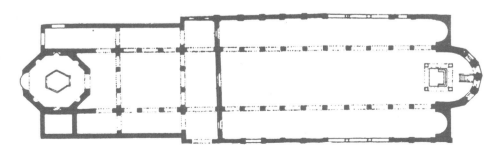

An earlier Pococke diary, dealing with the period immediately preceeding his visit to Parenzo in 1737, bears a later note in his father's hand: 'part of my sons travels Copyed for Mr. Jer. Milles'.[65] It is, therefore, very likely around 1737, when cousin Jeremiah was serving as cathedral precentor at Waterford, and in an excellent position to influence the course of architectural events there, that he was made aware of this obscure and unusual early Christian church and that he subsequently alerted Halfpenny to its dramatic potential as a model for a modern cathedral. Bishop Milles's untimely death on 12 May 1740 prevented the project coming to fruition.[66] This we can now see was a tragedy for the burgeoning classical style church in Georgian Irish architecture.[67]

———

DR TERRY FRIEDMAN is the author of the standard biography on the Georgian architect, James Gibbs, published in 1984. He has written widely on British architecture and is currently researching a book devoted to the designing and building of churches in England 1700-1799.

ENDNOTES

[1]   Shelf B3 (Jill Lever, *Catalogue of the Drawings Collection of the Royal Institute of British Architects*, vol. G-K (Farnborough 1973) 82-83, fig. 50), purchased 1965 from H.M. Colvin. The title derives from the first item, an engraved page referring to Thomas Hearne's *Ectypa Varia* (1737).

[2]   This is not the only such example. A poem in *The Gentleman's Magazine* (December 1738) 652, entitled 'To the Hon. Mrs Conolly, occasioned by the Monument she hath erected in Cellbridge, to the Memory of her late Husband, the Right Hon. William Conolly Esq; deceased', likened the deed to that performed in Antiquity by Queen Artemisia in building the tomb to her husband, Mausoleus, King of Caria, at Halicarnassus: 'Such were the thoughts which Caria's queen possess'd, / And such the anguish labour'd in her breast. / Not that, to tell posterity her woes, / Wonder of earth, the Mausoleum rose.' See Homan Potterton, *Irish Church Monuments 1570-1880* (Ulster 1975) 39, fig. 17.

[3]   On the title page of *The Art of Sound Building* (London 1725). Howard Colvin, *A Biographical Dictionary of British Architects 1600-1840* (New Haven and London 1995) 446-48.

[4]   Timothy Mowl, *To Build the Second City Architects and craftsmen of Georgian Bristol* (Bristol 1991) 58, who attributes other local work to him.

[5]   Katherine Eustace, *Michael Rysbrack Sculptor 1694-1770* (Bristol 1982) 91-92, pl. 22.

Halfpenny also designed the altarpiece (Colvin, *A Biographical Dictionary*, 447, 931-32; Mowl, *To Build the Second City*, 19, 37-38, 46-47, 57).

[6] Eileen Harris, *British Architectural Books and Writers 1556-1785* (Cambridge 1990) 218-28.

[7] 'The Cit's Country Box', *The Gentleman's Magazine* (September 1756) 445.

[8] William Halfpenny, *The Art of Sound Building* (London 1725) inscribed 'This Church is of my Invention for Leeds in Yorkshire'. For details of this episode see Terry Friedman, *Church Architecture in Leeds 1700-1799*, Publications of the Thoresby Society, Second Series, vol. 7 (1997) 73-78, fig. 16.

[9] Terry Friedman, *James Gibbs* (New Haven and London 1984) 57-70, pl. 27. Zacharia Pearce's *A Sermon Preached at the New Parish Church of St. Martin in the Fields* (London 1727) includes 'An Essay on the Origin and Progress of Temples'.

[10] Joseph Bingham, *Origines Ecclesiasticae: or, the Antiquities of the Christian Church* (London 1708-22), quoting from Robert Bingham, ed., *The Works of The Rev. Joseph Bingham, M.A.* (Oxford 1855) iii, 49-50, 'Contents of the Eight Nine, and Tenth Books of The Antiquities of the Christian Church', first published in 1711.

[11] Giacomo Leoni, *The Architecture of A. Palladio; In Four Books* (London 1715-20) book 4, chapter 8.

[12] *An Essay In Defence of Ancient Architecture; or A Parallel of the Ancient Buildings with the Modern: shewing The Beauty and Harmony of the Former, and the Irregularity of the Latter* (London 1728) 2, 20, 23 and xiii, respectively. Morris's 'great Protectors of Antiquity' were Palladio, Lord Burlington and Sir Andrew Fountaine (the dedicatee of Halfpenny's *The Art of Sound Building* (London 1725)). For links between Morris and Halfpenny see Harris, *British Architectural Books and Writers*, 219-22, 317.

[13] James Ralph, *A Critical Review of the Publick Buildings, Statues and Ornaments, In, and about London and Westminster* (London 1734) 6, 9.

[14] *Practical Architecture* illustrates doors and windows taken from Palladio and Vitruvius; *Magnum in Parvo: or The Marrow of Architecture* (London 1728) demonstrates 'how to draw a Column ... According to the Proportions laid down by the most celebrated PALLADIO'; *The Builder's Pocket-Companion* (London 1731) includes the orders 'taken from the Immortal Andrew Palladio, and laid down after Will. Halfpenny's Practical Method', and so on.

[15] Leslie Stephen and Sidney Lee, eds, *The Dictionary of National Biography*, xiii (Oxford 1921-22) 432-33, 436; xvi (Oxford 1967-68) 12-14.

[16] British Library, Add. MSS 15776, ff. 27-31, 55-56, 73. The Ms. carries Milles's bookplate. Peterborough choir was surveyed in 1734 by Robert Wright, the surveyor to the Dean and Chapter (Colvin, *A Biographical Dictionary*, 1098).

[17] Sarah Markham, *John Loveday of Caversham 1711-1789, The Life and Tours of an Eighteenth-Century Onlooker* (Wilton 1984) 203.

[18] *The Gentleman's Magazine* (June 1735) 325.

[19] Brian de Breffny and George Mott, *The Churches and Abbeys of Ireland* (London 1976) 105-8, 136.

[20] Eusebius, *The History of the Church* (London 1709) subtitled *Made English from the Edition of these Histories, which Valesius published at Paris in the Years 1659, 1668 and 1673*, Lib. X, chap. iv, 184-85.

[21] Lever, *Catalogue of the Drawings Collection*, 83; f 8.

[22] Prints and Drawings 7.x.1977. I am grateful to David Griffin of the Irish Architectural Archive, Dublin, for drawing my attention to these latter items (letter to the author, February 1996). One view is reproduced in Breffny and Mott, *The Churches and Abbeys of Ireland*, 75. Charles Smith, *The Antient and Present State of the County and City of Waterford* (Dublin 1746) 175-76, describes the building briefly. Christ Church was the common dedication of the cathedral.

[23] John Mannion, 'Vessels, Masters and Seafaring: Patterns of Voyages in Waterford Commerce, 1766-1771', in William Noland and Thomas P. Power, eds, *Waterford History & Society* (Dublin 1992) 373-98.

[24] Halfpenny's drawings for the Exchange are datable 1738-40 (Walter Ison, *The Georgian Buildings of Bristol* (London 1952) 96, pl. 15; Mowl, *To Build the Second City*, 42). He had published an earlier design for the Exchange in *Perspective Made Easy* (London 1731) (Mowl, *To Build the Second City*, 49). The Exchange and Market was built 1741-43 to the design of John Wood Sr.

[25] Colvin, *A Biographical Dictionary*, 447.

[26] 'The South Prospect of the Cathedral Church of St. Flannan in Killaloe', Co Clare, inscribed 'I. Blaymires delin. L. Dempsy Sc.' is initialled 'W.H. A.D. 1738'; 'Ecclesiae Cathedralis Armachanae Facies Australis' and a view of St Carthag, Lismore, Co Waterford, are initialled 'W.H.'; 'The North West Prospect of the Church at Clonmacnoise', Co Offaly, and views of the cathedrals at Kildare and Derry are both dated 1738, and St Mary, Limerick, dated 1739; 'The Ground Plan of ye Cathedral Church of St Canice in Kilkenny' and St Coleman, Cloyne, Co Cork, both neither signed nor dated. There is also a miscellany of views of Saxon and Gothic churches from John Leland's *Itinerary Collectanea* and 'The Ichnography or Plan, of Glastonbury Abby' with an elevation of the octagonal Kitchen.

[27] Folios 1a to 6a (Lever, *Catalogue of the Drawings Collection*, 82-83; John Harris, *The Palladians* (London 1981) 100, pls 103-04). Bishop Milles's successor, Charles Estes, rebuilt the palace from 1741 to a design attributed to Richard Castle (Mark Girouard, 'The Noblest Quay in Europe', *Town and Country* (New Haven and London 1992) 155-56, pl. 133).

[28] This plan, with the diagonally placed pulpit and desk attached at the angle, the steeply pitched roofs crowned at the crossing by bell turrets, and the odd tracery of the pediment window in Plate 9, are features commonly found in seventeenth-century Dutch churches, for example, the Noorderkerk, Amsterdam (1620-22), illustrated in Hendrick de Keyser, *Architectura Moderna* (1631) (W. Kuyper, *Dutch Classicist Architecture, A Survey of Dutch Architecture, Gardens and Anglo-Dutch Architectural Relations from 1625 to 1700* (Delft 1980) fig. 3, pls 28-30, 31, 42, 44). This leads me to think that Halfpenny was aware of this Netherlandish tradition. Of course, Waterford city enjoyed close trade links with Holland (Mannion, *Vessels, Masters and Seafaring*, 316, 374, 376, 395).

[29] Bingham, *Origines Ecclesiasticae* (1711) iii, 65.

[30] Folio 4 is illustrated in Harris, *The Palladians*, 99, cat. no. 102, and Lever, *Catalogue of the Drawings Collection*, fig. 50; f 2 in Mowl, *To Build the Second City*, 52.

[31] Compare Plate 2 to Richard Castle's design, now in the Irish Architectural Archive, probably for rebuilding, 1743, Maynooth church, Co Kildare, previously said to be for the similar Newton Breda church, 1737, Co Down (*Quarterly Bulletin of the Irish Georgian Society*, xi (April September 1968) 23). I am grateful to David Griffin for drawing my attention to this new attribution.

[32] Smith, *The Ancient and Present State*, 80. See Lord Killanin and Michael V. Duignan, *The Shell Guide to Ireland* (London 1989) 303, and Girouard, 'The Noblest Quay in Europe', pl. 134.

[33] John McVeagh, ed., *Richard Pococke's Irish Tours* (Dublin 1995) 108: 'These Churches were order'd in this manner & adorned under the care of Dr Thomas Milles.'

[34] Smith, *The Ancient and Present State*, 181, also recording Milles's legacy (1740) to the city which involved 'repairing and rebuilding churches' (190). William Ven der Hagen (fl.1720-45) painted a view of Waterford (Homan Potterton, *Irish art and architecture* (London 1978) 166; *Irish Houses and Landscapes* (Belfast 1963) 17, no. 24.

[35] McVeagh, *Richard Pococke's Irish Tours*, 112. See Killanin and Duignan, *The Shell Guide to Ireland*, 308.

[36] Rolf Loeber, 'Early Classicism in Ireland: Architecture Before the Georgian Era', *Architectural History*, 22 (1979) 60, pl. 11a; Jacqueline O'Brien and Desmond Guinness, *Dublin, A Grand Tour* (London 1994) 37. Robinson rebuilt (1679 onward) St Carthage's Cathedral, Lismore (Rolf Loeber, *A Biographical Dictionary of Architects in Ireland 1600-1720* (London 1981) 90, 95; Smith, *The Ancient and Present State*, 53).

[37] Richard Hewlings, 'Chiswick House and Garden: Appearance and Meaning', in Toby Barnard and Jane Clark, eds, *Lord Burlington Architecture, Art and Life* (London 1995) figs 8a, 41.

[38] Fourth Book, chapter II, 'Of the forms of Temples', 82, where, however, S Giorgio is not illustrated.

[39] Ralph, *A Critical Review*, 29.

[40] Smith, *The Antient and Present State*, opposite 52.

[41] Gloucestershire Record Office, D2663/28, letter to Bishop Milles, 13-24 May 1734.

[42] British Library, Add. MSS 15776, f 110. SS Peter and Paul was built 1735-39 to the design of John and William Bastard (*Royal Commission on Historical Monuments, Dorset*, iii, pt. 1 (London 1970) 19-21, frontispiece, pl. 98). Milles described the chapel of Emmanuel College, Cambridge, which was beautified in 1735 by the local Palladian architect, Sir James Burrough, as 'very neat' (f 36; Colvin, *A Biographical Dictionary*, 194). Milles thought the Baroque style of St Alkmund, Whitchurch, Shropshire, designed and built 1711-13 by John Barker and William Smith, 'a very handsome modern church' (British Library, Add. MS 15,776, f 166, dated 1743). Bishop Milles had subscribed £2 2s 6d in c 1711 towards its construction (K. and B. Barnard, *Monumental Inscriptions of St Alkmund's Church Whitchurch Shropshire* (1987) typescript in church, CH7).

[43] Halfpenny, *Practical Architecture*, 26. See also *The Art of Sound Building*, pl. 14, fig. 76. A second edition of *A Book of Architecture* was published in 1739. This feature appeared with increasing frequency in Irish churches after 1740 (Alistair Rowan, *The Buildings of Ireland: North West Ulster* (Harmondsworth 1979) 123-24, 191-92, pls 63-64, John Aheron, *A General Treatise of Architecture, In Five Books* (Dublin 1754) in Marcus Whiffen, *Stuart and Georgian Churches* (London 1948) 34.

[44] Gloucestershire Record Office, D2663/28, letter to Bishop Milles, 15-26 May 1734. They also visited Ravenna Cathedral (built before 425 and demolished in 1748), 'an old Dark, & disagreeable building' with the nave 'supperted by 56 marble pillars' and the 'Tribune ... all mosaick', which 'They are at present repainting ... & digging up ye pavement', and S Spirito. See Richard Krautheimer, *Early Christian and Byzantine Architecture* (London 1989) 181-83, 185-87, 277-78, 481-82 note 35, pls 144-46, 149, 239-40. Another letter from Milles to the

bishop, dated 30 May-10 June 1734, reveals that the travellers had been in contact with the French scholar, Bernard de Montfaucon (1655-1741): at Modena 'We were recommended here by father mountfaucon to one Muratori a very learned man & Library keeper to ye Duke. He shew'd us ye Library.' Montfaucon was author of *L'Antiquité Expliquée* (1719; English edition 1721-22), a massive compilation of illustrations of classical artifacts from early Greek to Theodosius II, including octagonal structures. Among the engravings in the RIBA album is a seventeenth century view of the east exterior of St Bartholomeo de Insula on Tiber Island, Rome, with its austere, apsidal chancel, built in the tenth century on the ruins of the Temple of Aesculapius, and later much altered; see Emile Mâle, *The Early Churches of Rome* (London 1960) 103-7).

[45] See Samantha Mussells, 'Architects, Travellers and the Revival of the Early Christian Basilica' in Pierre de la Ruffinière du Prey, ed., *Architects Books & Libraries* (Kingston, Ontario 1995) 9-15, citing Rev Sir George Wheler, *An Account of the Churches and Places of Assembly of the Primitive Christians* (London 1689) and Henry Maundrel, *Journey from Aleppo to Jerusalem* (Oxford 1703) illustrated by Nicholas Hawksmoor.

[46] Bingham, *Origines Ecclesiasticae*, iii (1711) 42, 39-40, respectively.

[47] Quoting from Bingham, as in note 46. An untitled tract dated 14 June 1678 condemned 'the sumptuousness and magnificence of Churches [as] not at all suitable to the times of the Gospels' (British Library, 816.m.9, *Tracts Relating to London*, item 92).

[48] Kerry Downes, *Hawksmoor* (London 1959) 162-63, pl. 52a; Pierre de la Ruffinière du Prey, 'Hawksmoor's "Basilica after the Primitive Christians": Architecture and Theory', *Journal of the Society of Architectural Historians*, xlviii, no. 2 (June 1989) 38-52, fig. 1, item marked B. At St Anne, Limehouse (1714-31) the baptistery is a semi-projecting, domed rotunda at the west end (Downes, *Hawksmoor*, 171-73, fig. 33, pl. 55a).

[49] Bingham, *Origines Ecclesiasticae*, iii (1711) 117, 119.

[50] The auditory advantages of this form is the subject of Robert Morris's design for an 'octangular Chapel' (*Rural Architecture* (London 1750) 5, pls xxxi-xxxii): 'It has been objected to, that the inner Part should have been a Circle in the Plan, and the Roof spherical, that the Sound striking in the Angles, will render it confused, and reverberate from a Roof Octangular in the Plan, very unintelligible to the Audience; but as the Angles are small, and nearly approaching to a Circle, I think the Objection of little Weight.' 'Mr. William Halfpenny, Surveyor' is listed (p ii) as a subscriber to this publication.

[51] RIBA album, f 6a.

[52] Sir John Soane's Museum, London, MSS 'A Manuscri by Mr. Gibbs Memorandums, &c.', 20, referring to *I Quattro Libri*, book four (Venice 1570) chapter xvi, 61-62, which also appears in Ware, *The Four Books*, fourth book (London 1738) 96-97, pl. xlii.

[53] Graham Parry, 'The John Talman Letter-Book', *Walpole Society*, lix (1997) 23-5, 47; John Ingamells, *A Dictionary of British and Irish Travellers in Italy 1701-1800* (New Haven and London 1997) 924-25; drawings in Victoria and Albert Museum. See Krautheimer, *Early Christian and Byzantine Architecture*, 176, figs 141-42.

[54] Gloucestershire Record Office, D2663/28, letter of 15-26 May 1734, adding that the statues 'are transported to Venice. There are ye names of them wrote on ye pedes.' See Krautheimer, *Early Christian and Byzantine Architecture*, 232-7,269-73, pls 187-92, 234.

[55] 'I saw the Cathedral Baptistery' (British Library, Add. MSS 22994, f 168). Ingamells, *A Dictionary of British and Irish Travellers*, 662, 779-80; Kenneth John Conant, *Carolingian*

and Romanesque Architecture 800-1200 (Harmondsworth, 1966) 373-75, figs 287-88.

56 Michael McCarthy, '"The dullest man that ever travelled"? A re-assessment of Richard Pococke and of his portrait by J.-E. Liotard', *Apollo*, 143 (May 1996) 25-29.

57 Richard Pococke, *A Description of the East, and Some other Countries*, ii (London 1745) part i, 14-15, pl. iii.

58 Pococke, *A Description of the East*, ii, part i, 39, plan following page 18, similar to Krautheimer, *Early Christian and Byzantine Architecture*, fig. 227.

59 For example, the 'large church' at Caesarea, Palestine, 'which probably was the cathedral of the archbishop [and] seems to have been built in the style of the Syrian churches, with three naves, which ended to the east in semicircles, where they had their principal altars', and the similarly planned cathedral at Tyre (Pococke, *A Description of the East*, ii, part i, 59, 82). The latter is described in Eusebius, *The History of the Church*, Lib. X (London 1709) chapter iv, 189.

60 Pococke, *A Description of the East*, ii, part i, 120, 170, pls xxi, xxxiv, respectively. See Krautheimer, *Early Christian and Byzantine Architecture*, 144-51, figs 100, 102-04.

61 Pococke, *A Description of the East*, ii, part iii, 263, 276.

62 British Library, Add. MSS 19939, f 74, recording a journey between 14-25 August 1737, repeated in Add. MSS 22997, ff. 66v-67. For 'Gothick' read 'Goth'.

63 British Library, Add. MSS 22994, f 47.

64 Krautheimer, *Early Christian and Byzantine Architecture*, 278-80, figs 241-42.

65 British Library, Add. MSS 19940, first page, covering May-June 1737.

66 *The Gentleman's Magazine* (May 1740) 262, of 'stone in bladder'.

67 Pococke reported in 1752 that Waterford's medieval 'Quire has lately been much ornamented if intermixture of Grecian with Gothick Architecture can be called an Ornament by a Corinthian Altar piece, which is the gift of Mrs. Susannah Mason & cost £200;- by a very handsome Canopy over the seat of the Mayor & Aldermen, & by the same over the galleries, & the seats of the families of the Bishop & Dignitaries, by making a Gallery to the north for the Soldiers, to the west over the Organ for the Charity boys, – by adorning the Galleries with handsome Ballustrades, & New seating the Church & paving it with black & white marble, to which besides the white marble The Revd. Dr. Jeremiah Milles, Chantor of the Cathedral of Exeter as he was likewise formerly of this Church & Treasurer of Lismore, gave the sum of fifty pounds' (McVeagh, *Richard Pococke's Irish Tours*, 108). This was undertaken by Charles Este, Bishop Milles's successor in 1740. The medieval cathedral was demolished and rebuilt between 1774 and 1792 in a handsome Palladian manner to the design of John Roberts, a local architect (Girouard, 'The Noblest Quay in Europe', 159-60, pl. 13).

—

1 – The artist at work in his Dublin studio
(photo: Reeves collection)

The works of Oswald Reeves (1870-1967) artist and craftsman: an interim catalogue

PAUL LARMOUR

As the story of the Arts and Crafts Movement in Ireland of the late nineteenth and early twentieth centuries has unfolded in recent years, the importance of one of its central figures, Oswald Reeves (1870-1967) has become apparent.[1]

Recognised in his own lifetime but largely forgotten until re-discovered in the 1980s,[2] his special place in the history of the movement as one of the really outstanding individual art-workers is secure. What has not yet been committed to print, however, is a comprehensive catalogue of his works. The task of recording his output is not yet complete, but an attempt at an interim list of works may be considered a useful step on the way, and may help to unearth further works as well as establish the whereabouts of some known only from archival sources. The materials are in some cases incomplete, but it is possible to construct a chronologically arranged list which covers most of Reeves's working years.[3] As an introduction to it, it may be worthwhile recounting briefly something of the artist's life and career, and to take the opportunity to illustrate some lesser known examples of his work.

PERCY OSWALD REEVES

Percy Oswald Reeves was born in 1870 in Birmingham, the son of a schoolmaster. Starting at the age of fifteen, he attended evening classes at Birmingham School of Art where he obtained his Art Teacher's Certificate. He went on to teach for four years at Southport School of Art, from 1892 to 1895, before gaining a scholarship to the Royal College of Art in London. Little is known of his time at the RCA save that he won a book prize in 1897 and went on to be awarded his degree and Art Master's Certificate in 1900 for studies in architecture, painting, and craft work. Following that, he joined the London studio of Alexander Fisher (1864-1936) as an assistant.

Fisher was an accomplished artist – skilled as a jeweller, sculptor, silver-smith, enameller and metalworker. He had taught enamelling at the Central School of Arts and Crafts in London from 1896 and also wrote extensively on the subject in *The Studio* magazine. Through not only his teaching and his writing but also the exemplary quality of his own works, he had become the most influential figure in enamelling in Britain at the turn of the century. Reeves was to learn much from Fisher, artistically as well as technically, as something of Fisher's evocative and symbolist treatment of figures was to pervade his own designs for most of his career, and an element of Fisher's distinctive use of leafy ornament is also apparent in some of Reeves's work.

Details of Reeves's period with Fisher are scant, but he was officially credit-ed by Fisher with assisting him on a jewel box which was shown at the English-based Arts and Crafts Exhibition Society in 1903. In the same exhibition the catalogue also listed a 'silver tankard, in repoussé silver with enamels ... executed by Alexander Fisher and assistants in his workshop'. Among Reeves's collection of his own designs and photographs of his own finished works is an illustration of just such a silver flagon, with an enamel inset depicting a dove, surrounded by interwo-ven vine tendrils in repoussé work. Its date and authorship are not recorded in his notes but it can be identified as a piece designed and made by Fisher.[4] It could well be the tankard exhibited by him in 1903, and it may be supposed that Reeves's apparent personal interest in it suggests that he was involved in its manufacture.

In view of Reeves's eventual departure for Ireland it is interesting to reflect on Fisher's occasional use of Celtic interlaced and zoomorphic ornament apparent in some works from about 1896 onwards. Reeves himself was never to embrace the Celtic ornamentalist tradition wholly, but his possible encounters with its heritage of historic ornament in Fisher's studio may well have opened his mind to opportunities in Ireland. At any rate, by 1903, Reeves had left Fisher's studio, to take up a teach-ing appointment at the re-formed Metropolitan School of Art in Dublin.

With the success of the Central School of Arts and Crafts set up in London in 1896 and the revolutionising of the Royal College of Art in London in 1898, reor-ganised on 'arts and crafts' principles by Walter Crane, the crafts had become an integral part of British art educational thinking, and a clear direction had been given to the various schools in Ireland. The 1899 Agriculture and Technical Instruction (Ireland) Act had brought about a change in the control of the Metropolitan School of Art in Dublin, and it passed from the jurisdiction of the Science and Art Department in London to the control of the new Department of Agriculture and Technical Instruction for Ireland on 1 April 1900. The new department was commit-ted to the design aspect of art, with crafts its firm priority, and a number of specialist classes were established as a result. One of the first classes was in enamelling allied to art metalwork, set up in 1903 with Oswald Reeves appointed as instructor.

Reeves's classes proved very popular, and in the years that followed, under his expert direction, the work of the Dublin school in enamels was to gain an international reputation. Some of his pupils were successful in the national competition for schools of art in Britain and Ireland held annually at South Kensington, and their work was illustrated in such popular journals as *The Studio*. Their work was shown regularly at exhibitions in various cities in Europe, and on one occasion, at an exhibition in Vienna, the Austrian government reportedly bought the entire collection of Dublin enamels as models. They were also prominent in the *Exposition de l'Art Decoratif de la Grande Bretagne et d'Irlande* held at the Louvre in Paris in 1914, and by 1916, when the Metropolitan School was featured in a special number of *The Studio* and a number of pieces by Reeves's pupils were illustrated, the power of his influence was evident.

Reeves was to marry one of his former pupils, Dora Allen, in 1913. Dora Allen (1885-1981) was born in Monkstown, Co Dublin, to a Quaker family. She was one of Reeves's best pupils, winning a silver medal in the 1908 National Competition and having her work illustrated in *The Studio* that year and in the official record of the 1914 exhibition at the Louvre in Paris. She also contributed to the Arts and Crafts Society of Ireland exhibitions of 1904, 1910 and 1917. They had two children, both daughters, born in 1918 and 1920.

By 1920 Reeves was appointed Second Master at the school of art, and he was to remain in post until his official retirement in 1936. In fact, due to difficulties in replacing him, he continued to teach at the school in a temporary capacity until his eventual retirement in 1937.

Throughout his career as a teacher, and also during the early years of his retirement, Reeves practised as an artist and craftsman in his own right. Many of his works were shown at the various exhibitions of the time, both in Ireland and further afield. His exhibited pieces attracted the attention of discriminating private collectors early on, as exemplified, for example, by the enamel plaque entitled *A Falling Star*, which was singled out for purchase by King Edward VII at the Irish International Exhibition in 1907, only for the King to be informed that it had previously been sold to Lady Dudley.[5]

Once Reeves's credentials as a craftsman had been established, he received a steady flow of commissions, the first important one after his arrival in Dublin being for a repoussé silver cover with enamel inset panels for a presentation album[6] to Sir Horace Plunkett in 1908. In both its central panel of a female figure and the intertwining Art Nouveau borders, it showed its author's debt to Alexander Fisher. Unlike many of Reeves's early works whose present whereabouts are unknown, its eventual fate has been recorded: it perished in the malicious fire which destroyed

Plunkett's home at Foxrock, Dublin, in 1922.

Over the years, Reeves received many other commissions for a wide variety of works, including enamelled panels, jewellery, badges, medals and trophies, for both religious and secular patrons. One notable high point in his early career was when he was chosen to design and make a silver and enamel pendant as a gift from the British Section of the Fourth International Art Congress to the city of Dresden in 1913, as a memento of the hospitality extended by the city to the members of the congress the previous year.[7]

Much of Reeves's early work was of a figurative and symbolist type, frequently of 'faerie' subjects, as testified by the romantic and evocative titles given to many of the pieces, but in the 1920s and 1930s it generally became more stylised and geometrical than previously. It took on a more modernistic look, with a restrained use of Art Deco ornament. Indeed, the span of Reeves's career was sustained enough, and his abilities as a designer enduring enough, that he was responsible for some of the most memorable examples of Art Deco design in Ireland, as well as some of the best examples of Art Nouveau and Symbolism.

Not only as an influential teacher and as one of the outstanding individual craftworkers of his era was Reeves important. He was also a keen and indefatigable organiser in the Arts and Crafts Society of Ireland, which was the main focus of the movement here from the 1890s to the 1920s. From 1907 he took a leading role in the society's affairs. First, as joint honorary secretary with James Brenan, he helped organise an impressive 'Arts and Crafts Sub-Section' on behalf of the society at the Irish International Exhibition of 1907, and then as sole honorary secretary he organised the society's own exhibitions of 1910 and 1917. He was also the founder and first master of the Guild of Irish Art Workers in 1909, a position he held until at least 1917. He went on to become a leading spokesman for the movement in Ireland, responsible for instance for a valuable review of its achievements published in *The Studio* in 1917.[8] The advent of extra responsibilities at the school of art appears to have curtailed his work for the society to some extent in the 1920s when he stepped down as honorary secretary, but he remained on the council and executive committee and wrote the foreword to the catalogue of the seventh exhibition. After that seventh exhibition, held in 1925, the society went into a decline for a variety of reasons, but although both the society and the 'movement' may have been moribund during the 1930s and 1940s, Reeves himself was still busy producing an impressive array of works, mainly memorials and trophies, but also some more functional objects. The trophies in particular were of especial interest as they marked a break away from the conventional silver cups that were, and still are, commonplace for competitions in Ireland.

Despite his quiet retirement, Reeves was still a figure of some significance in the 1950s, re-emerging to become the figurehead of the revived Arts and Crafts Society of Ireland. He was its president from at least 1955 to 1962, and although he was by then very elderly and no longer a practising craftworker, his special place in the history of the society was understood. As the chairman of its council, Brigid Ganly wrote in the catalogue of the fourteenth exhibition, held in 1962:

> few can have had a longer or more devoted connection with the Society than our President, Mr Oswald Reeves, ARCA, whose name appears over and over again as an outstanding exponent of fine metal work and enamelling, besides his continued support and encouragement of the work of the Society through the difficult times associated with two World Wars and a Civil War.

That recognition in 1962, though belated, was timely however, as by the time of the next exhibition Reeves was dead. He died on 12 April 1967 at his home in Wentworth Place, Wicklow, aged 96. Along with him went the name of the society itself, changed by that year's exhibition to the Irish Society for Design and Craftwork, but the legacy of a lifetime devoted to arts and crafts ideals in Ireland still remains in his record of achievement and the impressive list of works undertaken over a period of almost half a century.

———

2 – Oswald Reeves, panel designed for the Arts and Crafts Society of Ireland and Guild of Irish Art Workers (1910)

LIST OF WORKS BY OSWALD REEVES

The following list has been compiled from contemporary exhibition catalogues and from the artist's work account book, drawings, watercolour designs, photographs of completed works, undated press cuttings, and undated notes amongst the artist's papers. Works are generally undated and unsigned unless otherwise noted. Any measurements recorded are as expressed in Reeves's notes. Titles of works as recorded by Reeves are not necessarily inscribed on the actual pieces.

Abbreviations
ACSI – Arts and Crafts Society of Ireland
RA – Royal Academy
RHA – Royal Hibernian Academy

1904   *The Opal Queen*
Enamelled copper plaque. Exhibited St Louis World's Fair, 1904.

The Lady of the House
Painting. Exhibited RHA, Dublin, 1904.

Self lost; self found
Enamelled copper plaque; originally set in a wood frame in 1904; re-set in a silver-plated copper frame, with cast feet, standing upright, in 1906. [Job no. 1 in work book, where referred to as *Self found; self lost.*] Exhibited RHA, Dublin, 1904 (unfinished and in wood frame), priced at £40; Dublin Castle, per Lady Dudley, 1905 (in unfinished state); RA, London, 1906 (in finished state); Walker Art Gallery, Liverpool, 1906; City Art Gallery, Leeds, 1907; Irish International Exhibition (Fine Art Section), Dublin, 1907; Finsbury Technical College, City and Guilds of London, per A. Fisher, 1907; ACSI, Dublin, 1910, priced at £45.

A falling star
Enamelled copper plaque, 8" x 4$\frac{1}{8}$", depicting a female figure descending from the sky; originally set in a wood frame. Exhibited ACSI, Dublin, 1904, where bought by Countess of Dudley, £30. Framed in silver with crutch, in 1905, for 8 guineas; frame measuring 11$\frac{3}{4}$" x 6$\frac{1}{2}$" x 16G, including feet $\frac{3}{4}$" high. [Job no. 2 in work book.] Exhibited Lady Dudley's Exhibition, Carlton Gardens, London, December 1906; Irish International Exhibition (Arts and Crafts Sub-Section), Dublin, 1907.

A Message
Large silver and enamel jewel for hair or front of dress. Four wings, champlevé, and jewel centre. [Job no. 3 in work book: price £8.] Exhibited ACSI, Dublin, 1904.

1906   *Undine*
Enamelled copper plaque, 11$\frac{1}{4}$" x 4$\frac{3}{8}$" in silver-plated copper frame, with crutch, 14$\frac{5}{8}$" x 5$\frac{7}{8}$" x 16G, including feet, $\frac{7}{8}$". [Job no. 5 in work book.] £50. Exhibited at RA, London, 1906; Lady Dudley's Exhibition, Carlton Gardens, London, 1906, where

bought by Lord Brassey; lent to Irish International Exhibition (Fine Art Section), Dublin, 1907. *In collection of Cecil Higgins Art Gallery, Bedford, England.*

1907   ### *The Hunter's Moon*

Enamelled copper plaque, in silver plated copper frame, with crutch. [Job no. 6 in work book.] Given to the Countess of Dudley.

Silver box with enamel on copper, entitled *Plenty with Blessing*

and priced at £8. [Job no. 7 in work book, recorded at 1910.] Exhibited at Irish International Exhibition (Arts and Crafts Sub-Section), Dublin, 1907, priced at £10; ACSI, Dublin, 1910, priced at £8, where bought by the Countess of Aberdeen.

1908   ### The Plunkett Album

Album with illuminated address and copies of signatures, bound in silver, enriched with repoussé work and with one large centre enamel, six small enamels, four 'jewel' enamels in border, and champlevé enamels in the four corner bosses. Made to commission for the officers of the Department of Agriculture and Technical Instruction, Dublin, and presented by the officers and staff to Sir Horace Plunkett on his retiring from Vice-Presidentship of the Department. [Job no. 8 in work book] £70. Exhibited RA, London, 1908; ACSI, Dublin, 1910. Destroyed by fire in Plunkett's house in Foxrock, Dublin, in 1922.

1909   ### *A double star*

Slipcase in silver with *baisse-taille* enamel, with leather-bound book. Title page of book inscribed in ink 'Days to be Remembered'; final page inscribed in ink 'This book with silver and enamel case designed and executed by P. Oswald Reeves ARCA. Lond., Dublin 1909'. [Job no. 4 in work book.] Exhibited ACSI, Dublin, 1910, priced at £30. *Private collection, Dublin.*

Illuminated address

in painted wood frame, for presentation to Mrs Michael Gunn on retiring from Gaiety Theatre, in watercolour and gold on Whatman's paper. Done to commission from Mr Gill and committee, £7.10s. [Job no. 9 in work book.] Exhibited ACSI, Dublin, 1910, lent by Mrs M. Gunn.

1910   ### Presentation album

Illuminated address with one page figure design 'Good Wishes' on Whatman's paper, bound in leather, with enrichment on tooling, velum panel, and coloured; binding done by Miss Fitzpatrick, Dun Emer Guild, in 1911. Done to commission of committee, through Michael Drury, for presentation to Dr Walsh. [Job no. 10 in work book.]

Cover design for exhibition catalogue

for the Arts and Crafts Society of Ireland and Guild of Irish Art Workers. The figurative panel design was also used as a headpiece device in *The Irish Architect and Craftsman*. (Plate 2)

c 1910   **Drawing of copper and enamel stall-plate**

depicting arms of the Earl of Arran. Exhibited ACSI, Dublin, 1910.

1911   **Two pendants**

Silver and enamel. Heart-shape enamel on copper; silver setting with chains to pendant. Made to commission of Mr Gill; copies of a pendant supplied by him. £2.5.0. [Job no. 13 in work book.]

Cover design, headpieces and initial letters for
The Irish Architect and Craftsman

Cover depicts a figure holding a model of a church, flanked by a mason and a metal-worker; signed with monogram. The design used for the first volume was slightly modified for the second volume, and by January 1913 Reeves's design had been replaced. Headpieces varied from stylised leafy branch devices to an elaborate medievalist tableau depicting a dragon being slain by knights on horseback. (Plates 3, 4)

1912   **Silver and enamel box, entitled** *Twilight fairy*

$3^1/_2$" x $2^7/_8$" x $1^5/_8$" box with round corners and enamel top depicting figure with moth's wings bringing stars. Bought from the artist in January 1913 by Mr Fayle. £6. [Job no. 14 in work book.]

Copper and enamel box, entitled *Pansy faces*

$3^9/_{16}$" x 3" x $1^7/_8$" box with square corners and enamel top. £4. Bought by Mr Mitchell of Blackrock. [Job no. 15 in work book.]

Circular copper box, entitled *Pansy*

Circular copper box, $2^1/_{16}$" diameter x $1^1/_8$" deep unhinged, with enamel top. £1.10.0. Bought by Mr Fayle. [Job no. 16 in work book.]

Cushion design

Watercolour drawing depicting 'Forget-me-not—Rose'. [Job no. 19 in work book.]

The Spirit of the Willow

Watercolour, $10^1/_2$" x $3^1/_4$", in wood frame. [Job no. 20 in work book.] Exhibited ACSI, Dublin, Belfast, and Cork, 1917, priced at £8.8s.

1913   **Circular copper box, entitled** *Plenty with love*

Circular copper box, $2^9/_{16}$" diameter x $1^1/_2$" deep unhinged, with enamel top depicting a broken leaf with briar and rose blossoms. £1.15.0. Bought by Lady O'Neill on 13 December 1913. [Job no. 17 in work book.]

Memorial tablet

Copper plate, with inscription in repoussé with ornamental capital letter T. Fixed on stand of lantern at Friends' Meeting House, Eustace Street, Dublin. Done to commission. £3.10.0. [Job no. 18 in work book.]

Oswald Reeves
3 – Headpiece for The Irish Architect and Craftsman *(1911)*
4 – Figure panel drawn for cover of The Irish Architect and Craftsman *(1911)*

1913   **Ink pot**

Copper and enamel. Enrichment on sides, three fairy figures with stars (thoughts); on top, a winged flaming star. Wedding present for Mr Sheridan (solicitor) per G.P. Sheridan. £5. [Job no. 11 in work book.] Exhibited ACSI, Dublin, Belfast and Cork, 1917, lent by W.T. Sheridan.

The Dresden pendant

Silver, enriched with repoussé work and a circular enamel, suspended from a flaming crown. Inscribed on back 'From the British Section of the Fourth International Art Congress, Dresden, 1912', and signed with monogram superimposed on 'Dublin'. Made to commission of the British Section of the congress for £15, and presented to the city corporation of Dresden as a memento to hang on the silver 'tree' centre-piece in the Rathhaus. [Job no. 12 in work book.] *Private collection, Dublin.* (Plate 6)

Slipcase for wedding certificate

Silver with enamel enrichment, signed on cover with monogram. Made to contain the marriage certificate record and signatures of the guests on the occasion of the artist's marriage to Dora Allen on 7 August 1913. [Job no. 24 in work book, July 1913.] Exhibited ACSI, Dublin, Belfast and Cork, 1917. *In possession of the artist's heirs.*

1914   *Fairy fantasy*

Enamel plaque, framed in copper. £45. [Job no. 21 in work book.] Rejected at RA, London, 1914.

Instruction

Panel picture, pastel, 4' x 1'8", in wood frame. [Job no. 22 in work book.]

Badge for President of Architectural Association of Ireland

Enamel on copper and gold foil, $1\frac{1}{2}$" diameter; silver setting and gold rings (9c) gilt; Irish poplin band with gold hook and eye; leather case. £5. To commission of Professor W.A. Scott ARIBA, 45 Mountjoy Square South, Dublin. [Job no. 23 in work book.] The badge depicts two draughtsmen seated either side of a tree, surrounded by a ribbon: based on a device designed for the association by R.C. Orpen in 1896. Exhibited ACSI, Dublin, Belfast and Cork, 1917. *In possession of Architectural Association of Ireland.*

1915   **Badge for President of Dublin Building Trades Employers' Association**

Enamel on copper and silver foil, $1\frac{3}{8}$" diameter; gold setting and rings (22c), 2" diameter, with name of association around the enamel in repoussé and 'Presented by John Good 1915' on the back; St Patrick's blue ribbon, with gold hook and eye; leather case. £15.15.0. To commission of John Good. [Job no. 25 in work book.] The badge depicts tools and a wreath. Exhibited ACSI, Dublin, Belfast and Cork, 1917.

Oswald Reeves

5 – The Bird of Truth *(1915)*
6 – *Design for the Dresden pendant (1913)*
7 – *Seal design for the National Gallery of Ireland (1919)*

1915 **Ring**

Silver with carved cherub. For T.K. Moylan. £1.1.0. [Job no. 26 in work book.]

Circular nickel box

Box of nickel, with silver feet and mount for enamel, $2^{1}/_{2}$" x $1^{1}/_{2}$" deep, unhinged, velvet lined, with enamel top depicting 'Badge of the Royal Irish Fusiliers'. £2.2.0. Sent to Irish Literary Society Exhibition, London. Given for the War Fund sale, November 1915 (Bennett's); returned. Given for the War Funds to Blackrock Work Depot. [Job no. 27 in work book.]

Circular nickel box

Box as job no. 27, but with enamel top depicting 'Pansy' design as in job no. 16. [Job no. 28 in work book.] Given by Reeves as wedding present to Evans Perry.

The Response of the Rose: enamel plaque

[Job no. 29, November 1915.] Enamel on copper, with silver all over, and gold, $6^{1}/_{4}$" x $2^{5}/_{8}$" framed in copper, plain with crutch. To commission of Mr N.A. Sumerling. £7. Exhibited ACSI, Dublin, Belfast and Cork, 1917, lent by N.A. Sumerling.

The Response of the Rose: watercolour drawing

[Recorded as part of job no. 29 in work book, November 1915.] Exhibited ACSI, Dublin, Belfast and Cork, 1917, priced at £4.4.0 and sold at Belfast to Mr R.S. Lepper of Elsinore, Crawfordsburn, Co Down.

Courtown Harbour

Oil painting in gilt frame. [Job no. 30 in work book.].

The Bird of Truth

Point engraving on copper plate. [Job no. 31 in work book, which records that it was 'sent out for Xmas. 1 print sold per Miss K. Fox. 10s. 6d. April 1916'.] Exhibited ACSI, Dublin, Belfast and Cork, 1917; price £3.3s. *Private collection, Dublin.* (Plate 5)

1916 **Gold watch chain**

(incorporating old gold chain supplied). End pieces and clasps engraved with sun, sheaf, moon, daisy, lyre and poppy. For Rt. Hon. L.A. Waldron, P.C. of Dublin. £12. [Job no. 32 in work book.]

Tabernacle door and panel
for Honan Collegiate Chapel, Cork

Repoussé silver and enamels, gilt, with bronze surround (door panel re-enamelled after damage in gilding). Door panel depicting 'The Adoration of the Lamb'; panel over door depicting 'The Blessed Trinity'. To commission of Sir John Robert O'Connell. [Job no. 33 in work book, May 1916.] Door panel exhibited ACSI, Dublin, Belfast and Cork, 1917, lent by Sir J.R. O'Connell.

c 1917 **Copper box with enamel top**

Exhibited at ACSI, Dublin, Belfast and Cork, 1917, priced at £4.4s.

Design for headpiece

Exhibited at ACSI, Dublin, Belfast and Cork, 1917.

1919 **Seal for National Gallery of Ireland**

Design made and submitted in competition; £21 offered; selected and awarded the prize. Wax model made also. [Job no. 34 in work book.] This is presumably the 'Design for a Seal for Impression in Paper' exhibited at ACSI, Dublin, 1921. (Plate 7)

Enamelled copper arms of Archbishop Peacock

Part of memorial in Christ Church Cathedral, Dublin (per R.C. Orpen). Repoussé and champlevé enamel. £30. [Job no. 36 in work book, which records payment to K. Quigly for the work.] Design in watercolour by Reeves exhibited ACSI, Dublin, 1921.

**Design for scheme of war memorial
for St Andrew's College, Dublin**

Watercolour drawing. [Job no. 39 in work book.]

1920 **Enamelled copper device**

for top of brass memorial plate, depicting cross, crown, wreath and rays, in repoussé and champlevé work (per George Atkinson). £5. [Job no. 35 in work book.]

Design for memorial stone

(inscription) for Earl of Mayo. Executed in grey Irish limestone by Sharp and Emery of Dublin. [Job no. 37 in work book.]

Finial and inscription for banner pole

for St John Ambulance Brigade Flag for Mrs Rowlette. Copper, silver plated. [Job no. 38 in work book.]

Response of the Rose

Enamel plaque in copper frame (replica of 1915 design, revised). To commission of Miss Isobel Knox. £23. [Job no. 41 in work book, November 1920.]

Copper inscription plate for crucifix

with Irish inscription, head and tail enrichments repoussé. For Major General Sir William Hickie. £12. [Job no. 42 in work book, October 1920.]

Tabernacle panel for Newry Cathedral

Painted enamel, depicting the 'Sacred Heart', together with blue background plate. For Ashlin and Coleman, architects, Dublin. £18. [Job no. 43 in work book, November 1920.]

1920   **Triptych war memorial**
for All Saints' Church of Ireland church, Grangegorman, Dublin

Design by Reeves submitted in competition; £5 offered; design selected and commissioned per R.F. Jones at £70. Executed in ebony, gold, silver, oxidised copper, and enamels. Woodwork by James Hicks; lettering of wing panels by George Atkinson; metal work by John F. Hunter and James Wallace; enamelling by Reeves. [Job no. 40 in work book.] Exhibited ACSI, Dublin, 1921. (The watercolour drawing for the enamelled panel is in a private collection in Dublin.) (Plate 8 and cover illustration)

8 – Oswald Reeves and others, Triptych War Memorial (1920)
All Saints' Church of Ireland church, Grangegorman, Dublin

1921   **Stall plate of Earl of Bessborough**

for St Patrick's Hall, Dublin. Repoussé copper, enamelled champlevé. Adapted design by Sir Neville Wilkinson. [Job no. 44 in work book, March 1921.]

Stall plate of Viscount French

for St Patrick's Hall, Dublin. Enamel champlevé, copper oxidised. Design by Sir Neville Wilkinson, adapted. [Job no. 45 in work book, April 1921.]

***Bel-broid lingerie* shop sign**

Two butterflies in champlevé enamels on copper. [Job no. 46 in work book, March 1921.]

1922   **Design for postage stamp**

for Irish Free State; not adopted. For Hely's Ltd (Frank A. Lowe). £8. [Job no. 47 in work book, March 1922.]

**Designs for cover and doublures
for *Ireland's Memorial Records 1914-18***

for the committee of the Irish National War Memorial; binding and tooling carried out by William Pender; the records privately printed in eight volumes by Maunsel and Roberts Ltd, Dublin, 1923.

c 1924   **Tabernacle door panel**

Repoussé silver gilt. Exhibited at *Aonach Tailteann Exhibition of Irish Art*, Dublin, 1924, priced at £95; won silver medal for gold and silversmith's work.

Tabernacle door panel

depicting 'Our Lord in Benediction'. Solid silver, parcel-gilded, chased and tooled. Exhibited at South Kensington, London, 1924; illustrated *Irish Builder and Engineer*, 14 June 1924. (Plate 9)

**Tabernacle door panel
for the Roman Catholic church, Maguiresbridge, Co Fermanagh**

Silver, gilded and enamelled. Depicts 'The Pelican feeding its young'.

1924   **Tabernacle door panel
for the Convent Chapel, Foxford, Co Mayo**

Silver, parcel-gilded and enamelled.

c 1925   **Panel in coloured plaster**

Exhibited at ACSI, Dublin, Belfast and Cork, 1925, priced at £30, and replicas advertised also at £30.

Design for a book plate

Exhibited at ACSI, Dublin, Belfast and Cork, 1925.

Oswald Reeves
9 – Tabernacle door panel depicting
'Our Lord in Benediction' (c 1924)
(photo: Reeves collection)

opposite
10 – The Nugent Memorial (1933)
St Bride's Church of Ireland church,
Mount Nugent, Co Cavan

c 1930   **Candlestick in enamelled copper**

Exhibited at *Exposition d'Art, Irlandais*, Musées Royaux des Beaux-Arts de Belgique, Bruxelles, 1930. *Private collection, Dublin.* (Plate 11)

1931   **Cover design for *Popular Astrology***

Black and white drawing, inscribed as for vol. 1, no. 1, October 1931; signed with monogram.

1933   **Nugent Memorial**
in St Bride's Church of Ireland church, Mount Nugent, Co Cavan

Low relief sculpture in plaster, coloured; 4' x 2'; depicting an emblematic figure with birds and a cup. Signed with monogram. (Plate 10)

1934   **Altar cross**
for St Vincent's Hospital Chapel, Dublin

Copper, with panels of beaten gold and enamel, champlevé enamelling and repoussé work. Height 4' 8". Signed with monogram. Adapted for use as a processional cross also, being able to be withdrawn together with its knop from the stand, to be attached to a staff. Presented by the members of the visiting staff of St Vincent's Hospital to the mother rectress and the community on the occasion of the first centenary of the foundation of the hospital. Later figure affixed to cross, not by Reeves. *In possession of St Vincent's Hospital, Dublin.*

Mullingar Town Trophy

Oxidised copper with silver and gold details, enamel, and marble. Reeves assisted in work by James Wallace. Made for presentation by the traders of Mullingar to the Westmeath GAA to commemorate the golden jubilee year of the association in October 1934. Presented in 1935; replaced in 1953 when won outright.

1935   **Irish Army Challenge Trophy**

Copper, brass, silver, gold, champlevé enamel, and marble. Signed with monogram. Made for presentation by the Irish Government to the National Horse Show Association of America.

Military Tattoo Trophy

Copper, with silver and gold inlaid and chased in the form of a plaque on a stand. Made for presentation by the Military Tattoo Committee to the Royal Dublin Society. Depicts a harpist with a horse and butterflies. Signed with monogram. *In possession of the Royal Dublin Society.* (cover illustration)

c 1935   **Drinking horn trophy**

Silver, with gilt bands, with a stand of bronze and ebony. Design founded on the Kavanagh Horn, a model of which is in the library of Trinity College, Dublin. 23" in length. Presented by the Minister for Defence to the Royal Dublin Society, for military jumping competition. *In possession of the Royal Dublin Society.* (Plate 12)

Oswald Reeves
top left   *11 – Candlestick in enamelled copper (c 1930)*
(photo: the author)
top right   *12 – Drinking horn trophy (c 1935)*
(photo: Reeves Collection)
13 – Plaque in St John's College Chapel, Sydney, Australia (c 1935)
(photo: Reeves collection)

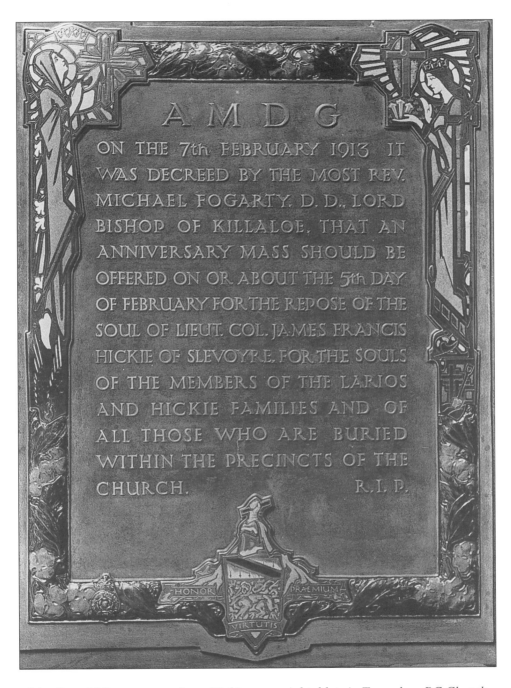

*14 – Oswald Reeves, one of two Hickie memorial tablets in Terryglass RC Church,
Co Tipperary (c 1935) (photo: Reeves collection)*

c 1935   **Memorial tablet**
in St John's College Chapel, Sydney, Australia
Sculptured bronze, inlaid with copper, gold, silver, and enamel. Commission of Mrs
F.B. Freehill. The design for the tablet was exhibited at the ACSI Tenth Exhibition,
Dublin, 1955. (Plate 13)

Hickie Memorial Tablets
in Terryglass RC Church, Co Tipperary
Two memorial tablets for members of the Hickie family commissioned by Major-
General Sir W.B. Hickie, K.C.B. of Slevoyre, Co Tipperary. Cast bronze in relief,
inlaid with copper, silver, gold and enamels; one tablet bearing the arms of the Hickie
family with figure subjects of the Assumption, and St Helena and the finding of the
Holy Cross; the other bearing the arms of the Larios family, with figures of Mary and
St Clare. Lettering on tablets by George Atkinson. Reeves assisted in execution of the
work by James Wallace. (Plate 14)

President's Badge, Belvedere College Union
Gold and enamels.

Plaque for presentation to Senator W. Quirke
Copper inlaid with gold, silver, and enamels, chased and engraved, in copper frame
and stand.

Large candlestick for dinner table centrepiece
Hammered copper with silver, brass, champlevé enamel enrichments.

1943   **President's Trophy for the Irish Red Cross**
Copper, silver, and brass with gold inlaid panels; in the form of a font with hinged
enamelled lid; figurative panels depicting scenes of healing after the legendary battle
of Clontarf. Signed with monogram. Exhibited at ACSI Tenth Exhibition, Dublin,
1955. *In possession of the Irish Red Cross Society.* (Plate 15)

c 1949   **Design for medal**
for Grand Master's Lodge Bicentenary 5749-5949. Carved plaster model for com-
memorative gold medal.

undated   **Hammered copper bowl**
Exhibited ACSI Tenth Exhibition, Dublin, 1955.

Bookplate for Julia, wife of Edward W. Allen
Signed with monogram. [Print among Reeves's papers.]

Enamelled metal coat of arms
mounted on the marble memorial to Lt. Henry Grove Mansel-Pleydell, M.C. of
Whatcombe and 1st Batt. Dorset Regiment, killed near Thiepval, France, 17 May

Oswald Reeves

15 – Design for a panel of the President's Trophy for the Irish Red Cross (c 1943)

16 – Design for enamel plaque on stand (n.d.)
(not known if executed)

1916. Location unknown. Presumably by Reeves. [Photograph among Reeves's papers.]

Circular metal box with enamels mounted on sides and lid
[Photograph among Reeves's papers.]

Enamelled metal plaque on stand
depicting a central female figure with arms upraised, flanked by attendant male figures bearing produce, with doves at their feet. [Photograph of poor quality among Reeves's papers.]

Tabernacle door panel
depicting 'The Pelican feeding its young'; design similar to that of Maguiresbridge R.C. church but with leafy branches framing the central panel. [Photograph among Reeves's papers.] (Plate 17)

Design for a tabernacle door panel, in coloured enamels
depicting 'Our Lord in Benediction'. [Coloured drawing among Reeves's papers.]

Design for an enamelled silver box
depicting winged horses and stars. [Coloured drawing among Reeves's papers, signed with monogram.]

Design for enamel panel
depicting a female figure with garland and doves. [Watercolour formerly in possession of Doreen Dickie, a pupil of Oswald Reeves in the 1920s; now in a private collection in Dublin.] (cover illustration)

Design for a plaque on stand
depicting a female figure with harp, doves, and fruit trees. [Drawing among Reeves's papers.] *Private collection, Dublin.* (Plate 16)

Reeves's notes, compiled sometime between *c* 1935 and *c* 1938, also list the following:

Pendant Cross, privately owned in New York, of silver.

Plaque, in collection of Duke of Bedford; painted enamel in silver frame.

Plaque, in collection of Earl of Dudley; painted enamel in copper frame.

Plaque, in private collection in Singapore; painted enamel in copper frame.

Plaque, in private collection in Canada; painted enamel in copper frame.

Plaque, presented to the German 'Flyers' when in Dublin; painted enamel in copper frame

———

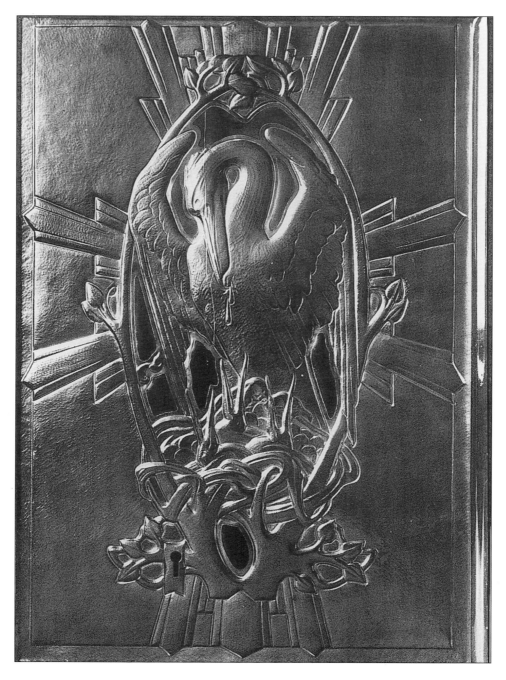

17 – Oswald Reeves, tabernacle door panel depicting
'The Pelican feeding its young' (n.d.) (photo: Reeves collection)

Dr Paul Larmour is Reader in Architecture at Queen's University, Belfast. His publications include *Celtic Ornament* (Dublin 1981), *Belfast: An Illustrated Architectural Guide* (Belfast 1987), and *The Arts and Crafts Movement in Ireland* (Belfast 1992).

ACKNOWLEDGEMENTS

The author wishes to thank Peter Lamb for his invaluable help in the preparation of this article and his generosity in allowing access to the Reeves collection and permitting items from it to be copied and reproduced here; and also to acknowledge the use of the Research Fund of the Queen's University of Belfast.

ENDNOTES

[1] See Paul Larmour, *The Arts and Crafts Movement in Ireland* (Belfast 1992); and Larmour, 'Arts and Crafts Movement', in B. de Breffny, ed., *Ireland: A Cultural Encyclopaedia* (London, 1983) 36. Biographical information on Reeves, compiled by the artist himself, and later by his widow, is contained in a small collection of papers, photographs, designs, undated news-cuttings, and his work book, formerly in the possession of his heirs, and now in a private collection in Dublin.

[2] In 1938 one of his works (the Grangegorman War Memorial) was illustrated in the section on enamelling in *Encyclopaedia Britannica*. In 1980 his work was acknowledged by Jeanne Sheehy in her book *The Rediscovery of Ireland's Past: The Celtic Revival 1830-1930* (London), and in 1983 he was accorded a brief biographical entry by this author in *Ireland: A Cultural Encyclopaedia*. Since then he has been discussed more fully, and a number of his works illustrated, in Larmour, *Arts and Crafts Movement*. See also Theo Snoddy, *Dictionary of Irish Artists: 20th Century* (Dublin 1996).

[3] Reeves's own work account book spans the years 1904 to 1922, but appears to have been compiled retrospectively as it is not in strict chronological order. It also contains some anomalies in dating.

[4] The flagon was illustrated in *The Studio*, March 1902, 117.

[5] The plaque entitled *A Falling Star* is illustrated in Larmour, *Arts and Crafts Movement,* 172. It should not be confused with the plaque entitled *Undine* in the collection of the Cecil Higgins Art Gallery in Bedford. The two plaques have been confused from time to time, as for example in the article 'Symbolism in Turn-of-the-century Irish Art', in *Irish Arts Review Yearbook 1989-90*, and again more recently in *The Arts and Crafts Movements in Dublin and Edinburgh* (Dublin 1998) 173, pl. xxi. *Undine* was previously illustrated in *Victorian and Edwardian Decorative Art: The Handley Read Collection* (Royal Academy of Arts, London 1972) 100 (cat. no. E109) but its title was not identified and it was wrongly attributed to Reeves's wife.

[6] Illustrated in Larmour (1992) 174.

[7] Illustrated in *ibid.*, 173.

[8] 'Irish Arts and Crafts', *The Studio*, October 1917, 15-22.

———

1 – Belsize House, c *1720*
(courtesy Conway Library, Courtauld Institute of Art)

The Irish in London:
post-Restoration suburban houses

CAROLINE KNIGHT

CONSIDERABLE RESEARCH IS BEING UNDERTAKEN INTO IRELAND'S ARCHITECT-
ural history, but there is another aspect that is sometimes overlooked: the
houses which aristocratic Irish families leased, bought, or inherited in
England. This article is concerned with a particular type of house, which could
loosely be described as a suburban villa, that is, neither the London house nor the
country estate of a family, but a moderately sized house and garden in the vicinity of
the capital. Defoe sums up their purpose:

> These fine houses ... are not, at least very few of them, the Mansion-Houses
> of families, the Ancient Residences of Ancestors, the Capital Messuages of
> Estates; nor have the rich possessors any Lands to a considerable Value about
> them; but these are all Houses of Retreat ... Gentlemen's meer Summer-
> Houses, or Citizen's Country Houses, whither they retire from the hurry of
> business ... to draw their breath in a clean air and to divert themselves and
> their families in the hot weather.[1]

Combined with this sense of privacy and retreat was the advantage of proximity to
London and to the court. Many of the Scots who accompanied James I to London
after 1603 had established themselves in and around London during the early seventeenth century; the Irish were to do so slightly later.

As England became increasingly prosperous through the sixteenth century,
villages within about ten miles of the capital were scattered with the fine houses of
rich City merchants and of courtiers. Some areas were particularly fashionable,
especially Hackney and Highgate to the north of the City, and the easily accessible
villages along the Thames such as Chelsea, Chiswick, Kew and Richmond. The
later Stuarts and the Hanoverians no longer favoured the royal palaces to the east of
London such as Greenwich or Eltham; instead, when not at Whitehall or St. James's
they moved westwards along the Thames to Richmond and Hampton Court, each of
which had gardens and two large hunting parks. Londoners followed, and by the

early eighteenth century it was the Thames-side villages which became the favourite retreats of the rich.

The three houses with which I am concerned all belonged to Irish courtiers in the period between the restoration of Charles II in 1660 and the death of Queen Anne in 1714. They are Daniel O'Neill's Belsize House in Hampstead, the 1st Earl of Burlington's Chiswick House, and the 2nd Duke of Ormonde's Ormonde Lodge in Richmond (Plate 2). Apart from their Irish owners and their proximity to London, these houses have little in common architecturally: Belsize was a new house, rebuilt after the Restoration and leased from the Church; Chiswick was a Jacobean house, which had already had many different owners when Burlington bought it in 1682; and Ormonde Lodge was a royal hunting lodge, altered by Ormonde before reverting to the Crown at his downfall in 1715. All three of these houses have gone, although the villa we see today at Chiswick was an addition of the 1720's to the Jacobean house. Belsize was demolished in the mid-eighteenth century and the site redeveloped a century later with substantial stuccoed houses; Ormonde Lodge was demolished in 1772 and the grounds incorporated into what is now the Royal Botanic Gardens at Kew. This is fairly typical of the fate of such houses: many were demolished and their grounds covered with speculative building; sometimes the house went but the gardens were made into a public park; and just occasionally – as at Chiswick – a building of exceptional architectural interest has been saved, together with its immediate surroundings.

2 – Map of the environs of London
showing the relative positions of Belsize House, Chiswick House and Ormonde Lodge

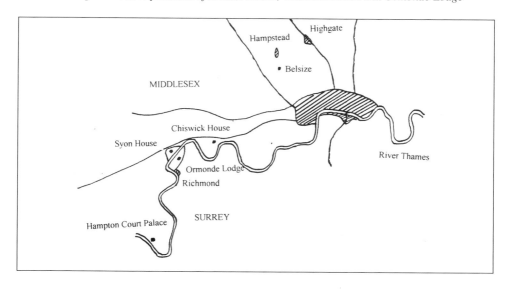

BELSIZE HOUSE

Daniel O'Neill (1612?-1664) was one of the few Irishmen to make his fortune directly through the sinecures he held as a result of his favour at court.[2] He belonged to an ancient Irish family who had been kings of Ulster but whose circumstances were greatly reduced. His father, Con O'Neill of Clandeboye, had already lost part of his estates through dubious dealings with two Scots who successfully claimed the remainder of the land over the next few years. Meanwhile Daniel was made a ward in Chancery to ensure his father's loyalty to the crown, and was taken to England to be brought up as a Protestant. He was the only member of his family not to be a Roman Catholic. This English upbringing gave him useful connections, and with his charm, intelligence and good looks he was able to make full use of them. Clarendon described him:

> Daniel O'Neile ... had a natural insinuation and address, which made him acceptable in the best company. He was a great observer and discerner of men's nature's and humours, and was very dexterous in compliance where he found it useful ... And though his inclinations were to ease and luxury, his industry was indefatigable, when his honour required it, or his particular interest ... made it necessary or convenient.[3]

As the younger son, Daniel had to make his own living and he decided on a military career, dividing his time between Britain and the Netherlands, where he was in contact with Elizabeth of Bohemia and fought bravely at the capture of Breda. By the outbreak of the Civil War he was an experienced soldier, diplomat and courtier, indispensable to the King. After many adventures during the war – imprisonment, escape, missions abroad, accompanying Charles II in his invasion of Scotland – he ended up in The Hague with the influential position of Groom of the Bedchamber to the exiled Charles II.

At the Restoration, O'Neill's loyalty was amply rewarded with sinecures, and it was these which made him wealthy enough to rebuild Belsize 'at vast expense', according to Evelyn.[4] His considerable income derived entirely from royal favour as he and his brother had been unable to reclaim their Irish inheritance, and even after his brother's death in the Civil War he had an income of only £160 per annum. As well as an annual pension of £500, he was given the monopoly of manufacturing gunpowder for the Crown, and was part of a syndicate with the right to mine north of the Trent and in Wales, but, most lucrative of all, he was made Postmaster-General in March 1663 – a post which he could not have held unless he were a member of the Church of England. For farming the posts he paid the Crown the considerable sum of £21,500 per annum, and was then entitled to any profits he could make. He also had a rich wife, having recently married the beautiful widow Katherine Wotton, created Countess of Chesterfield in her own right in 1660. She too was a courtier, having been part of the royal household in The Hague since 1641.[5] She had inherited her father's fine house at Boughton Malherbe in Kent, which she and O'Neill used as their country house. In addition, she had a London house at Spring Gardens in St. James's where her married daughter lived. As Lady Chesterfield was Lady in Waiting to Catherine of Braganza, they were also entitled to lodgings in Whitehall Palace, and it was here that O'Neill died.[6] So Belsize was for occasional use as a retreat from London.

Belsize House, when O'Neill took it over, was a large brick courtyard house, dating from about 1496. As its name implies, it enjoyed a fine position on the southern slopes of Hampstead Hill, sheltered, sunny and comparatively accessible, unlike the remote and as yet unfashionable village of Hampstead perched on the hill above (Plate 1). The property belonged to the Dean and Chapter of Westminster but had been leased to the distinguished Waad family from the mid-sixteenth century until they had lost possession under the Commonwealth. In spite of their efforts to reclaim it at the Restoration, they failed to dislodge the Parliamentarian Colonel Downes, and it was Daniel O'Neill who took out a new lease. This has usually been dated to about 1663, but it was actually on 28 January 1661 that the Chapter ordered that a lease be drawn up for twenty-one years 'for Mr.Oneale under the old rents and Covenants'.[7] Another Westminster document records an indenture of February 1661 made between 'Daniell Oneale one of the Grooms of his Maiesties Bedchamber' and the Dean and Chapter of Westminster of

> their Mannor ... and messuage of Bellsess situate ... in the parish of Hamsteed in the Countie of Middlx. together with all and singular the houses Tenemts Buildings lands Tylehouses meadows pastures hedgerows woods underwoods with sufficient Timber to bee taken from time to time for the maintenance of the aforesaid houses and all the ponds orchards and gardens with all and singular their profitts ...'

He paid the Dean and Chapter an annual rent of £38 5s 8d.[8] Usually these suburban houses had perhaps ten to thirty acres of gardens and fields, but Belsize had enough land to be a modest estate. The acreage is not given in these documents, but a map of 1713 shows the same estate with land stretching south into St John's Wood in the parish of Paddington, and gives the acreage as 233 acres.[9]

Documents relating to his new house are sparse, but there are two pieces of visual evidence: a map of 1679 and a print of about 1720 (Plate 1). This print shows

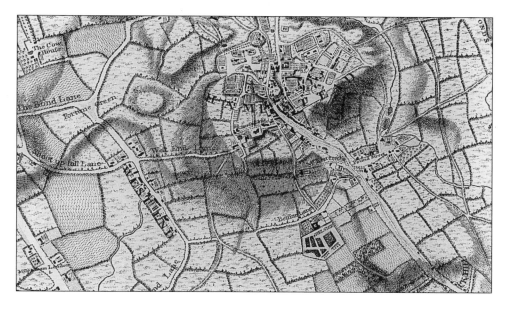

3 – Detail of Belsize and Hampstead from Rocque, 12
(courtesy London Topographical Society)

4 – Detail from 'A Mapp of the mannor of Belsize ... by Will. Gent Surveyor 1679'
pen and ink with some coloured wash outlines
(courtesy Camden Local Studies & Archives Centre)

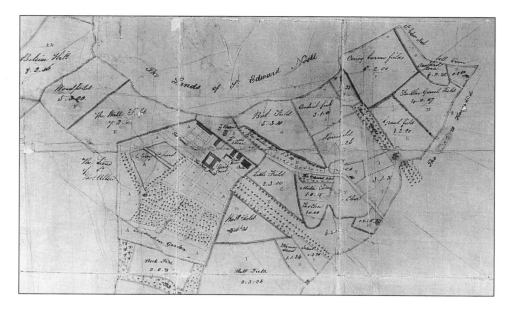

a typical Restoration house, presumably built of brick with stone quoins, rather Dutch in style, with two equal storeys over a semi-basement and with attics in a high hipped roof, the centre of which is crowned by a cupola. But this façade is deceptive: the 1679 map shows that it is only one side of a large courtyard house. This must be a rebuilding on the same site of the fifteenth-century house. The map allows us to work out its size: it was a substantial house approximately 40 x 37 metres (121 x 110 ft). The staircase seen in the print which clumsily connected the first floor to the gardens is the product of its conversion in 1720 into a place of entertainment, but otherwise there are few obvious changes from O'Neill's time. The Hearth Tax returns are a useful guide to the size of a house, but the 1664 returns (the most detailed for the late seventeenth century) register only sixteen hearths, suggesting that work was still in progress then.[10] O'Neill died in 1664 leaving Belsize to his wife. When she died there in 1667 she left to her younger son

> Charles Henry Lord Wootton all ... the Lease and Estate of and in the mannor of Belsize ... and my House scituate in the parish of Hampstead and all the money plate Jewells and ffurniture that I shall leave therein ... and all ... my Lease and Estate in the said Woods called St. John's Wood...

The will has a codicil which gives a little information about her belongings and her considerable wealth. She left to the King and Queen two of her most precious possessions: Charles II was to receive the 'Greate Pourslane Pott which is in my Gallery at Belsize and my blacke Indian Skreene', and the Queen was to receive 'my two Wyreworked candlesticks and a silver perfuming pot', though these are not specified as being at Belsize.[11] This impression of exotic furniture is confirmed by Evelyn: 'The furniture is very particular for Indian cabinets, Porcelane and other solid and noble moveables, the Gallery very fine.'[12]

Like so many of these suburban houses, the twenty-five acres of gardens were lavishly laid out, and we can get some idea of them from the map drawn by William Gent in 1679 (Plate 4). This shows the double avenue flanking the drive from Haverstock Hill (replanted with plane trees, this survives today as Belsize Avenue), the courtyard house behind a walled forecourt, and the irregular wall enclosing the gardens. Beyond the house was a straight walk, with the orangery marked as the long, low building facing south. To the south side of the house were formal areas, with the less formal 'Wilderness' beyond. The former consisted of grassed squares with a vase or statue in the centre of each, and below that the Wilderness was divided by straight paths with a fountain at the intersection. The service buildings were to the north-east of the house – a laundry, water house and stables inside the main enclosure and a barn outside. Pepys described the gardens in 1668 as 'wonderful fine; too good for the house, the gardens are; being endeed the most noble that ever I saw – and rare Orange and Lemon trees',[13] while Evelyn was less complimentary, describing in 1676 'the Gardens very large but ill-kept, yet Woody and chargeable; the mould a cold weeping clay, not answering the expense.'[14]

The splendid house did not last long. The Earl of Chesterfield sublet it in 1704 to an unscrupulous entrepreneur called Charles Povey, who extracted as much profit as he could by stripping the place of such assets as its timber and even the leadwork of the house.[15] Povey in turn sublet it to James Howell in 1720, and it briefly flourished as a fashionable place of entertainment such as Ranelagh Gardens was later to become. In 1733 the Chesterfields applied to the Dean and Chapter for permission to demolish Belsize 'which is by length of time and many accidents so decayed as to be brought into a ruinous condition and not to be supported without a very great Expense.' Permission to demolish was granted, but on condition that the house be replaced.[16] The exact date of demolition is not known: Rocque's map was prepared between 1741 and 1745, and still shows the courtyard house with its walled gardens, orangery and outbuildings (Plate 3). At some stage during the 1740s, a much smaller Belsize House was built, possibly incorporating part of O'Neill's house. In the early nineteenth century the land was split into smaller parcels and a new house was built on a different site, much closer to Haverstock Hill. From 1853 the site of the house and grounds was gradually developed with a mixture of detached and terraced houses, and today only a clutch of street names such as Belsize Park and Belsize Square record the existence of the house and gardens.

This house was only very briefly in Irish ownership, being left at O'Neill's death to his widow and then to his stepson, but it was O'Neill who made the decision to rebuild the old house and make it more splendid and up to date. In contrast, the Earl of Burlington was content to leave the old house he bought at Chiswick comparatively unaltered, and it was only about 1726 that his descendant, the 3rd Earl of Burlington, added the present Chiswick House to the earlier one.

———

CHISWICK HOUSE

Richard Boyle, 1st Earl of Burlington (1612-1698), was also 2nd Earl of Cork in the Irish peerage. Unlike O'Neill but like Ormonde, he was immensely rich through the rent roll of his huge estates. He was born and brought up in Ireland, the eldest surviving son of the powerful Richard Boyle, 1st Earl of Cork, a Protestant who had gone to Ireland in the late six-teenth century and had acquired enormous estates in Munster, with Lismore Castle as his main seat. He arranged good marriages for his large family, but Richard's was perhaps the most financially rewarding, his marriage to the English heiress Elizabeth Clifford bringing him vast estates in the north of England, including the Londesborough, Skipton and Bolton Abbey estates in Yorkshire. This Yorkshire link was recognised in his English peerage that he was given in 1665, as Burlington was the alternative name for Bridlington in the East Riding. With these vast estates and the local responsibilities which went with them – Burlington had two spells as Lord Lieutenant of the West Riding of Yorkshire – and a seat in the English House of Lords, he increasingly spent his time in England, although regularly visiting Dublin and keeping a careful watch over his Irish estates. In 1667 he bought the partly built Burlington House in Piccadilly, next to Lord Clarendon's splendid new town house, and soon after gave up his Dublin house. With his country estates far away in Ireland and in the north of England he also needed a house near London for his growing family, and in 1682 he paid Sir Edward Seymour, the Speaker of the House of Commons, the substantial sum of £4,800 for 'a Messuage and severall Lands ... at Chiswick in ye County of Middlx'.[17] The outbuildings included new stables and a coach house which Seymour had built that same year.

The house at Chiswick had been built in the early years of the seventeenth century by Sir Edward Wardour, and had then changed hands many times before Burlington bought it.[18] The riverside village of Chiswick was half a mile away to the east, and the house faced a quiet lane which skirted the water-meadows by the Thames.[19] It was a courtyard house, slightly smaller than Belsize, described by Bowack in 1706 as

> a noble antient Seat ... after the antient manner very regular and Strong. It has very many spacious rooms in it, and large gardens behind. In this Seat for-merly dwelt James Duke of Monmouth, it afterwards was purchas'd by the Right Honourable the Earl of Burlington where he Liv'd and Dy'd; his son the late Earl us'd commonly to dwell there during the Summer Season.[20]

Its site was much more 'suburban' than Belsize. Chiswick House was flanked to the west by Sutton Court, Lord Fauconberg's house, and to the east, Sir Stephen Fox's house, rebuilt by Hugh May in 1682-84, was even closer.[21] This meant that the gardens were mainly behind the house, and amounted to only fifteen acres, with a few other scattered plots of land which were rented in the parish.

As so often with lost seventeenth-century houses, there is little visual evidence for the original house, no known plan or inventory, and practically no contemporary comment. The house was demolished by the 5th Duke of Devonshire in 1788 to make way for the new wings he added to the 3rd Earl's villa.[22] The main source for the early house is the Kip engraving of about 1710 (Plate 5). Kip shows a substantial brick courtyard house of two storeys with attics; the attic windows are set in shaped gables and the roofline is punctuated by tall chimneys. A small walled forecourt opened onto the road, beyond which an avenue led down to the water-meadows by the Thames. Service buildings, rebuilt by Kip's time, were to the side, and a formal garden was laid out behind and beside the house. The boundary with Fauconberg's house was a small stream, the Bollo Brook, which was enlarged into the present lake by the 3rd Earl. There appear to be no garden buildings; the large orangery to the right of the house belonged to the adjoining property. The axis of the gardens behind the house is preserved in the gardens of Chiswick House today, where the eighteenth-century villa is not aligned on the main avenue.

It seems unlikely that the 1st Earl made any important alterations to the house. He was notoriously frugal in his habits and unlikely to spend large sums on Chiswick, which he must have considered as much less important than his country seat. Having completed his London house, he began major works on both house and grounds at Londesborough in 1672.[23] This substantial late-sixteenth-century house was finely sited on the southern slopes of the Yorkshire Wolds. Robert Hooke was possibly employed by Burlington to update and enlarge it, and to lay out the large formal gardens on three sides of the house. A Kip view of about 1700 shows the formal gardens, possibly also designed by Hooke, on three sides of the house. The 6th Duke of Devonshire demolished the house in 1818, but as so often there was no incentive to level the gardens, so some of the hillside terraces can still be seen, and traces of avenues.[24]

———

page 70   5 – *Kip, view of Chiswick, c 1710*
             (*courtesy Conway Library, Courtauld Institute of Art*)

page 71   6 – *Thomas Sandby, Ormonde or Richmond Lodge, Kew, c 1770?*
             (*The Royal Collection, Her Majesty Queen Elizabeth II*)

ORMONDE LODGE

The lack of information about Chiswick is in stark contrast to the records of Ormonde Lodge, where, due to the impeachment of the Duke of Ormonde, a full inventory was made of the saleable contents of his house and garden in 1716. This house was Crown property, attached to Richmond Palace on the Thames (Plate 7). This is a detail of Rocque's 1746 map (and was therefore surveyed after alterations to the gardens made by Queen Caroline). It shows the position of the house – it is across the Thames from 'the Duke of Somerset's Syon House', and about a mile north of the village of Richmond. The Palace at Richmond was no longer in royal use during the reign of William and Mary. Instead William III, who loved hunting, improved the lodge in the Old Deer Park, known as Richmond Lodge, for himself, and also updated the gardens.[25] These lodges were often held by the Ranger of the Park, and it was through his post as Ranger that Ormonde had the opportunity to take out a lease after William's death.

James Butler, 2nd Duke of Ormonde (1665-1745) was much more closely involved with Irish affairs than either O'Neill or Burlington. He came from one of the great Irish families, most of whom were Roman Catholics, although he was a Protestant, and a patron of Swift.[26] The Ormondes had large estates at Kilkenny, Dunmore and Clonmel, with a rent roll estimated at £25,000 per annum in 1688. His main country house was the ancient Kilkenny Castle, but he also had lodgings in Dublin Castle. As Lord Butler of Moore Park he was also entitled to sit in the English House of Lords, and from 1685 to 1688 he was a Gentleman of the Bedchamber to James II.[27] In spite of this, he supported his cousin William of Orange in 1688 – Ormonde's mother was Dutch – and fought for him in Ireland, Flanders and Spain. With the accession of Queen Anne he was made Lord Lieutenant of Ireland, and later replaced Marlborough as her Commander-in-Chief. He remained high in the Queen's favour, so much so that she insisted he did not risk his life nor her armies while in command in Europe. The manner in which he followed her secret instructions and failed to support the allies – which included Hanover – was later to be the one of the charges against him. After the accession of George I he was immediately dismissed, and the House of Commons voted by a narrow majority to impeach him. He avoided his trial by fleeing to Paris in 1715, where he joined the court of the Old Pretender. He died in Avignon in 1745.

In 1682 – the year in which he married his first wife, Lord Burlington's niece – he bought a fine London house in the newly developed St James's Square. He also had lodgings in Whitehall Palace. Richmond, 'the prettiest place in the world',[28] would have been a convenient retreat between Hampton Court – much used by Queen Anne – and London. He was granted a ninety-nine year lease on the lodge and various pieces of ground in May 1704.[29] When he went into exile in 1715 and was later impeached in his absence, his property and goods were forfeit, and it is due to the detailed inventories drawn up for the Forfeit Estates Commissioners that we know so much about his house and its furnishings. There are no known depictions of the house in Ormonde's time, but a later eighteenth-century watercolour of the south front gives us some idea of its appearance (Plate 6). It was a brick house with two ranges divided by an entrance forecourt on the east side, a service court-yard to the west, and a central core of hall and staircases. The advantage of this plan was that all the main rooms overlooked the gardens, either north to the Thames or south towards Richmond; the disadvantage was the rather awkward circulation.

As a busy man, constantly on the move between his Irish estates, court duties and military commands, Ormonde could not oversee the alterations he wished to make to his new house, so various Irish friends and relations supervised the work. There are references to his brother-in-law and cousin, the 1st Earl of Grantham, and in one of the latter's letters is a tantalising entry which might be to the architect Sir John Vanbrugh. Grantham writes, '*J'ay paye, selon vos ordres, a M. Van Brugh cinquante guinées.*' [30] Grantham was helped in his supervision by the Earl of Arran, Ormonde's younger brother, and by the Earl of Ranelagh. The latter described himself as Ormonde's *surintendant*, although his history of financial mismanagement and extravagance makes him seem a brave choice.[31] Their letters to Ormonde throw some light on the expensive works on both house and gardens which, in spite of William III's recent expenditure, were begun at once. There is no mention of the Duchess of Ormonde making any contribution to the changes, [32] nor are there any references to an architect (apart from the payment above to Vanbrugh), but a carpenter called Churchill was in charge of the works. This was almost certainly John Churchill, Master Carpenter at the Office of Works from 1706 to 1715. Ranelagh went down from London for occasional visits on site, dealt with the accounts and with payments to the various bricklayers, plumbers, slaters, smiths and carpenters, and reported back to Ormonde on progress.

The garden front of the house was to be redesigned with Churchill in charge of the estimates. In December 1704, Ranelagh sent Ormonde a 'draught for the garden front ... under the upright of the front you will find as much of the grounde plotte as is necessary to make everything cleare.' Another letter explains that this was simply a refacing of the existing front, 'a new coat', as Ranelagh puts it, with arched 'sachée windows' in rubbed brickwork. This probably means the north front, overlooking the more important riverside gardens; the arched windows may be similar to the arched second-floor windows which can be seen in the Sandby water-colour of the south front. (There is no known illustration of the north front.) A letter from Grantham in February 1705 tells Ormonde that

> *Tous s'avance beaucoup a Richemont; on a abattu tout ce qu'il y avoit a abattre et toutte la peinture est presque finie. My Lord Ranela a été hier avec moi pour ordonner votre ameublement, on nous a promis que tout servit fait dans un mois; esperre que vous trouverrés a votre gré.*[33]

Expensive work in the gardens included building two new 'green houses' to shelter orange trees. As at the exactly contemporary Kensington Palace orangery, these were to be wainscoted and well floored to serve as summer rooms when the trees were outdoors. Ranelagh suggests using best Swedish marble for the floors 'much handsomer [than tiles] when your orange trees are removed', but it turned out to be unobtainable in London that year, so an inferior stone was used instead. When the contents were inventoried in 1716 there were one hundred large and eighty-four small orange trees, worth a total of £48, as well as pomegranates, 'Malibo nutt trees', myrtles and bay trees.

Creating a terrace and a pond in the gardens involved considerable amounts of earth-moving, and Ranelagh had to point out to Ormonde how high wages were compared to Ireland, 'particularly in the digging and removal of earth, for there hands are cheap, but here very deare, especially soe neare London as Richmond is'.[34] In charge of the garden alterations were 'Ingeneer O'Brien', who seems to have been in overall charge of the garden works, and Reading 'the leveller' with his team of labourers. They dug a 'great pond' to be fed from springs beneath it, which was then to be stocked with fish. The river walk had a summer house overlooking the Thames, which can be seen on Rocque's map, almost opposite the gardens of Syon House. According to the Forfeit Estates Commissioners, this was comfortably furnished, with '8 leather chairs' and a couch worth £7, two Dutch 'sea-peices' worth £4, an overmantel mirror and sconces and '2 small oval tables'. There were also '18 Leaden Gilt flower potts' worth £22 arranged along the wall of the 'Little Garden', perhaps that to the south of the house.[35] Outside the immediate garden was a 'plantation' stocked with young trees, fenced off with pales and 'planted with quick sette which will hinder rabbits and hares from attaquing them'. Macky described the gardens in 1722:

> There is a fine avenue that runs from the Front of the house to the Town of Richmond, at half a mile's distance one way, and from the other front to the River-side, both inclosed with Ballustrades of Iron. The Gardens are very spacious and well-kept. There is a fine Terrace towards the River. But above

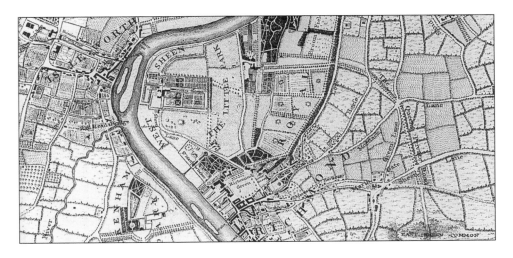

7 – Detail of Richmond Old Park and Thames from Rocque, 15
(*courtesy London Topographical Society*)

8 – The ground floor of Ormonde Lodge, Kew, together with its service buildings
(*The Royal Collection, Her Majesty Queen Elizabeth II*)

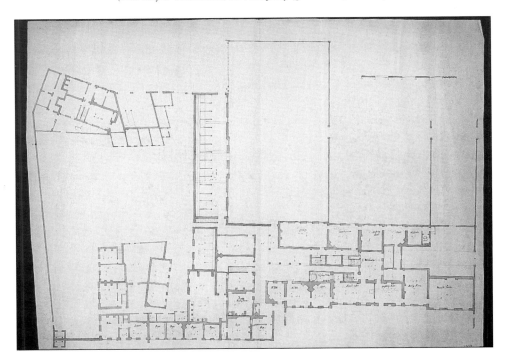

all the Wood cut out into Walks, with the plenty of Birds singing in it, makes it one of the most delicious Habitations.[36]

The house would need furnishing, and in January 1705 Ranelagh had begun considering 'the furnishing [of] your apartment at Richmond' together with Grantham and the craftsmen. By mid-June he was able to tell Ormonde that

> he will find his Marly ready to receive him ... Your four commissioners [Ranelagh, Grantham, Kendall and Arran] dined [at Richmond] yesterday to see your own apartment entirely furnished ... Your bathing apartment will also be ready and furnished by the end of next week, and though we cannot assure you as yet that you shall not see workmen there when you first visit it, yet you may depend upon it they shall not trouble you with their noise.[37]

Turning to the inventory prepared by the Forfeit Estates Commissioners, we can get some idea of the layout and furnishing of this house.[38] There is also a series of plans of the house and service buildings in the Royal Library which probably date from about 1771-72, that is, just before its demolition (Plate 8). Combining the information from these two sources, we can build up a picture of the house, which with all its alterations was curiously haphazard in its planning. The Sandby watercolour shows an addition to the right, marked on the plan as 'Musick Room' and the plan shows another large room marked 'Library' on the north front; both of these rooms were probably added by George III, as was the narrow entrance hall. Other changes, such as the 'Bagnio' which projected into the colonnaded service courtyard, were probably made by Queen Caroline, but the other rooms seem little changed from Ormonde's time.

In 1716 Lord Grantham was living in part of the house and had signed an agreement with the government not to remove any contents; he had brought in a few pieces of his own furniture, which are noted in the draft but omitted in the final copy. Although not large, Ormonde Lodge was luxuriously furnished, with a valuable Tompion clock in the entrance-cum-staircase hall, marked 'Antichamber' on the plan.

The great dining room, marked 'Dining Room' (to the west of the music room addition) was furnished with a set of twelve crimson damask chairs, and would have been brilliantly lit by '7 large oval glass sconces double branch't'. The paintings here were considered important enough to list specifically; as usual these are described by subject matter rather than by artist. There were two overdoor paintings with half-lengths of Dutch admirals, a 'large picture of the Holy Family' over the chimney-piece and another one opposite, and portraits, including one of the 1st Duke of Ormonde. Adjoining, marked 'Dressing Room', was the Little Dining

Room, and a small 'Sideboard Room' could be used for either. This had a 'white marble cistern & black marble Stand' and the 'Japan Iron cistern' may have been fitted into the niche marked on the plan.

The ground-floor apartment of yellow damask bedchamber, dressing room and closet had the most expensive furnishings, with the bed protected by case curtains and the matching settee, chairs and stools by covers. The dressing room had specified oil paintings: '2 sea pieces and a still life'. Beyond it another 'Closet within the dressing room' contained a number of 'Indian pictures' as well as a glazed bookcase of walnut and several maps, and beyond was the 'Closet for Necessary House' with its close stool. These rooms were probably the 'Dressing Room' and 'Closet' on the north front, and the two small closets beyond. The rather male furnishings – sea paintings, maps and a bookcase – suggest that this may have been Ormonde's own apartment.

On the south front was the well furnished 'Room leading to the Garden' which had a 'flowered damask couch' and matching stools, and no less than four pier glasses 'in glass frames'. This was probably the room marked 'Bedroom' on the south front, between the little dining room and the closets beyond. There is no saloon in the inventory, but this room, with its expensive furnishings and tapestry hangings, may well have served as the withdrawing room. Beyond lay the 'Bagnio' with its expensive 'blew and white calico bed lin'd', but with no information as to the bathing arrangements.[39]

The staircase was lit by a hanging lantern, and was decorated with '5 Indian pieces in Pannells'. This may have been similar to the almost contemporary Japan Room in Buckingham House, where black lacquer panels were inset as part of the decorative scheme.[40] At the top of the stairs was hung a plan of the house. On the first floor was the 'First bed chamber' which had a bed hung with green flowered silk, walls hung with silk and white damask curtains. This was followed by 'My Lord's bedchamber' probably referring to that used by Grantham, and 'My Lady's Closet'. There is no identifiable reference either to the Duke's or Duchess's bedchambers, dressing rooms or closets, again suggesting that Ormonde's rooms were below, the only other well furnished room being that of Lady Frances Coote with its tapestry hangings and blue damask bed with matching window curtains. The rest of the first-floor bedrooms were more modestly furnished and apparently belonged to members of the household. Footmen slept in the garret.

Only three rooms had tapestry: the 'Room leading to the garden,' Lady Frances Coote's bedchamber, and the housekeeper's room. None is described, but they were respectively valued at £18, £3 and £4, the latter two presumably of indifferent quality. The high value of the tapestry in the 'Room leading to the Garden' again suggests it was the withdrawing room, for which tapestry would have been a suitable wall-covering. The house was full of pictures – oil paintings, prints, maps, and at least sixty-seven 'Indian pictures' in various of the main rooms. There is no clue as to the subject matter of these, and only one reference to size – the little dining room had '16 Indian pictures Great & Small'. The latter could possibly have been Indian miniatures; certainly some were imported into Europe during the seventeenth century, especially via the Netherlands, and Ormonde with his Dutch connections and military service abroad could have inherited or bought them. But the term Indian is used so loosely at this time that it is also possible that they were Chinese, though these would have been much rarer.[41] He clearly shared the fashionable taste for the exotic oriental style as the inventory listed sets of japanned furniture as well as the staircase panels. Not surprisingly, there was also a strong Dutch influence in the furnishings, with a Delft pot in the great dining room fireplace, Dutch chairs and Dutch paintings.

After the sale of Ormonde's goods, his brother the Earl of Arran was allowed by Parliament to buy his estates, but he did not keep Ormonde Lodge, selling it in July 1719:

> Yesterday the house of the late Duke of Ormonde at Richmond was put to sale at Auction before the Commissioners of forfeited estates and bought by the Prince [of Wales and later George II] for £600. No body bid upon his Royal Highness.[42]

Macky describes it at this time as 'a perfect Trianon ... It does not appear with the Grandeur of a Royal Palace, but is very neat and pretty.'[43] It became one of the favourite retreats of George II and Queen Caroline, and in 1727 it was settled on the latter as her dower house. It was after this that Queen Caroline laid out her celebrated gardens with the help of William Kent, keeping some features of the older layout but adding winding walks and curious garden buildings such as the Hermitage and Merlin's Cave.[44] The house was demolished by George III in 1772 when he planned his great new palace at the northern end of Kew Gardens.

These three owners were the earliest Irish courtiers to establish themselves near London, but later in the eighteenth century there were a few other Irish aristocrats who acquired houses in the vicinity of the capital. The Earl of Grantham, whom we have already seen advising Ormonde on his building projects, bought Grove House in Chiswick, probably in the late 1740s. He died in 1754. Another Irishman, Lord Dunkerron, joined him in the same parish, buying Heathfield House in 1747. He died three years later. The common factor with both these owners was their age – these men found the environs of London both peaceful and convenient; they did not need large family houses such as Belsize or Chiswick House, nor elaborate and expensive gardens such as those at Ormonde Lodge.

CONCLUSION

The cult of the country house and the expansion of London have combined to diminish the importance of these suburban houses to us today. But in their time they were conspicuous and well known. Kip's views included several of these suburban houses as well as many substantial country seats. Belsize was unusual in not being on a main route out of London, but Chiswick and Ormonde Lodge could be seen by anyone travelling along the Thames. Throughout the eighteenth century, foreigners described seeing them: Saussure, 'going down the river from Hampton Court to London', mentioned Chiswick as one of the principal houses which could be seen along the river. Ormonde Lodge he referred to as 'small, but in good taste', and praised its gardens.[45] Modest in scale some of them may have been, but they were lavishly and comfortably furnished, as we have seen from Ormonde's inventory. It was easy to see the latest fashions in London, simple to order fine quality goods, less expensive to redecorate and furnish a comparatively small house than a great country one. Perhaps there was also a sense in which the state rooms of a great country house should display a formal and traditional style, while in a lesser house decoration could be both more informal and more fashionable.

For garden enthusiasts also there were many advantages over the country. The landscape along the Thames might be too flat for dramatic views, but the houses along its banks themselves provided the interest: Ormonde Lodge looked across the Thames to the park and ancient silhouette of Syon House. The gentle climate of the Thames valley allowed the cultivation of exotic plants, and nurseries such as that at Brompton were set up to supply native plants, as well as those imported from Holland or newly discovered in more remote places.[46] Garden enthusiasts could meet to discuss the latest botanical discoveries, and could easily visit each other's gardens, just as Evelyn called in to look at Belsize. Lastly, it is worth considering whether these three houses – owned, altered and embellished by Irish owners – are in any way recognisably Irish in their appearance, furnishings or surroundings. They are not. Houses like these were changing hands throughout the seventeenth and eighteenth centuries, and were bought by royalty, courtiers and merchants, whether of Continental, Scottish, English or Irish origin. These suburban houses reflected the personal preferences of their owners, not their origins.

———

Caroline Knight is a freelance lecturer specialising in seventeenth and eighteenth-century British architecture and patronage. Her research project on the history of Kensington Palace led to her current research into suburban houses near London.

ACKNOWLEDGEMENT

I am grateful to Dr Jane Fenlon for drawing my attention to the inventories of Ormonde Lodge, and for her help on various aspects of the patronage of the Duke of Ormonde.

ABBREVIATIONS

HMC	Historic Manuscripts Commission
Kip	*Britannia Illustrata*, or *Views of several of the Queen's Palaces and also of the Principal Seats of the Nobility & Gentry of Great Britain* (London 1714)
LMA	London Metropolitan Archives
PRO	Public Record Office
Rocque	John Rocque, *An Exact Survey of the City's of London & Westminster ye Borough of Southwark & the Country 10 Miles round London* (London 1746; reprinted London Topographical Society 1971)
WAM	Westminster Abbey Muniments

Dates are new style.

ENDNOTES

[1] Daniel Defoe, *A Tour through the Whole Island of Great Britain* (London 1724) 126.

[2] D.F. Cregan 'An Irish Cavalier:Daniel O'Neill', *Studia Hibernica*, 3 and 4 (1964) and 5 (1965). These articles contain detailed research into O'Neill's family background, education and politics, as well as covering his exploits as a soldier both before and during the Civil War. The coverage of his last few years is relatively cursory.

[3] Edward, Earl of Clarendon, *The History of the Rebellion & Civil Wars in England*, 8 vols (Oxford 1826) v, 98-99.

[4] Guy de la Bédoyère, ed., *The Diary of John Evelyn* (Bangor 1994) 239. Entry for 21 June 1676.

[5] Katherine Wotton married first Henry Stanhope, by whom she had one surviving son who later inherited Belsize. She married secondly the Dutch Jan van der Kerchhove; their son Lord Wotton inherited Belsize on his mother's death. Kerchove died in March 1660, and his widow was given her title in May, *Complete Peerage* (1913) ii, 106; iii, 180-81. The exact date of her marriage to O'Neill is unknown, but was probably soon afterwards.

[6] He was buried at Boughton Malherbe, and there are fragments of his splendid tomb in the church. See J. Newman, *West Kent & The Weald, Buildings of England* (1969)167. In her will the Countess of Chesterfield asks her son Philip Earl of Chesterfield to erect the monument,

the total cost not to exceed £300.

[7] WAM Chapter Act Book, 1660-1662. This entry proves that Bushell's lease, given in 1642 to his wife Lady Anne Waad for twenty-one years, had not expired when O'Neill's lease was granted.

[8] WAM Lease Book XVI, *A Register booke of all Leases & grants...* f 173.

[9] WAM Map no. 12450 by Grove. This was probably commissioned by the Dean and Chapter of Westminster at the death in January 1714 of Philip Stanhope, 2nd Earl of Chesterfield, who had inherited Belsize after the death of his step-brother, Lord Wotton.

[10] LMA MR/TH/3 has the 1664 Hearth Tax returns for Hampstead. Colonel Daniel O'Neill heads the list with sixteen hearths. The largest house in the parish is Lady Vane's with twenty-four hearths. A large courtyard house such as Belsize would be likely to have about that number. T.J. Barratt in his *Annals of Hampstead*, 3 vols (London 1912) iii, 366, gives O'Neill's as seven, and misreads Lady Vane as Lady Ware.

[11] PROB/11 323 Will of the Countess of Chesterfield. She also left a considerable amount of gold and silver plate, cash and jewellery. £1,000 at Belsize she had set aside to renew the lease of Belsize, and this was bequeathed to her son Lord Wotton for that purpose. O'Neill's will (PROB/11 315) leaves Belsize to his wife but gives no further details.

[12] *Diary of John Evelyn*, 239.

[13] R. Latham and W. Matthews, eds, *The Diary of Samuel Pepys*, 11 vols (London 1970-1983) ix, 281. Pepys visited it when it was owned by Charles Henry Kirkhoven (as he anglicised his name), the son of the Countess of Chesterfield by her second husband. Charles was created Lord Wotton in 1650 and given the Irish title Earl of Bellomont in 1680 (although he was not Irish by birth, his father being Dutch). Entry for 17 August 1668.

[14] *Diary of John Evelyn*, 239, as above.

[15] WAM 16486. An anonymous letter of complaint about Povey's depradations was sent to Chesterfield in 1714. WAM 16483 is Povey's letter refuting this.

[16] WAM Lease Book XXXIV, f 577.

[17] The 'Bill of Sale & Surrender for the Estate at Chiswick' is dated 11 December 1682. See Devonshire MSS, Chatsworth, L/32/1.

[18] These constant changes of ownership are a feature of these suburban houses. Between Sir Edward Wardour and Sir Edward Seymour, the house was owned by Robert Carr, Earl of Somerset; Philip Herbert, Earl of Pembroke; John Poulett, Lord Poulett; John and Elizabeth Ashburnham; James, Duke of Monmouth; Charles, Lord Gerrard; and Richard Jones, Lord Ranelagh (who was Burlington's nephew and who features in this article supervising works at Ormonde Lodge). See *Victoria County History, Middlesex* (Oxford 1982) vii, 74. After being bought by Lord Burlington it passed by descent to the Dukes of Devonshire, and remained in their possession until they sold it in 1929 to Middlesex County Council.

[19] The present Chiswick House used to be much closer to the road. Under the 6th Duke of Devonshire, the road was moved towards the Thames to give the house more privacy.

[20] John Bowack, *Antiquities of Middlesex* (London 1706).

[21] Both Sutton Court and Sir Stephen Fox's house were later absorbed into the grounds of Chiswick House.

[22] There is also a Rigaud drawing of *c* 1728 which shows the old house with the alterations to the façade and to one side carried out by the 3rd Earl of Burlington, but we can still see the Jacobean features of the old brick house.

[23] Information on Burlington's finances and estates are taken from T.C. Barnard, 'Land & the Limits of Loyalty', *Lord Burlington: Art, Architecture & Life* (London 1995) 167-200.

[24] The Kip print is reproduced in N. Pevsner & D. Neave, *Yorkshire: York and the East Riding, The Buildings of England* (London 1995) 603.

[25] See H.M. Colvin, ed., *The History of the King's Works*, 6 vols (London 1976) v, for a general history of Richmond Lodge and its surroundings.

[26] His grandfather, the 1st Duke, had been taken to England like O'Neill and brought up as a Protestant. See J.C. Beckett, *The Cavalier Duke: A Life of James, Duke of Ormonde 1610-1688* (Belfast 1990).

[27] Vicary Gibbs, ed., *The Complete Peerage* (London 1913) x, 157-61. In 1661 his grandfather had bought Moor Park in Hertfordshire as his suburban house, but was so deeply in debt that it was sold in 1670.

[28] *HMC New Series* (London 1920) viii, 79. Letter from Sir Richard Coxe to Ormonde dated 25 May 1704.

[29] *Calendar of Treasury Books 1704-1705* (London 1938) ixx, 169.

[30] *HMC New Series*, viii, 140. Letter from the Earl of Grantham to Ormonde, dated 24 February 1705. Vanbrugh was Comptroller of the Office of Works at this time, and it is therefore possible that he would have been involved in the project.

[31] Richard Jones, 1st Earl of Ranelagh (1641-1712), also Irish, had been a powerful figure at the court of Charles II and under William and Mary. While Treasurer of the Royal Hospital, Chelsea, he built Ranelagh House for himself on adjoining land. He was in charge of royal parks and their buildings from 1700-1702, and would therefore have been responsible for the lodge and Old Deer Park. In 1703 he had been expelled from the House of Commons for misappropriation of funds. He 'hath no great Estate, yet hath spent more money, built more fine Houses, and laid out more on Household-Furniture and Gardening than any other nobleman in England.' J. Macky, 'Characters', *Roxburghe Club* (1895) 67.

[32] The Duke of Ormonde in 1685 had married his second wife Mary Somerset, daughter of the Duke of Beaufort and a Lady of the Bedchamber to Queen Anne. She died in 1733.

[33] *HMC New Series*, viii, 140, as above. Henry d'Auverquerque, 1st Earl of Grantham (c 1672-1754) was born in Holland and was related to Ormonde through the latter's Dutch mother, Emilia van Beverwaert; he would have been equally fluent in Dutch and French. He explains that the work is progressing well, painting is nearly finished, and that he and Ranelagh have been ordering furnishings. He hopes the work will be completed to Ormonde's satisfaction within a month.

[34] *HMC 7th Report*, ii, appendix, 774-76. Reading was to be paid two instalments of £100 each in 1705, with the balance later.

[35] This and other references to the appraisals drawn up for the Forfeit Estates Commission come from PRO FEC 1/879, and FEC 1/887. The former is a draft for the latter (see note 32).

[36] John Macky, *A Journey through England* (London 1723) 66.

[37] *HMC New Series*, viii, 160. Letter from Ranelagh to Ormonde in Ireland dated 16 June 1705.

[38] PRO FEC 1/880 'An exact appraisment of the Goods of the late Duke of Ormond in his late Dwelling House at Old Richmond Park in the County of Surrey Viz. August 4th 1716.'

[39] The inventory records 'In the Yard. An Engine with pipes and cocks to fling up ye Water for the use of the house' valued at £21. There is a bath clearly marked on the plan, but this was probably installed by Queen Caroline.

[40] These panels were recorded by Pyne in 1820, and are illustrated in D. Watkin, *The Royal Interiors of Regency England* (London 1984) 86.

[41] I am grateful to Robert Skelton for his help over imports of Indian works of art into western Europe during the seventeenth century.

[42] Pue's *Occurrences*, xvi, no. 58, 14 July 1719.

[43] Macky, *Journey*, i, 66.

[44] William Kent's garden buildings are described in Colvin's *History of the King's Works*, v, 221-24.

[45] C. de Saussure, *A Foreign View of England in the Reigns of George I and George II*, translated and edited by von Muyden (London 1902) 143, 146

[46] Stephen Switzer in his *Gardener's Recreation* (1715) 49, states that London & Wise's business at the Brompton Nursery was valued at £30-40,000 per year.

———

1 – Portumna Castle, Co Galway, built by Richard, 4th Earl of Clanricard, c 1610-18
(courtesy Dúchas the Heritage Service, Dept of Arts, Heritage, Gaeltacht and the Islands)

Some early seventeenth-century building accounts in Ireland

JANE FENLON

T HIS INTRODUCTORY ARTICLE SETS OUT TO EXPLORE, THROUGH THE MEDIUM OF documents, some of the facts about building in Ireland during the early years of the seventeenth century. Material is taken from account books and from contracts drawn up between employers and their workmen. A selection of relevant documents is reproduced at the end of this text.

According to Rolf Loeber, 'buildings were erected at an unprecedented rate', in Ireland during the first three decades of the seventeenth century.[1] Large tracts of land had changed hands and newcomers like Richard Boyle, later 1st Earl of Cork, and Sir Laurence Parsons, with his brother William and others, were busy acquiring property. Once settled, building would help consolidate their claims on lands. Initially, many of the settlers enlarged and improved old buildings on the site; later new houses were built. Long-established landowners such as the Earls of Clanricard were also building at this time. A splendid new house was erected at Portumna, and improvements were carried out to other Clanricard properties at Loughrea and Tir Oileán (Terryland) (Plate 1). Others, like Walter, 11th Earl of Ormond, were making improvements to their ancestral castles. The O'Briens were also busy building, and at Bunratty Castle there are traces of the fashionable decorative plasterwork that was installed at that time (Plate 2).[2] Many other houses of varying sizes were being built or altered during the period, but these do not concern us for the purposes of this article.[3]

SOURCES AND METHODS

Two account books dating from about the 1620s or 1630s have been consulted. The first, a meticulously detailed book of accounts at Birr Castle, Co Offaly, which provides the basis for this article, was kept for and by Sir Laurence Parsons from the time he took over the O'Carroll castle at Birr in 1620 until his death eight years

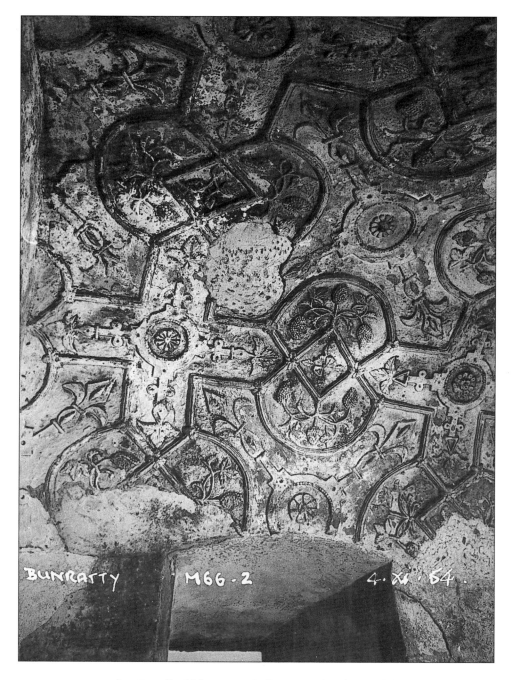

2 – Detail of Plasterwork, Bunratty Castle, c 1600
(courtesy Dúchas)

later.[4] The second, an account book kept by John Shee, Steward, probably for Walter Butler, 11th Earl of Ormond, includes payments for work at Kilkenny Castle and other Ormonde properties.[5] In addition, from the huge archive of Cork papers, a few entries have been extracted in order to provide comparisons with those of Birr.[6]

The Birr accounts record that Sir Laurence took over extensive buildings from the O'Carrolls; a castle, gate-house, flanker, dungeon and bawn are mentioned. These structures were extensively remodelled for their new owner, additions were made, and several new buildings were erected on the site (Plate 3). All of this activity, and more, is described on page after page of the account book. Written contracts are recorded in the same book.[7] A wealth of material about the settling in of a new landowner is available here; for instance, how Parsons arranged his finances, and how, as the years went by, his expenditure increased on his building projects. The Ormond account book contains far less information on buildings. Most of the entries are concerned with day to day spending on clothes, medicines, transport and suchlike.

Lord Cork's voracious acquisition of lands meant that he was engaged in a massive building programme that continued for most of his life.[8] This activity con-

3 – Birr Castle, Co Offaly, pen and ink drawing 1668
(courtesy the Earl and Countess of Rosse)

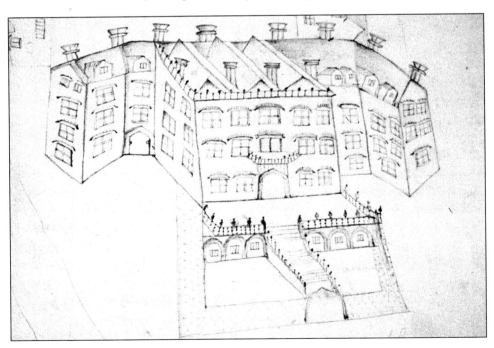

tinued even during the later 1630s when Cork was spending more time at his English properties.[9] In Ireland, many of his building projects consisted of altering existing structures, as at Dublin, Youghal, Askeaton, Maynooth and other sites. He also spent a considerable amount of money on new building. There are accounts for the building of a church, school, five almshouses, and work on two market houses, the walls and other structures in the town of Bandon.[10]

In his work on building history in England during the sixteenth and seventeenth centuries, Malcolm Airs charts the changes from the medieval system of direct labour to the more modern method of piece work.[11] He describes the principal methods by which workmen were paid. The direct method, generally, was when the employer undertook to supply all materials and equipment and workmen were hired on a daily basis to carry out tasks under instruction. Contracts formed the basis for a second type of arrangement, which often incorporated elements of the earlier direct method. Such contracts might sometimes be for the whole building, but more usual was the contract with a master craftsman who often had men working under him. The third method of organising payment was by measurement, whereby a craftsman would be paid for each foot or unit of work carried out. This last method grew in popularity as the seventeenth century progressed.[12] From the sources under discussion, it would seem that methods in use in England were also prevalent in Ireland at that time.

The sample contract documents presented here – for convenience listed as Docs 1-12 below – show that the different categories were not clearly defined; rather they flowed one into the other. On the occasion when Sir Laurence contracted with John Symons to transport stones, he supplied the horses (Doc. 1).[13] Symons was required to find his own help in the form of a boy to load the stones; he was then expected to pay the boy and also give him food.[14] In the next contract Parsons contracted with the mason, Coghlan, to build up the old castle and to carve springers for it (Doc. 2). He was to hire as many masons as he could get, and this was to be done with the approval of the agent Francis Morley.[15] Coghlan was to be paid at the higher rate of 15d per day, compared to the 13d, 12d and 10d daily rate of the other masons.

Transport of materials was a major charge on building work in both Ireland and England, as confirmed by information contained both in the Birr and the Cork papers.[16] During the extensive alterations and additions carried out at Birr Castle in the period 1620 to 1628, numerous payments were made for the transport of stone, sand and gravel from nearby quarries. The rate paid in 1627 to John Symons was 3s 6d per hundredweight for drawing stones to Birr castle, using a garron [small horse] (Doc. 1). During the early days of his building campaign, Sir Laurence made numerous payments for the hire of men and horses to draw materials. Some entries record the hire of just one man and his horse, others are for four men and four horses at a cost of 3s 4d per day, while twenty-two horses and twenty-three men cost 18s 3d for a day.[17] Labourers and horses were also engaged to draw wood and help with repairs on the bridge at Birr. In 1636, Lord Cork paid £39 15s for 'the drawing and carriage of stone' over one thousand loads a distance of about three miles, for his building at Bandon' (Doc. 12).[18]

Due to the cumulative high costs involved in transport, it is not surprising to find that Sir Laurence gave instructions for the salvaging and reusing stones from earlier buildings on the site at Birr. Two contracts drawn up for this purpose give detailed information about the methods used. In the first (Doc. 2), instructions are given 'to sort the coins [coignes] and wallstones by themselves, turning those all into the bawn'.[19] But it was not only the stones that were salvaged from the old castle; the mortar was also reused. Later, as noted in Doc. 3, when the masons were contracted to pull down part of the bawn wall they were required, in addition to saving the stones, 'to save and screen the sand or old lyme comeing thereout'.[20]

Another method for reducing costs was to transport materials by water. At Birr, 'a bargain' was made with joiners to cut rails for wainscotting and to leave them ready for carriage by water (Doc. 5).[21] This method of transport was also used where possible in England, and for the same reasons. During the building of Woolaton in Nottinghamshire, the carriage of a ton of glass for two miles overland cost 4s, while the eighty-five miles by water for the same load was estimated at 7s 6d.[22] Another frequently occurring expense was payment for the cutting, debarking and transport of wood for building purposes. In 1621 Sir Laurence was paying 7d per tree for the felling of forty oaks and a further 8d each for 'barking'.[23] The various contracts for wainscot are interesting because they inform us about the labour intensive nature of this task (Docs 5-8). Descriptions of the huge footage of rails, of five thousand and three thousand feet cut to various lengths, are recorded, and to these were added punchions and panels.[24] All the various sections were then transported to the site where the joiners would assemble them to line the walls of designated rooms.

Fitting-out work such as plastering, glazing and painting were carried out by a variety of craftsmen. Sometimes masons worked on plastering, as can be seen from the contract cited in Doc. 9, where William Denman and James Henderson agreed to plaster the church by the yard. Their contract also specified that 'they must also be paid for any jobs of masons work to be done'.[25] An interesting and detailed memorandum concerned with the glazing and painting of Sir Laurence's 'English House' and other buildings at Birr was drawn up in 1627 (Doc. 10). In this, the glazier, one Roger Peirce [?], contracted to 'colour and putty all my windows and doors and stairs now made ... and also to refresh again with colour and oil all windows, doors and stairs in my castle called the gate-house'.[26] Peirce was also sworn not to 'embezzle, sell or exchange any of my stuff or in any sort to misspend the same'. For this service, he was to be paid 40s for the work and was expected to supply the putty. It seems, however, that Pierce had managed to obtain payment in advance, and when he absconded without finishing the work, he owed 15s.[27]

In the Ormond account book, few tradesmen are named.[28] Several recorded payments suggest that much of the work carried out at various Ormond properties was for maintenance purposes. Some small items listed include payment of 5s to masons, 'for payment for mending ... at Coolnagary', and another of 1s 'for lyme for the tyler of Doonmore' [Dunmore].[29] During the year 1630, masons were paid £7 for work at Kilkenny Castle, and a tiler was paid £1 3s for slating 'the new building at Kilkenny' (Plate 4).[30] In the same year, John Sweete, the glazier, received a number of payments for glazing several rooms at the castle, '£1 5s for 44 foot of glass ... and 60 quarrells'[small panes], and '14 sheete ledde ... of six pounds and a half'.[31] The lead was used for making a framework for the quarrells. Work on windows at Kilkenny, and also at Ormond Castle in Carrick-on-Suir, continued on throughout the year (Plate 5). It is not entirely clear, but items in the accounts would suggest that wooden casements were being fitted, and several payments were made to a carpenter for his work on windows.[32] Payments were also made to joiners for building furniture in situ. Items recorded include payments 'to the Joyner for 3 bedsteades £1.15s', and £1 was paid for two cupboards.[33] Several payments for furniture were also made at Birr; among the items made by the joiner there were a drawing table, cupboard and stools for £3.[34]

A preliminary list of craftsmen and others employed at Birr is included with the documents at the end of this article. Sir Laurence Parsons employed craftsmen from both Ireland and England to work on his building schemes. In the Birr archives there are several references to workmen with English names, and some of these men, with their families, became tenants in the town. Richard Roose [Rouse], Carpenter, was a tenant of Sir Laurence in 1628. One of the conditions of his lease was that he would build a stone chimney in his house, and for this purpose, he was to be supplied with lime and stone to carry out the task.[35] Other names on the list are obviously of Gaelic Irish origin. Many of these men seem to have worked as labourers; others such as James Bourke, Brian McHugh Coghlan and John O'Hogan are described as masons. The appropriately named O'Gowan and O'Gowna are recorded as blacksmiths.[36] The pool of craftsmen working in Ireland must have been fairly small, and further research will probably show that the same workmen moved about from site to site as they did in England, and, indeed, as they do to the present day. As more information becomes available it should be possible to ascertain how many were native to Ireland, what their particular skills were, and how many came in specially to work here, some to stay and some to return to their own countries.

This brief examination of account books may serve to sketch some of the background to the process of building and methods used in Ireland during the seventeenth century. It also provides facts about costs and about contracts with the workmen involved. A more thorough analysis is needed, but a careful reading of the contracts, as published, will, it is hoped, supply some useful material in this neglected area of research.

———

4 – Kilkenny Castle, c 1814

(courtesy Miller/Robertson Papers, Royal Society of Antiquaries of Ireland)

5 – Ormond Castle, Carrick-on-Suir, Co Tipperary
(courtesy Dúchas)

THE DOCUMENTS

Documents 1 to 11 and names of workmen are taken from Birr Archives MS A/8, Birr Castle, Co Offaly. The contracts and accounts are written into a book, bound in a parchment cover. Accounts run from pages 1 to 88, and pagination is in pencil. Contracts occupy a section of twenty pages, which also contains details of leases, purchases of livestock, etc. The first pages at both ends of this book have corners missing, and the handwriting, which is in pale to paler brownish ink, is difficult to decipher. The contract documents were originally transcribed by Miss Frances Wilson in 1983. Amendments have been made to some of her transcripts. The accounts section of the manuscript had not been transcribed. Some of the transcripts of the contracts have modern spelling; I have inserted the original punctuation. Where words were difficult to decipher, I have sometimes suggested alternatives, using square brackets [ ] to indicate my interventions. The list of names is incomplete; it is a sample and does not purport to include all of the workmen named in the account book. The reader is directed to footnote 4 for further information.

CONTRACTS

1. Transport of Materials   [In margin] (15th December 1627. For drawing stones Jo[hn] Symons with my garrans.) I have agreed with him to draw stones to my castle of Birr from twelftide next, till Michaelmas next dayly when weather serves, with two garrons of mine, at the rate of 3s 6d for every 100 load, for which he is to be paid as every 100 loads is brought in, And I am to find him truckles and gear and meat for the said garrons. And he is to find a boy and to load the stones and to give the boy meat, drink and wages. [100 load = hundredweight, 112 lbs]

2. Masonry   [In margin] (For pulling down part of the old castle and of the bawn wall – Paid them in hand 30s. Paid William McWalter 6d. Paid them in full of this contract £2.10s) 1st March 1627, It is contracted betwixt me on the one part and Brian McHugh Coghlan, W[illia]m McWalter Bourke, Ja.[mes] O Hogan and Dermot Reogh McCoghlan and James B... Hearn, on the other part, that they shall out of hand take down xii foot of the south east angle of the old castle, the dungeon there, and the west wall within the old castle in the western end thereof; to take down also the inside wall of the north side of the old castle so low as may serve for the loft to be layed thereon: to take down the little flanker and that part of the bawn wall that reacheth from thence to the dungeon: To sort the coins [coignes] and wall-stones by themselves, turning those all into the bawn: to turn the lime and gravel of the old castle walls inward within those walls, and that gravel and stones preceeding [?] of the dungeon within the walls thereof likewise, And that of the bawn wall inward likewise. To rid the foundations for the new work sufficiently And all the aforesaid works are by all our agreement to be done as Fra:[ncis] Morley shall appoint; for which works I am to pay them four pounds sterling.

3. Masonry [In margin] (for ridding the foundation of the stable: Jo.[seph] Palmer and Edw.[ard] Reynolds whereof they have a note) The 24th September 1627, they have contracted in the presence of Richard Roose [Rouse] with me, to pull down my bawn wall all along betwixt the old castle and the storehouse tower and to cast or carry the earth outward without the bawn and the stones inward into the bawn and to save and screen the sand or old lyme coming thereout, And to rid the foundations for the stable and privy; in such length, breadth and depth as Rich: Roose shall appoint them aforehand and allow of after it is done, for which I am to pay them £4 as the work proceeds.

4. Masonry [In margin] (24th February? 1627, For building the old Castle Brian McHugh) I contracted with Brian McHugh Coghlan mason, that he should undertake the building up of my old castle in such part as he should be prescribed in writing, and make a watchtower there for me, to stand upon 13 springers on the outside: He is to bring as many masons under him as he can get, and to set on the work the first day of March next, and not to leave it till it be finished, And his own wages is to be xvd a day and such other chief , as he and Fra[ncis] Morley think worthy thereof, are to have xiiiid a day, and the rest xiid a day or xd as Morley can agree with them, And Morley is to have vid a day to oversee that work, and I am to provide and bring in place all materials; and I gave Brian McHugh Coghlan vid in earnest to bind the bargain and the masons and to be p[ai]d every Saturday.

5. Wainscot [In margin] (Walter Hand and Hugh Fullon) [No date], I have agreed with them to hew for me 5000 of rails for wainscotting, some to be 4 foot long at 4s for 120: 5s for those of 5 foot long, and 6s for those of 6 foot long. And I am to draw them to the water side, and they are to bring them by water to Clonahan [Clonahill] within the bargain, each rail to be four inches broad and inch and half thick on each side

6. Wainscot [No date] for wainscotting, Burrows hath contracted with me to cut half a thousand more half inch boards with the grain before All Saints for which he is paid in corn beforehand and he is hereby to cut 1500 more of like half inch boards with the grain before Christmas next, for which he is to have 2s 8d the hundred, and 3,000 foot of rail to be hereby sawed by Christmas next at 2s 9d per hundred: he is to fell, square, break and make the sawpits and when they are brought into the bawn by Francis Morley, he is to pitch the rail and pin the boards and he is to begin the work on Wednesday next and not leave it till all this be done, nor to take any other work in hand till this be finished.

7. Wainscot [In margin] (John Langtree Joiner:) I have contracted with him 21st April 1628 to wainscot as many rooms in my castle of Parsonstown as I shall appoint him at the rate of 15d a yard measure and Cipher I finding him timber, and I have lent him 20s as ... to be deducted out of his work

8. Wainscot [In margin] (For wainscotting: Walter Hammon pd them xxs for one thousand upon condition they shall make ... to bring them on land paid them 18s and 25s more Paid them by Barnes 18s ?more, which is all) 5th August [?October] 1627, I have contracted with Walter Hammon and Hugh O Folan Carpenters to make for me 3000 of punchion and panel by Candelmas next, 500 of each sort the punchion to be 20ins long at least, and the panel to be xviii inches long, 11 or 12 inches broad, for which I am to pay them xviiis a thousand, and their payment to be made as soon as they have made ready a thousand and so for every thousand. And when a thousand are ready; they are to give notice thereof to Richard Barnes that he may measure, and pay them, and fetch them away.

9. Plastering [No date] I have contracted with William Denman and William Mathews plasterers, that they shall plaster divers rooms in my castle such as Fra. Morley shall appoint for 1d per yard, and they are to make their mortar, and to have a labourer to carry up the same, and to be p[ai]d weekly as their work is measured.

10. Plastering [No date] [In margin] (Denman and Henderson for plastering ye Church ... in toto...): They have agreed to plaster all the Church within for 37 yards at ?s a yard. And they must be paid weekly as they proceed in their work... And they must also be paid for any jobs of masons work to be done as Richard Rouse Carpenter shall pay betwixt us.

11. Glazing [In margin] (for colouring my windows. Pd him 10s in hand. Paid him 5s more paid him more 10s 6d paid Jo. Evans for him Barnes pd him more 10s so he is overpaid 3s 6d & .. 18d he ran away before Christmas 1627 15s in my debt at least) 24th September 1627, Memorandum that Roger Peirce[?] glasier hath contracted with me the 24th September 1627 not only to colour and puttogh [putty] sufficiently; all my windows and doors and stairs now made in my English house, the 3 great towers [flankers crossed out] for the buttery, storehouse; and flanker, but also to refresh again with colour and oil all the windows, doors and stairs in my dwelling castle called the gate-house and not to cease the work till all be finished, without my leave or direction. And for his pains therein I am to pay him 40s and to find him all stuff except puttogh [putty] Which he is to provide at his own charge. And he is sworn not to imbeazill, [embezzle] sell or exchange any of my stuff, or in any sort to mispend the same.

12. Transport of Stone 21 March 1636/37

'A Note of what materials are prepared for the Right Honoble. My Lorde the Earle of Corke his new building of a Schoolhouse and five Almes houses in Bandon Bridge and the charges disbursed about the same.' [Chatsworth, Lismore papers, vol. xviii, no. 153]

'Paid to John Webbe for drawing and carriage of stone for the building £39 15s for this he ath brought all the freestone from the quarrie being about three miles from the town: and hath reddy for the work 1000 loades or upwards of good hard stones which he hath drawen out of the quarrie and brought for the worke which he the most part of them ... reddy for the worke ... certaine plans where the building should stand being then unknown.

He is more to provide and bring in ... all other stones to finish the worke; for all of which he is to have ... the ... for every small p[ar]t of the wall of the building.

Craftsmen

Masons
Bourke, James, Mason
Coghlan, Brian Mc Hugh, Mason
Crosby, Laurence, Mason, 1626
Davis, Thomas, Mason
Denman, William,
      Mason, Plasterer 1626
Hammond, [Hammill] Edward,
      Agent for Masons hired 1626
Henderson, James, Mason, Plasterer
Hogan, Donal, Mason
Lowry, John, Mason, 1626
O Hogan, John, Mason

Carpenters and joiners
Burrows
Hamon, Walter
Langtree, John
O Folan [Fullon], Hugh
Tailor [Taylor], Ben, Carpenter
Williams, Morgan [Wainscot]

Glaziers
Sweete, John Glazier, Kilkenny
Pollard, William, Glazier

Smiths
O Gowan Dermot, Smith
O Gowna Eoin, Smith

Labourers
Clarke, Thomas, General Labourer

Plasterers
Denman, William
Mathews, William

Not designated
Ball, William – Supplies timber
Bennett, H?
Clarke, William
Condon, Patrick
Duffy, William
Evans, Thomas
Fuller, Bennett
Hogg, James
Humphrey, George
Jones, Taige
Mc Colgan, Donal
Mc Donagh, Teig
Mc William, Philip
Millburne [Willburne], William
O Donnell Taige,
O Duggan, Philip
O Hogan, Donogh
O Hogan, Thomas
O Kennedy, ?Borris
O Kennedy, Darby
O Logan, Dermot
O Logan James
O Logan, Teige
O Lynn [Lynham, O Lyne], Edmund
O Shea, John
Parving, George
Reynolds, George
Saddler, Liam
Stockdale, William
Tailor, Thomas
Wallace, John, Labourer
Walter [Waller, Mc Walter], William
Wilson, William
Willburne [Millburne], William

JANE FENLON specialises in the study of Irish art and architecture from 1550 to 1700. She is currently working as a Consultant to Dúchas the Heritage Service, Department of Arts, Heritage, Gaeltacht and the Islands.

ACKNOWLEDGEMENTS

I would like to acknowledge the work of Frances Wilson who originally transcribed some of the contracts, and to Cathal Moore for allowing me to use his MA report (Courtauld Institute, University of London, 1990) on 'The Patronage of Richard Boyle First Earl of Cork in Ireland and England'. I am grateful to the Earl and Countess of Rosse for their support and for providing access to the archives at Birr Castle. To my colleagues Grainne Carr for her assistance with the transcription of the Building Accounts, and Claire Gapper, London, for alerting me to the presence of the archival material at Birr Castle. My thanks also to Tony Roche of Dúchas for his assistance with photographs for this article.

NOTES

[1]   Rolf Loeber, 'Early Classicism in Ireland', *Architectural History*, 22 (1979) 49-63, 49. Maurice Craig, *The Architecture of Ireland from the earliest times to 1880* (London and Dublin (1982) 1989), especially chapter 8, 111-134. Harold G. Leask, 'Early seventeenth-century Houses in Ireland', and D.M. Waterman, 'Some Irish Seventeenth-Century Houses and their Architectural Ancestry', in E.M. Jope, ed., *Studies in Building History, Essays in Recognition of the work of Bryan H. St. J. O'Neil* (London 1961) 243-250, 251-274.

[2]   C.P. Curran, *Dublin Decorative Plasterwork* (1967) 10.

[3]   See note 1 above.

[4]   Birr Archives MS A/8. 'Receipts and disbursements 28 October 1620-7 June 1628', 1-88. [Acs.] There seems to be some confusion in the descriptions of this manuscript. It is described as both MS A/8A, missing 1620-21 Account Book and as MS A/8, 'Sir Lawrence Parsons' account book recording accounts and contracts mainly for the upkeep and maintenance of the castle and estate...' The latter description is correct. Most of the entries in the account book section of the MS would seem to be in Sir Laurence's own hand. This book also contains contracts between the various workmen and Sir Laurence. [Contracts]

[5]   National Library of Ireland (NLI) MS 2528, Ormonde Papers. 'The Book of Disbursements beginning February 21st 1629[30]'. This account book is signed by John Shee, Stewarde, 26 January 1632[33]. These accounts were probably kept on behalf of Walter Butler, 11th Earl of Ormonde and Ossory, born 1569, died 24 February 1632[33].

[6]   Papers relevant to Lord Cork's building schemes are at Chatsworth, Lismore Papers xviii, xxv, xxvi, xxvii, and in the National Library of Ireland MSS 6897, 6898, 6899, 6900, 6241, 6243. Some of these papers have been published in Alexander Bullock Grosart, ed., *The Lismore Papers*, 1st series, 5 vols (London 1886) and 2nd series, 5 vols (London 1888).

[7]   See note 4 above.

[8]   See note 6 above. Evidence for this is contained in page after page of building accounts covering a period of forty years.

[9] Grosart, *The Lismore Papers*, 1st series, iv, 203. In 1636 Lord Cork purchased Stalbridge House, Dorset.

[10] *ibid.*, 1st series, i, 102, 203, 216, 251.

[11] Malcolm Airs, *The Tudor and Jacobean country House, A Building History* (United Kingdom 1995), especially chapters 4 and 11. Mark Girouard, *Robert Smythson & the Elizabethan Country House* (New Haven & London (1983)1985) 8.

[12] *ibid.*, p 63. Examples of payments by measure are contained in the documents cited as Docs. 7, 8, 9 and 10.

[13] Birr Archives MS A/8, Contracts 12.

[14] *ibid.*

[15] *ibid.*, 7.

[16] Airs, *The Tudor and Jacobean country House*, 136-143.

[17] MS A/8, Acs. 8.

[18] Chatsworth, *Lismore Papers*, xviii, no. 153.

[19] MS A/8, Contracts 14.

[20] *ibid.*, 8.

[21] *ibid.*, 16.

[22] Airs, *The Tudor and Jacobean country House*, 138.

[23] MS A/8, Acs. 10.

[24] *ibid.*, Contracts 9.

[25] *ibid.*, 5.

[26] *ibid.*, 7.

[27] *ibid.*

[28] NLI MS 2549, 10.

[29] *ibid.*, v11.

[30] *ibid.*, 2.

[31] *ibid.*, The name John Sweete, glazier, Kilkenny appears also in the Birr Contracts, 3.

[32] *ibid.*, 12, v12, 13, v13.

[33] *ibid.*, 4, 5.

[34] MS A/8, Acs. 72.

[35] *ibid.*, Contracts 15.

[36] O Gowan and O Gowna, Gabhann, is the Gaelic word for Smith.

———

1 – The Exhibits of the Donegal Industrial Fund
(The Queen, *28 July 1888)*

The Irish Exhibition at Olympia, 1888

BRENDAN ROONEY

O RGANISED AND FINANCED BY MEMBERS OF THE NOBILITY AND PERSONS DISTIN-guished in the fields of politics, literature, science and commerce, the Irish Exhibition in London was held at Olympia, Addison Road, West Kensington from 4 June to 27 October 1888. It was a large-scale, ambitious affair, and, located in fashionable central London, was well placed to draw the attention of the British public and press alike. It happened to coincide with other major events taking place that summer, namely the triennial Handel Festival at Crystal Palace, the Italian Exhibition, and the vast Glasgow International Exhibition (which ran from the beginning of May to the end of October), but exhibitions of this kind were very much part of Victorian urban society, and audiences were used to dividing their attentions between 'rival' events.[1]

The Irish Exhibition occupied the vast covered building itself called Olympia – the largest exhibition building in Britain – and six acres of adjacent grounds. It was easily accessible to visitors arriving on foot, by train (West Kensington Station was nearby) or by carriage. For the standard entrance fee of half a crown, they were presented with an array of Irish attractions, ranging from displays of Irish arts and crafts, to industrial demonstrations, military manoeuvres and performances of Irish music.[2] The floor space in the main hall was divided among the exhibitors who, at stalls and in show cases, displayed and sold Irish wares. The grounds outside were given over to structures intended to evoke the Irish landscape and the activities, culture and history of its people. Irrespective of its minor status, and indeed scale, when compared with contemporary international exhibitions, it was a significant undertaking – both in terms of administration and engineering – and the bodies responsible for its success were understandably large. Though these bodies had no explicit political agenda, the exhibition was more than simply a commercial and cultural festival.

THE ORGANISERS

The party allegiances of many of the organisers was the most obvious link between the Irish Exhibition and politics. All major parties in the House of Commons featured on the list of organisers and patrons. The primary planning body, the Executive Committee, counted numerous MPs among its members. Lord Arthur Hill, Honorary Secretary of the committee and MP for Down West, and Lord Charles Beresford, former MP for Co Waterford, represented the Unionists.[3] Sir R.N. Fowler, MP for London and former Lord Mayor of the City, and the Earl of Latham were the Tory MPs on the council. The Liberal Unionists were Sir John Lubbock and the Duke of Westminster. Lubbock, MP for London University and honorary graduate of Trinity College, Dublin, was also an important member of London County Council.

Significantly, Irish Home Rule interests were also well represented, albeit from varying perspectives. Liberal MPs Herbert Gladstone, son of the Right Hon W.E. Gladstone, then leader of the Opposition, and Sir Charles A. Russell QC, advocated Home Rule. Russell, the Attorney General, was Irish born and educated. The sole member of the Home Rule Party itself was Mr Justin McCarthy, MP for Londonderry and soon to take over from Parnell as the leader of the party. Not only, therefore, was the input from major parliamentary figures considerable, but many of them could claim Irish connections and/or concerns.[4] Ernest Hart, editor of the *British Medical Journal*, and political campaigner, also sat on the Executive Committee.[5]

AMBITIOUS AIMS

The committee outlined its intentions in the catalogue accompanying the art gallery exhibitions. Curiously, not to say unrealistically, in view of the high number of politicians on the controlling council, all concerned wished that the exhibition would be 'non-political'. This was, at least, an interesting and, one assumes, philanthropic ambition. The reality was somewhat different. The aims of the exhibition were listed as being:

1   To place before the English public a clear view of the predominant industries in Ireland.

2   To awaken public interest in the efforts being made to revive her trade.

3   To exhibit to the many thousands of persons in England who have never

crossed the Irish Channel somewhat of her deeply interesting Historical and Antiquarian treasures.

4   To illustrate the worth and significance of Irish Art, and, finally to help to moderate the prejudices which, frequently tending to fetter the judgement, are at the very root of misunderstanding between people and people.[6]

All profits which might accrue from the exhibition were to be invested in the development and promotion of industrial technical schools and cottage industries in Ireland.[7] The committee asserted that if Englishmen were to actually go to Ireland, they would learn more than could be gleaned from 'all the speeches, books and pamphlets on Ireland ever made or printed'.[8] The Irish Exhibition, therefore, represented an explicit attempt to recreate Ireland in central London, thus educating, or perhaps more precisely re-educating, the English public. The most telling statement of all comes at the end of the introduction, where the organisers define themselves as belonging to a

> movement entirely outside the arena of politics; freed from all sectarian or class influence; initiated and undertaken with a worthy purpose; encouraged and directed by persons of energy and practical experience.[9]

An anomaly lies therein. Simply by attempting openly to depoliticise themselves, the committee was acknowledging the political dimension and politicising itself, or more correctly, the exhibition, in the process. This becomes more evident when the exhibition is viewed in the context of the prevailing attitudes in England towards the Irish and Ireland, and representations thereof by the British press. It took place at a time when Irish affairs were very much at the forefront of British government policy-making. The issue of Home Rule featured high on the political agenda, frequently splitting the main parties, and its cause was well served by some formidable members of parliament, both Irish and English. Many of these were vilified regularly by the press. The exhibition also coincided with the Parnell commission, which occupied column after column in the English broadsheets, and pages in the corresponding illustrated newspapers.[10] The Plan of Campaign, initiated in 1882, continued, and was viewed with much distrust in England, not least because of its suspected connection with militant nationalism.[11] At one level, therefore, one might view the Irish Exhibition as a rather extravagant public relations exercise, designed to appease the English public and amend their image of Ireland and the Irish in general. Therefore, though neither reactionary nor revolutionary, the exhibition was fundamentally political.

    In tone, it was quite different from the Irish exhibitions, both national and international, which had preceded it. The rhetoric, for example, which accompanied the Exhibition of Irish Arts and Manufactures in Dublin of 1882 was markedly different from that of the exhibition in Olympia. Held in the Rotunda in Dublin, this event was also concerned with defining an Irish identity through the arts and the manufacturing industries, but was essentially introspective.

In London, the challenge lay in redressing the Irish image amongst the English. In Dublin, no such distinction applied. Here, the emphasis lay instead on establishing a national cohesion, both economic and social. It was also much more clearly politically and historically defined. 'It was felt', wrote the organising committee of that exhibition 'that in spite of all opposition and difficulties an Irish Exhibition should be held in 1882, the year of the inauguration of the O'Connell monument, and the Centenary of the Volunteers'.[12] Even the site had a political significance, and the organisers made sure to point out that the Rotunda's walls 'echoed to the eloquence of all the great Irish leaders and thinkers': United Irishmen, O'Connell, Home Rulers, Nationalists, leaders of the Land Movement etc.[13] Finally the committee asked,

> Can these associations be more fitly crowned than by an Exhibition intended to mark the progress of Ireland in the paths of peace, to forward the cause of peaceful industry in the future, and to help to unite in common love and common duties all sections of Irishmen and Irishwomen?

No members of the Irish nobility or aristocracy featured among the committee members, and only one official was subsequently involved in the administration of the London event.[14]

'PATRICIAN VISIONS'

Ostensibly the committee took for its inspiration the Irish industrial exhibitions that had taken place in Ireland, and sought to transplant them onto English soil. However, the exhibition remained a singular venture in terms of its design and execution. Though one of its main purposes was to elevate the Irish peasant classes, both economically and socially, by focusing on the quality and individuality of their produce as well as their industrious character, it effectively realised the visions of a patrician and, therefore, largely detached community, motivated in many cases by a sense of *noblesse oblige*.

This detachment had a direct impact on the formation and presentation of the exhibition. Speaking of the supposedly authentic native villages which had become a standard feature of international fairs, and of which there was one at the Irish Exhibition, Paul Greenhalgh says that the presentations ... were less to do with accuracy or with the encouragement of tourism than with the relationship they were in with the English ... Ireland had to be different ... in order for the English to be able to differentiate themselves and rule.[15]

Despite the 'Irishness' of many of the organisers, this principle applied equally to the Olympia exhibition. What really interested the organisers was the presentation of a positive side of Ireland as they themselves envisaged it, which would be both intelligible and palatable to an English audience. It was therefore, always and necessarily, a simulacrum, an imposed, unavoidably subjective and narrow interpretation of Ireland.

A BROAD SCOPE

Irrespective of the possibly deluded approach of its organisers, the exhibition was an imaginative and wide-ranging project. As many elements of Irish industry and custom were incorporated into the exhibition as was feasible. Agriculture, engineering, mining, brewing and distilling, printing and book-binding, chemical and allied manufacturing were among the industries represented. Education and science also featured. These appeared alongside more entertainment-oriented attractions which were the *sine qua non* of any exhibition of this kind. There were, for example, both a switchback railway and a toboggan run, dramatic and musical performances and military manoeuvres (Plate 2).[16]

The Great International Exhibition in Dublin of 1853 had been ground-breaking in terms of the emphasis placed on the arts. This was repeated at subsequent exhibitions of its kind in Britain and further afield, and, once again, at Olympia. Here, an attempt was made to present an overview of Irish arts, both current and historical, through the acquisition of important and prestigious art works spanning the centuries. Attempts were made to obtain on loan for the Department of Ancient Irish Art both the Cross of Cong and the Book of Kells, but the requests were, understandably, refused by the respective custodians of these antiquities. However, the committee still managed to put facsimiles of both on display during the exhibition, as well as one of the Ardagh Chalice and other fine objects.

Under the direction of dynamic patrons and with the support of numerous local industrial funds, Irish arts and crafts had been revitalised in recent years. All

page 106   *2 – At the Irish Exhibition* (The Graphic, *4 August 1888*)

page 107   *3 – Irish Peasant Workers in Their Cottages* (The Queen, *28 July 1888*)

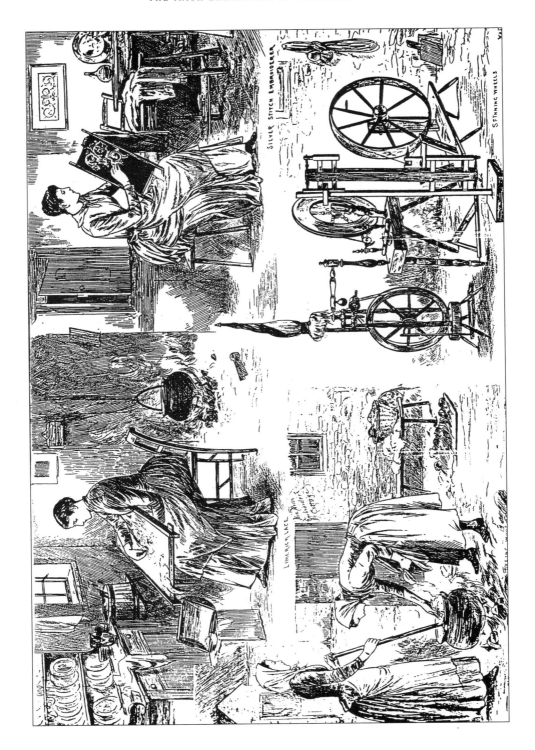

4 – Kells Embroideries Worked under the Direction of the Donegal Industrial Fund
(The Graphic, *9 June 1888*)

5 – A Village Street in Donegal
(The Queen, *7 July 1888*)

manner of crafts were on view to the public at the exhibition, and much of the produce was on sale for the duration. Traditional and modern crafts on show included spinning by hand and weaving of homespuns and linens, dyeing, carding, weaving of damasks, lace-making, sprigging (embroidering of sprigs on muslin handkerchiefs), knitting and hemstitching (Plate 3). Kells embroidery, a style that had been developed to be distinctly Irish in character, drawing its ornament from early Irish manuscripts, also featured strongly (Plate 4). Crafts proved to be one of the most popular attractions, thanks in no small measure to the endorsement and presence of important patrons, among them the irrepressible Lady Aberdeen. Essentially the figurehead of the Irish home industries movement, Lady Aberdeen had been committed to its development since her arrival in Ireland with her husband, the Lord Lieutenant, in 1886, and, as Jeanne Sheehy expresses it, had that 'romantic partiality for Ireland to which some English are prone'.[17] Mrs Ernest Hart, who had been instrumental in the development of Irish craft industries, setting up the Donegal Industrial Fund in the early 1880s, was even more directly involved. She and the Earl of Leitrim were responsible for the design of the Donegal Industrial Village, which was the largest single section of the exhibition, and emphasised both local industry and indigenous crafts (Plate 5).

Designed to be educational, faithful to reality and picturesque, the village was based on the layout of a typical Donegal hamlet. 'Authentic' Irish peasants were invited over from Donegal to inhabit its twelve thatched cottages and demonstrate their respective skills, which included many of the aforementioned crafts, as well as undergarment and shirt-making. A cross was placed at the centre of the village, and the ruins of an Irish tower formed the focal point of the western side. Attention to detail was of paramount importance, and even the fires inside the cottages were to be lit with Irish peat.

A subway passed from the Great Hall into the grounds, where one was presented with a reconstruction of Blarney Castle.[18] Further on, an old Irish castle was located in the centre, complete with portcullis, drawbridge and moat, and nearby stood what the *Freeman's Journal* described as 'that great mystery of the Irish antiquary, an old round tower'.[19] The organisers even went to the lengths of building an Irish dairy, housing sixty cows, in the grounds, which was worked by Irish dairymaids in national costume. The whole project was an undeniably ambitious undertaking, not to be outshone by larger or better funded alternatives. Ireland was to be presented as steeped in history, industry and creativity, but also commercially attuned and viable.

---

page 112   *6 – Old Irish Market Place* (The Queen, *7 July 1888*)

page 113   *7 – The Fancy Fair at the Irish Exhibition* (The Graphic, *28 July 1888*)

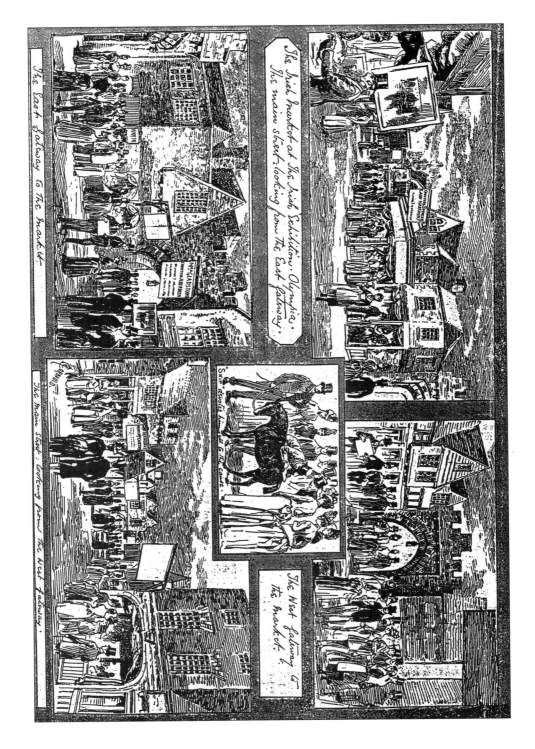

THE FANCY FAIR

Of all the individual events that took place during the four month duration of the exhibition, the Fancy Fair, held in the Old Irish Market Place for four days in mid-July, seems to have attracted most attention (Plates 6, 7). To some extent, it brought glamour to the proceedings and provided a counterpoint to the rustic village described above. The great novelty of the event was that 'Ladies of distinction', as they were referred to in the *Cork Examiner*, rather than the Irish peasants themselves, worked at the stalls.[20] The women taking part were among the most famous and fashionable personalities of their day, and it was believed that such a gathering would be sure to draw the crowds.

Again, many had Irish family connections, while for others contact was linked to their husbands' political career. In some more peripheral cases, their associations with Ireland may just have been through friendships. Prominent amongst the ladies was the aforementioned Lady Aberdeen. Her friend, Lady Gladstone was also on hand, as were the Countess Spencer, Lady Arthur Hill, the daughter of Mr Justin McCarthy, the Countess of Crawford, Lady Herschell, Countess Tolstoy (the wife of Leo Tolstoy), Constance Wilde, Lady Castletown and Lady Fanny Marjoribanks (Plates 8, 9). In claustrophobic and frenetic surroundings, they sold the produce of the Irish workers. The newspapers reported that many had dressed in Irish 'national costume'. In reality, they were dressed in highly fashionable and expensive dresses made from Irish materials, and any concessions to Irish traditional attire were made by some of the ladies' children who wore peasant-like clothing.

THE FINE ART SECTION

The fine art section of the exhibition, comprising of a north and south gallery, was housed in the main building. Both galleries were sub-divided into 'suitably draped' bays, which themselves were devoted to specific media and genres, including watercolour, oil painting, drawings, bas-reliefs, photography, and loan collections of silver and sculpture.[21] One of the bays was reserved for works by deceased Irish artists, another featured solely black and white illustration. The catalogues boasted that the collections represented an assemblage of some of the greatest masterpieces by major Irish artists, and elsewhere claimed, of another medium, that 'photography in Ireland is more successful than in England, owing to the clearer atmosphere'.[22]

The fine art galleries provided the audience with an excellent and unusual opportunity to enjoy and judge Irish artists as a group in their own right. Under normal circumstances in England, Irish pictures were hidden among all the other works

8 – Lady Salisbury's Stall
(The Illustrated London News, *28 July 1888)*

9 – Mrs Gladstone's Stall
(The Illustrated London News, *28 July 1888)*

in exhibitions of British or European art (as would have been the case at, for exam-ple, the Royal Academy or the Grosvernor Gallery). No doubt it was one of the aims of the organisers to illustrate through this show that one could speak of such a thing as an Irish school, distinguished by its vitality and originality. This was a com-mon refrain in the Irish press, though somewhat rash and misleading, as most of these artists were following a British or Continental artistic model for their style (if not necessarily the subject matter), and many were trained abroad. Nevertheless, it was certainly valuable for these artists to have a major platform on which to show their work and to be identified as a talented group with a particular culture and vision.

The limited number of exhibiting artists prompted the *Irish Times* to state, almost apologetically, that 'it would be unfair to say that the picture galleries at Olympia contain thoroughly typical specimens of Irish painting.' [23] Nevertheless, what remained was an impressive if not quite comprehensive collection. Above all, this exposure was of benefit to the younger generation of Irish artists. To exhibit with the likes of Maclise, James Arthur O'Connor, Catterson-Smith, John O'Connor, Alfred Grey and Sir Thomas Jones (then the president of the Royal Hibernian Academy) allowed them to define their work as continuing a distinctly Irish tradition. Thomas Jones was on the Dublin Committee of the exhibition, and is likely to have had a decisive influence over the choice of artists whose works were accepted for inclusion, and his endorsement would have carried considerable weight. The familiar names of James Brenan (Master of the Cork School of Art), William Henry and John Butler Yeats also featured prominently.

Many of the older, more established Irish artists were spoken of in customari-ly deferential tones in the Irish newspapers, but the real excitement was focused on the younger generation. Though there were notable absentees, not the least of whom was John Lavery, the group of young artists included a number who were destined to attract considerable plaudits and success in their careers, and in some cases to become major figures in the Irish artistic establishment. [24] Aloysius O'Kelly supplied a large selection of paintings, eleven in total, as did Richard Thomas Moynan, while William Gerard Barry, Margaret Allen, Col Egerton B. Coghill, Mildred Anne Butler, Edith Somerville and Walter Osborne collectively presented a strong selec-tion. An entire bay was reserved for works by students of the Cork School of Art.

Remarkably, the largest representation was reserved for Henry Jones Thaddeus. He was far and away the largest and also the most expensive living artist on show. With twenty-two of his paintings on exhibit at Olympia, he was the only single painter in oils to have had a bay devoted to his work in the main area of the exhibition. [25] Thaddeus's solid reputation within fashionable British society must go some way to explaining his strong showing. This is borne out by the fact that the

Irish Times deemed Thaddeus's reception of a party led by his old friend the Duke of Teck newsworthy. The article relates that the Duke was accompanied by Lieutenant Colonel Gore, the 6th Earl of Arran, and a distinguished and highly decorated soldier, Dr McNaughton Jones, Professor at Queen's University in Ireland and surgeon to the Cork Ophthalmic and Aural Hospital, the aforementioned Mr Justin McCarthy, Mr Robert Percy Ffrench, a high-ranking diplomat and a personal friend of Thaddeus, and George Faudel-Phillips, the son of a former Lord Mayor of London, who ultimately became Lord Mayor of London himself.[26] That such an apparently inconsequential event should have been recorded at such length says much of the social standing of both visitors and host.

In some cases, there was an interesting juxtaposition of the work of these young artists. One example was the hanging of an orientalist work, *Doorway of the Mohammedan Almshouse, Cairo* [no. 33] by Aloysius O'Kelly near Thaddeus's painting of the *Old Prison Annecy* [no. 32], a curiously and idiosyncratically coloured picture. Here, beside the more recognisably colourist O'Kelly, Thaddeus was able to present himself as perhaps more expansive than some might have expected. Not far away hung a painting entitled *Meditation* [no. 26], by Richard Thomas Moynan. Moynan's work was regularly singled out for praise by members of the Irish press, who admired his draughtsmanship and the atmospheric qualities that distinguished his work. His pictures often had a hazy, greyish tone, reminiscent of Bastien-Lepage and his followers, which was still so popular among critics and public alike at this time.

Appropriately, many artists exhibiting in the art section included works of Irish subjects. There was a predictably large selection of landscapes, but also a substantial number of genre scenes. Of the latter, scenes of Irish peasant life predominated, some purely descriptive, such as Hablot Browne's *Interior of an Irish Cabin* [no. 315] and *A Load of Turf, Connemara* [no. 42] by Aloysius O'Kelly, others with a pronounced narrative. The most challenging among the latter for a bourgeois, politicised audience were those pictures which referred directly to the 'Irish situation'. These included *Bad News in Troubled Times* [no. 97] by Margaret Allen, *The Village Politicians – A Scene from Real Life in Ireland* [no. 115] by Louisa d'Arcy, and *Notice to Quit* [no. 198] and *Bankrupt* [no. 98] by James Brenan.

None of these was what one could describe as subversive or revolutionary in concept, but they provided some commentary at least on a world with which the majority of their audience would have had limited knowledge and even less experience, and which was not represented elsewhere in the exhibition. Brenan's pictures, which echo themes he chose on numerous occasions, reflected the artist's personal sensibilities and heartfelt concern for the plight of the rural poor. Brenan, in fact, would have been very much in touch with the philosophy expounded by many of those involved in the exhibition with regard to the strengthening of the rural econo-my. Having taken over as headmaster of the Metropolitan School in Dublin, after serving as head of the Cork School of Art for over twenty years, he sought to extend its influence into the community, and promoted lace-making and weaving as cottage industries. His work in this area had begun some years earlier when he helped to establish lace-making classes in Co Cork.[27]

AN UNFORGIVING PRESS

Despite its association with so many members of British and Irish high society, the Irish Exhibition management came under constant criticism from the press for its adjudged ineptitude. Progress ran constantly behind schedule, and even as the lord mayors of London and Dublin led the opening ceremony, building work continued in the background, as it was to do for some more weeks. Even the *Irish Times*, which never wavered in its support of the exhibition, had to concede that all was not proceeding according to plan. However, it managed to do so in as positive a manner as could be expected. Speaking of the 'auspicious inauguration', it stated that the great hall, which was the scene of the opening ceremony, was very fine in appear-ance, and that the 'work of decoration so late of being taken in hand had been gone about with an energy and skill which reflect the greatest credit on the contractor'.[28]

Delays were, admittedly, a standard feature of exhibitions of this kind, and time invariably worked against the more extravagant projects. Some members of the press, however, were less forgiving than might have been the case in other circum-stances. Whether the logistical and administrative problems that plagued the event were oversights or symptoms of either inexperience or plain ineptitude on the part of the planners was largely a question of interpretation, but the exhibition's critics were unconcerned with such distinctions. 'Very Irish', wrote Florence Fenwick-Miller of the *Illustrated London News*, 'is much of the management of the Irish Exhibition. The grounds are, up to this moment, in a state of squalid looking dirt and disorder, the grand stand is yet in a process of building, and the special attrac-tions – feats of horsemanship and the like can hardly be presentable till the time comes for the whole affair to end.'[29] This vitriolic and essentially bigoted response, published almost two months after the opening of the event, evidently was not the kind of publicity that the executive committee had aspired to at the outset of the project.

In practice, the organisers were actually quite innovative in their handling of the delays, and managed to incorporate some of the construction work into the dis-plays. This was particularly effective in the case of the Donegal Peasants' Village, where visitors could watch roofs being thatched. They were thus afforded the opportunity of appreciating quite how dark the working conditions endured by some people were, as all they had to do was compare the light entering those houses with roofs and those without.

It seems that the art section suffered the same fate, although here the problems may have been rooted in procrastination as much as in poor organisation. Those responsible had simply not allowed themselves enough time to assemble a satisfactory collection. To compound this, the hanging of the collection, which had begun on the 7th of June, was not completed until the beginning of July, and the catalogue took even longer to become available.[30]

The correspondent for the *Irish Times*, with palpable regret, writes that the exhibition

> was far too hurriedly got up to admit of such a display as was witnessed on great occasions in Dublin. Justly to represent our artistic faculties, such bodies as the National Gallery, the Royal Dublin Society and the Royal Hibernian Academy should have been requisitioned for loans upon long notice, and Irish noblemen and gentlemen, in whose residences some of the rarest treasures of native art lie perdu, should have been approached.[31]

While it would be simplistic to suggest that some artists were encouraged to 'bring up' the numbers, it does seem reasonable that they were invited to submit as many pictures as was practicable at that time. It is noticeable how many works by the living artists on show were borrowed directly from the artists, and how few private collectors, relative to other major exhibitions, lent works. Richard Thomas Moynan, for instance, owned six of the seven paintings that he exhibited; Mildred Anne Butler owned all of her paintings on show, as did Margaret Allen. All eleven of the paintings by Aloysius O'Kelly in the galleries belonged to the artist.

SUCCESS AND SIGNIFICANCE

Despite the relative chaos that accompanied the setting up of the galleries, and the unorthodox nature of the collection itself, it was quite a success. Writers spoke of paintings being sold before they had even been put on display. It was hoped that the galleries would prove a focal point of the exhibition as a whole, which, contrary to expectation, attracted large crowds in its opening few days, and continued to do so throughout its duration.[32]

The success of the exhibition is difficult to gauge. Coverage in the Irish press was regular and generally positive, but in Britain it enjoyed, at best, a muted reception, at least among the papers with large circulation.[33] Attendance appears to have been more than reasonable, particularly in the early weeks, but whether or not it had a direct effect on the public's image of Ireland is another matter. It was certainly not a financial success. Realistically, such an exhibition, however ambitious, was never going to be able to compete for attention with larger, ongoing issues regarding Irish unrest and related governmental policy. However, at a more modest level, but very importantly, it served to maintain the momentum that had built up within the Irish arts and crafts movement, and which would continue well into the next century (Plate 1).

———

BRENDAN ROONEY is completing his doctoral studies in the History of Art department at Trinity College Dublin.

ENDNOTES

[1]   London had hosted major international exhibitions on a regular basis since the mid-century. Most recently, the Colonial and Indian Exhibition had run for six months in 1886. The Glasgow International Exhibition was opened by the Prince of Wales on Wednesday, 9 May 1888, and ran almost to the end of October.

[2]   Olympia stood 100 feet high and had an area of 232,200 square feet. There was an entrance fee for some attractions.

[3]   Lord Beresford was also the second son of the 4th Marquess of Waterford.

[4]   This list represents almost the full complement of members on the committee, but within that, the prime movers appear to have been the Earl of Leitrim, Lord Arthur Hill, Justin McCarthy, Ernest Hart and Herbert Gladstone.

[5]   Hart was also a collector of and a writer on art, particularly Japanese. The trustees of the exhibition were no less distinguished and included the bankers Alfred de Rothschild and Henry F. Slattery.

[6]   Irish Exhibition in London 1888 – Catalogue of Works of Art.

[7]   In practice, the exhibition made a significant loss, and members of the executive committee, including the impoverished Justin McCarthy, were held accountable.

[8]   ibid.

[9]   ibid.

[10]   This was a special commission appointed to investigate various charges made in The Times newspaper against Charles Stewart Parnell and others.

[11]   The Plan of Campaign was an attempt by the National League to pursue the Land War through agitation. Parnell had actually distanced himself from it in May of 1888, but related incidents remained a regular feature in newspapers.

[12]   Complete Official Catalogue of the Exhibition of Irish Arts and Manufactures (Rotunda, Dublin 1882).

13   *ibid.*

14   Mr John C. Rooney was Secretary of the Irish Exhibition Company in 1882, and Honorary Secretary of the Dublin Committee of the Irish Exhibition in London.

15   Paul Greenhalgh, *The Exhibitions Universelles, Great Exhibitions and World's Fairs, 1851-1939* (Manchester 1988) 107.

16   Most of the music was provided by bands of various Irish regiments. Invited musicians also played traditional Irish music. Theatrical productions included dramas with generic titles such as *Paddy's Wedding*. The army re-enacted famous battles as well as providing formal displays.

17   Jeanne Sheehy, *The Rediscovery of Ireland's Past: the Celtic Revival 1830-1930* (London, 1980) 103. Lady Aberdeen founded the Irish Industries Association in 1886. See also Nicola Gordon Bowe, 'The Irish Arts and Crafts Movement (1886-1925)', *Irish Arts Review Yearbook 1990-91*, and for a more personal account of Lady Aberdeen's involvement in the movement, We Twa, *Reminiscences of Lord and Lady Aberdeen* (London 1925).

18   Blarney Castle also featured in the Irish Industrial village designed by L.A. MacDonnell for Lady Aberdeen at the 1893 World Columbian Exposition in Chicago.

19   *Freeman's Journal*, 29 May 1888.

20   *Cork Examiner*, 14 July 1888.

21   *Freeman's Journal*, 2 July 1888.

22   Irish Exhibition in London, 1888 – Official Daily Programme, 10 October.

23   *Irish Times*, 4 July 1888.

24   John Lavery was otherwise engaged at the more prestigious International Exhibition in Glasgow. He and other members of the Glasgow School of painters who exhibited there were lionised by the Scottish press who were caught in a frenzy of national and civic pride. Ultimately, as Kenneth McConkey suggests, Lavery became 'a sort of artist in residence at the exhibition, painting all aspects of its daily life.' *Sir John Lavery* (Edinburgh 1993) 54.

25   Bay XIII in the Southern Gallery was occupied by views of Ireland by Miss Jane Inglis.

26   Faudel-Phillips' association with Ireland was made formal in 1894 when he was appointed Governor of the Irish Society, responsible for the managing the Irish Estates of the Corporation of the City of London.

27   See *Illustrated Summary Catalogue of the Crawford Municipal Art Gallery* (Cork 1992).

28   *Irish Times*, 5 June 1888.

29   *Illustrated London News*, 28 July 1888, 106. With a touch more humour, she proceeds to suggest that the Fancy Fair was 'quite properly prepared, no doubt because a committee of ladies managed it!'

30   *Freeman's Journal*, 2 July 1888.

31   *Irish Times*, 4 July 1888.

32   In the first week, roughly 20,000 visitors per day passed through the gates.

33   Coverage in the British press was rather infrequent and tended to focus on the social events – who was involved and who attended specific events – rather than on the content of the exhibition proper. *The Times* showed most interest when a furore developed following the refusal of the Barrack Street Band from Cork to play 'God Save the Queen' at the end of their performance.

1 – Castletown, Co Kildare, the great staircase, 1759-63

Castletown, Co Kildare:
the contribution of James,
First Duke of Leinster

DAVID J. GRIFFIN

ASTLETOWN WAS BUILT BETWEEN 1722 AND *c* 1725 FOR SPEAKER WILLIAM Conolly (1662-1729), most probably to the designs of Sir Edward Lovett Pearce (*c* 1699-1733). After Speaker Conolly's death in 1729, his widow Katherine continued to live at Castletown. Following her death in 1752, her nephew William Conolly moved to the house with his wife Lady Anne Wentworth, eldest daughter of Thomas Wentworth, Earl of Strafford. On the death of William in 1754, Lady Anne and family moved to Stretton Hall, Staffordshire. William was succeeded by his only son Thomas (1738-1803) who was then under age. On 30 December 1758, at the age of twenty-four, Thomas married Lady Louisa Augusta Lennox (1743-1821), third daughter of the second Duke of Richmond. Louisa had been brought up at Carton, the neighbouring estate to Castletown and home of her eldest sister Emily (1731-1814), wife of James, Earl of Kildare and later First Duke of Leinster (1722-1773). Thomas and Louisa finally settled at Castletown in October 1759, and Louisa was mistress of the house for the next sixty-two years. Being childless, she devoted her life to it. The work carried out to the main block during this period is the subject of this article.

Castletown's extremely complicated architectural history is well documented, at least by Irish standards. The Castletown papers, estate records and account books, together with Lady Louisa's correspondence with her sisters, provide a vital record of the building, decorative and furnishing works undertaken during this period. However, a great deal of what has been written about the house during the last thirty years has tended to concentrate on the written sources while neglecting the physical evidence provided by a study of the building itself. Research undertaken by the author has prompted a reappraisal of these documents, and the major restoration of the house itself currently being carried out by its new owners, the Office of Public Works, has already revealed much that is new about its architectural history.

Generally, recent research has suggested that Lady Louisa, with the backing of a band of skilful craftsmen, was in effect the architect or designer of the alterations carried out during this period.[1] However this is not the full story. While we already knew that Thomas and Louisa were persuaded by Louisa's brother-in-law James, Earl of Kildare, to settle in Ireland and at Castletown, the recent discovery of a letter dated 10 June 1766 from the Earl to his wife shows that his direct involvement with the house was much more extensive:

> I am glad you like what has been done at Castletown. I told Lady Louisa that, when she came to live there after the alterations were made, that she would be obliged to me as long as she lived for finding out that the alterations could be made without pulling down the house.[2]

The Earl was completing the interiors of Kildare (later Leinster) House, Dublin, to designs by Isaac Ware (1704-1766) from about 1759 onwards, and when one compares the two houses, similarities are soon noted, with various elements being repeated.[3] While it would be very tempting to suggest the hand of Ware directly at Castletown, it seems more likely that his various designs for Leinster House were used as a quarry for details which were then reassembled at Castletown, with a few additions under the Earl's direction. The Earl, who undertook the Grand Tour between 1737 and 1739, had a practical interest in architecture, which is demonstrated by his surviving sketch plans for rebuilding the main block of Carton dating from circa 1762,[4] and his extensive annotations on Isaac Ware's designs for the same scheme.[5]

———

2 – Early ground plan attributed to Sir Edward Lovett Pearce

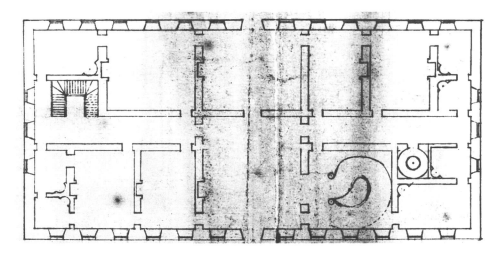

The influence of the Earl can also be detected in the choice of Philip Lafranchini (1702-1779) to decorate the walls and ceiling of the staircase at Castletown. This space was a shell when Thomas and Louisa arrived in the house in 1759, although a surviving early plan for the ground floor (Plate 2), possibly in the hand of Sir Edward Lovett Pearce, shows a circular staircase, probably of timber, reached through a colonnade supporting the first-floor landing, perhaps similar to that designed by Nicholas Dulois (c 1665-1735) at Chevening House, Kent.[6] A first-floor plan (Plate 3), dating most probably from 1759, shows the staircase as finally executed (Plate 1).[7] Lafranchini is first recorded as working at Castletown on 28 May of that year, when Lady Louisa wrote about him to her sister: 'Mr Conolly and I are excessively diverted at La Francini's impertinence, and if he charges anything of that sort to Mr Conolly, there is a fine scolding in store for his honour.'[8] From the wording of this letter it would appear that Philip was working alone. The choice of Lafranchini was not a particularly surprising one, and suggests again the probable input of the Earl of Kildare. Philip had already worked with his older brother Paul (1695-1776) on the decoration of the dining room (later salon) at Carton in 1739, and they may also have worked at Leinster House, Dublin. Philip Lafranchini's plasterwork recalls that executed c 1756 on the main staircase at no. 9 St Stephen's Green, Dublin. The main staircase at Wentworth Castle, Yorkshire, decorated by Artari and Bagutti, may also have provided inspiration. La Francini seems to have been treated as a member of the household, for the Conolly papers contain references to his room as late as 1774.

In the past it has been suggested that the plasterwork on the ceiling of the

3 – First-floor plan, c 1759-60

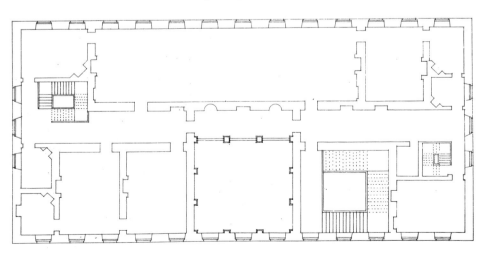

4 – The Long Gallery, Castletown

staircase dated from *c* 1730, and that the decoration of the walls alone was carried out by Lafranchini before the insertion of the staircase *c* 1760. The evidence cited for this suggestion is that the swaged mask below the second quarter landing does not line up with the door below. However the suggestion is not borne out by inspection. While the ceiling is similar to that in the adjoining hall, its decoration is stylistically later. Secondly it would be most unlikely to have decorated the walls of the room prior to the insertion of the staircase, with all the resulting disruption and risk of damage to the plasterwork. Finally the swaged mask is now off-centre because the doorcase has since been moved towards the window wall. Simon Vierpyl (*c* 1725-1811) was in charge of this work, as in the Long Gallery, as discussed below.

In December of 1760 Louisa wrote: 'Staircase is finished to putting up the banisters'. Three of the brass banisters are signed and dated by their maker 'A King Dublin 1760', and his bill for £280 survives.[9] This was Sir Anthony King, described as an 'eccentric brazier', who became Lord Mayor of Dublin in 1778.[10] The idea for the brass banisters had been taken from those at Wentworth House, 5 St James Square, London. This house had been designed by Matthew Brettingham, the elder (1699-1769), and built between 1748 and 1751 for the second Earl of Strafford (1722-91).[11] It was where Lady Anne Conolly had lived when Thomas and Louisa married. Brettingham had already worked at Goodwood, Sussex, and at Richmond House, London. The Castletown staircase was finally completed in 1763 (Plate 1), after which King was paid for five years to keep the banister clean.[12]

The design of the staircase was much admired by the architect Charles Robert Cockerell (1788-1863), who visited the house in August 1825. He wrote:

> The staircase is extremely handsome and the geometrical steps the boldest lightest and best I believe to have seen, the brass balustrade completes the whole giving an effect of elegance quite new to me.

Cockerell gives a sketch ground plan of the house, and an elevation of part of the staircase.[13] Staircases with brass banisters became very popular in Ireland in the early nineteenth century in the works of Sir Richard Morrison (1767-1849). Cockerell used them at Oakly Park, Shropshire and at Kinturk, Castlepollard, Co Meath.

To the same period as the creation of the staircase belongs also the creation of two small lobbies at first-floor level. These originally formed part of the east and west corridors and are not shown on the plan of 1759 (Plate 3). They are decorated with charming plasterwork by Lafranchini, featuring bearded masks above the arched doors similar to those designed by Isaac Ware *c* 1759 for the first-floor dining room (later saloon) at Leinster House. The mahogany doors, dado and floor also belong to this period.

The genesis of Louisa's interest in the first-floor Long Gallery at Castletown (Plate 4) can be seen in her interest in the gallery at Wentworth Castle, Yorkshire. Situated in the east wing of Wentworth, designed by Johann Von Bodt (1670-1745), the gallery itself was the work of James Gibbs (1682-1754). Writing in August 1757 from Wentworth Castle to her sister Sarah, Louisa commented that 'the house is very fine especially that long gallery you have heard so much off its really the finest room that can be.' [15] The Long Gallery at Castletown had originally been designed for Speaker Conolly as a picture gallery. It had six doors, two leading to the east and west corridors, while pairs of doors, each with one false and one real door, flanked the chimney-pieces at each end of the room and gave access to the adjoining rooms. Following her arrival at Castletown in 1759, Louisa seems to have wasted little time in turning her attention to this room. Referring to the gallery in a letter to her sister Emily in May 1759, she wrote 'We have sent by Lord Kildare the designs for finishing the Gallery.' [16] In July of the same year, she wrote:

> In one of your letters you mention that Mr Conolly had forgot to send over the finishing for the great room. He says they were to send the rest of it afterwards or else Mr Chamber's the architect had explained it to Mr Verpaille. [17]

Chambers was of course Sir William Chambers (1723-1796), the architect who, like Matthew Brettingham before him, worked for Louisa's brother, the 3rd Duke of Richmond (1735-1806), at Goodwood, Sussex, and Richmond House, London. Verpaille was Simon Vierpyl, the London-born sculptor and pupil of the Flemish sculptor Peter Scheemakers (1691-1786). Vierpyl settled in Ireland in 1756. He probably already knew Chambers, and subscribed to the first edition of Chamber's treatise on the *Decorative Part of Civil Architecture* published in the spring of 1759. A copy of this work, which was once held in the library at Castletown, now belongs to the author.

Vierpyl, with his foreman, a Mr Lambe, supervised the work at Castletown for Chambers. It is still not exactly clear what work was carried out at this time but it cannot have been very extensive, for by 15 December 1760, Louisa considered that it would be finished in a fortnight. [18] It is known that the original doorcases in the Long Gallery were flanked by columns which were later reused in the construction of a bathing or dressing house near the river. [19] It seems likely that Chamber's work consisted of replacing the original six doors and doorcases. Four remained in their original positions on the end walls, while the doorways on the south wall shown on the 1759 plan (Plate 3) were built up, converting them to niches and repositioning them as they are today, flanking a tall central niche (Plate 5). The gallery could now be entered from the first-floor gallery through a central door which had formerly been false. The east and west corridors could now be more private.

5 – Long Gallery doorcase repositioned by Sir William Chambers, 1759-60

6 – Long Gallery chimney piece (one of a pair), 1759, with later alterations

7 – Lady Louisa's boudoir

8 – Lady Louisa's boudoir, chimney-piece, 1760s

Chambers was probably also responsible for the window cases, dado and two new chimney-pieces of the Ionic order (Plate 6). Lady Louisa's comment,' I am vastly glad you like our chimney-pieces', in a letter to her sister the Countess Kildare of 28 May 1759 may refer to these.[20] They survive with minor alterations carried out in the 1770s.

———

Little of importance was done between 1760 and 1763, when the building work resumed with the refitting of Louisa's bedroom apartment on the first floor, above the present dining room. Daniel Conolly made a new chimney-piece for Lady Louisa's room, and in 1764 one Richard Brewer supplied 120ft of cornice for 'My Lady's Room'.[21] The chimney-piece (Plate 8), doors, doorcases, overdoors (since removed), window cases, etc., in the adjoining boudoir (Plate 7) probably also belong to this period.

This activity was the prelude to Louisa's most ambitious plan, namely, the remodelling of the ground-floor rooms carried out between 1764 and 1768: '[I] have been very busy about a plan for some rooms ... it employs my thoughts constantly.'[22] This work proved so disruptive that the Conolly household had to move to Leixlip Castle for seven months in 1766. During this period, the dining room was created, and the crimson drawing room, saloon or green drawing room, print room and adjoining room remodelled. Almost every window sash above the basement floor

9a – Ground-floor sketch plan, ideal date c 1730
(reconstruction by David J. Griffin, 1998)

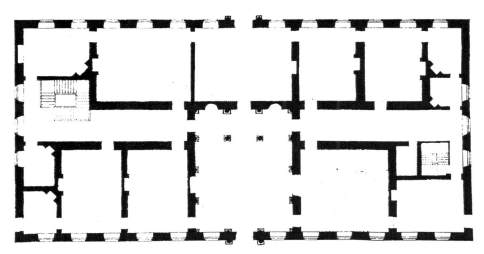

was replaced with those having fashionably slimmer glazing bars to a profile much favoured by Chambers.

The most drastic alterations involved the creation of the dining room (Plates 9a, 9b, 10). Formerly two rooms, the dividing walls were completely removed through three floors to the level of the main roof. A false wall was built to the west in order to centre the windows. Fireplaces and flues were repositioned, probably in 1763-64.

John Harris and others have suggested the hand of Sir William Chambers in the redecoration of the dining room, saloon or green drawing room and crimson drawing room.[23] While it is certainly true to say that Chambers is the only documented architect associated with the house during Lady Louisa's period, in the opinion of the author nothing particularly 'Chambers-like' is evident in any of these interiors. The clue to the actual designer may lie in a letter written from Castletown by Louisa, dated 5 May 1767:

> The Duke of Leinster and my sister dined here the other day it was the first time that he had dined here since our new dining room was made which he had the making of, I may say, for it was him that persuaded Mr Conolly to do it, he liked it vastly.[24]

In other words, it was the Duke of Leinster who advised on the decoration of the room which was completed in 1767. Furthermore, when one compares the ceiling (Plate 11) to that in the first-floor dining room (Plate 12) at Leinster House, Dublin,

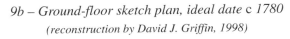

9b – Ground-floor sketch plan, ideal date c *1780*
(reconstruction by David J. Griffin, 1998)

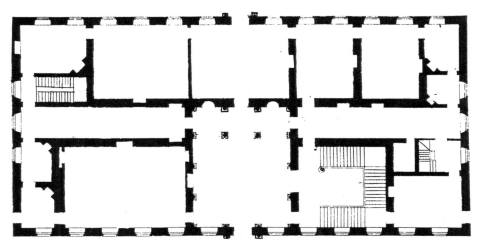

10 – Castletown, the dining room, completed 1767
bottom left   11 – Dining room, detail of ceiling, 1767

bottom right   12 – Leinster House, Dublin
first-floor dining room (later saloon) ceiling, designed by Isaac Ware c 1759

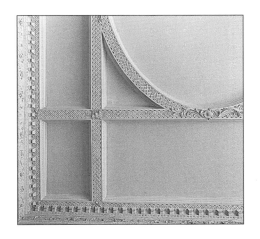

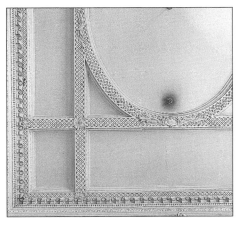

they are identical both in design and execution if not size. The design is in the style of Inigo Jones (1573-1652), and is loosely based on the ceiling of his banqueting hall, Whitehall, London, the most famous dining room in England. The dining room at Leinster House forms part of a suite of rooms designed by Isaac Ware.[25] The Duke's influence could also be found in the furnishings for the original dining room chairs, since sold. They were identical to a set last recorded at Carton.[26] The chimney-piece (Plate 13) may have been influenced by that originally created for the ground-floor dining room at Leinster House, though now to be found at Carton. The neo-classical swaged frieze is probably an alteration of the 1770s. Louisa mentions the arrival of chimney-pieces from England in February 1768. She is probably referring to those in the crimson drawing room (Plate 14), green drawing room or saloon (Plate 15), print room (Plate 16) and adjoining room (Plate 17). It would seem that these were supplied by the firm of John Devall and Son.

Lady Louisa wrote to her sister Sally from Castletown on 25 May 1768 stating:

> There are also gilders in the house, just came to new gild the frames of our pictures in the dining room, all this finishing work is so very entertaining, I am as busy as a bee, and that you know is mighty pleasant.[27]

Looking at the green drawing room or saloon (Plate 19), where the wall panelling was altered to form a backing to the 'pale green damask' silk hangings, in position by 1769, and the ceiling replaced, one can again detect the influence of Ware's work at Leinster House. The main doorcase is based on that in the first-floor dining room (Plate 20). The chimney-piece (Plate 15) is based on that in the first-floor drawing room (Plate 18) at no. 6 South Leinster Street, Dublin, built in 1761 on land let from the Duke. Another version was formerly in the library at Lucan House, Co Dublin.[28]

In the adjoining crimson drawing room (Plate 21), 'hung with a four colour damask predominately of red', the ceiling (Plate 22) is influenced by that in the supper room at Leinster House (Plates 23). Both are taken from designs published by Sebastiano Serlio (1475-1555) in Book Four of *The Book of Architecture* (London edition, 1611), as indeed was the dining room ceiling at Devonshire House, London, designed in 1734 by William Kent (1685-1748). An album of drawings formerly at Castletown contains a number of designs based on this source (Plate 24). The chimney-piece (Plate 14) is identical to that in Louisa's sister's dressing room at Leinster House. It is taken from Isaac Ware's *Designs of Inigo Jones and Others* of c 1735, and is also repeated at Carton and in the dining room at no. 6 South Leinster Street. The doorcases also have parallels at Leinster House. The original panelling was altered to form a backing to the silk hangings as in the adjoining saloon.

Relatively minor alterations to the structure were carried out in the print room (Plate 25) and adjoining bedroom (later library) (Plate 27). In both cases, the

13 – Dining room chimney-piece, 1767, with later alterations

14 – Crimson drawing room chimney-piece, 1768

15 – Green drawing room or saloon chimney-piece, 1768

*16 – Print room
chimney-piece, 1768?*

*17 – Ground-floor
bedroom chimney piece,
1768?*

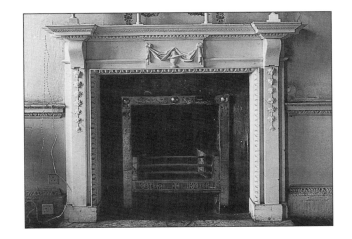

*18 – No. 6 South
Leinster Street, Dublin,
first-floor drawing room
chimney-piece, 1761*

19 – The green drawing room or saloon

20 – Green drawing room main doorcase by Richard Cranfield, c 1768

original coved ceilings were retained and new chimney-pieces (Plates 16, 17) installed, probably in 1768 when a William Heaton was paid for alterations to the woodwork in the print room. A drawing for the east wall of this room survives in the collection of the Hon Desmond Guinness, an early scheme for the hanging of the prints indicating that the original intention was to treat the door to the bedroom as a jib door, like that to the east corridor (Plate 26). The room was decorated with prints collected by Lady Louisa from 1762, and was completed by 1769 when Lady Shelbourne saw it and described it as 'a print room on the palest paper I ever saw and the prettiest of its kind'.[29] The background to the prints has since been repainted and the printed border painted out. In the adjoining bedroom, new window cases, doorcases and a chimney-piece were fitted, but, as noted, the original coved ceiling survives. This room was converted into a library in the nineteenth century.

Throughout all this alteration work to the ground floor, some of the original carved woodwork was retained, altered and reused. All of the new carved woodwork, skirting, window and door architraves, overdoors and chair rails were supplied by the well known Dublin carver Richard Cranfield (1731-1809), who was paid £223 1s 5d in 1768. While the panelled reveals are fully enriched, there is an obvious lack of carving on the mahogany doors installed at the time. This was probably caused by Thomas Conolly's financial problems, and perhaps it was intended that when finances improved the doors could be taken off their hinges and the work completed.

———

21 – The crimson drawing room

22 – Castletown, the crimson drawing room, detail of ceiling, 1768

23 – Leinster House Dublin, supper room, detail of ceiling, 1759

24 – Designs for ceilings after Sebastiano Serlio from an album of drawings formerly at Castletown

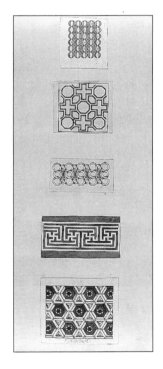

Little seems to have been done between 1768 and 1774 when Lady Louisa turned her attention again to the Long Gallery (Plate 4). Writing to her sister Lady Sarah on May 26 of that year, she stated:

> I am busy as usual but can't enjoy the out of doors work, as I do the gallery which is going so well, and I hope will turn out a very comfortable room, though not quite in the perfection that I could wish it. The ceiling is heavy, but the excessive slowness of the plasterers work comforts me for not having taken it down, as it must have been ages before we could have lived in the room, and to say the truth I have a great deal of impatience about having things finished for the Irish workmen try ones patience not a little.[30]

Her patience was to be tried even further. The stucco wall panels were removed in 1776 as they 'looked so very bad'.[31]

The gallery was redecorated in the Pompeiian manor by two English artists who had already worked at Louisa's brother's house, Goodwood in Sussex, Charles Reuben Riley (c 1752-1798) and Thomas Ryder (1746-1810).[32] Riley, who commenced work in 1775, seems to have executed the paintings set in decorative plaster panels, with Ryder executing the wall decoration. The subjects are mostly taken from d'Hancarville's *Antiquities Etrusques, Greques, et Romaines* (1767) and de Montfaucon's *L'antiquite et representee en figures* (1719).

A Thomas Ryan carver was at work on bookcases for the room. His bills covering the period October to December 1774 survive.[33] Where did these stand? Remembering that there were still doors at either side of the fireplaces of the end walls, the most likely place would be against the four blank piers between the windows on the north wall. The mahogany bookcases (Plate 27), incorporated in the ground-loor library in the nineteenth century,[34] had friezes decorated with fluting and roundels matching the frames of the Long Gallery mirrors which were in position by January 1775.[35] Surely these are the bookcases originally made by Ryan for the gallery. The bookcases were sold in 1965. Doors and doorcases in the end walls are mentioned by Lady Caroline Dawson who visited in 1778. They survived into the nineteenth century, when they were removed and reused elsewhere in the house.

The eight white marble portrait busts on carved and gilded consoles were in position by August 1776, and are probably the work of Simon Vierpyl.[36] The consoles, carved by Thomas Ryan in 1775, seem to have been fitted with candle branches.[37] The small statues which stand in niches formed when the doors from the landing were moved probably also date from this period, while the full-length statue of Diana, an antique, stands on an early nineteenth-century pedestal.

The chimney-pieces installed during the first phase of decoration were altered when painted plaques were added to tie them in with the Pompeiian wall

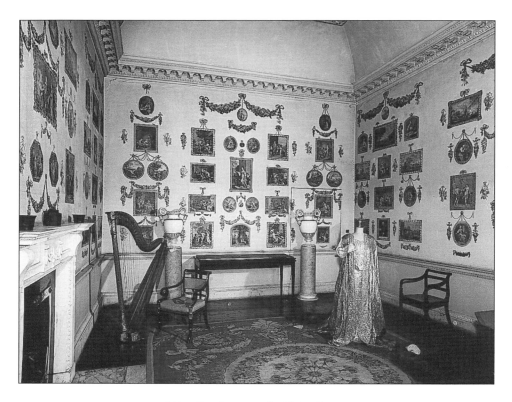

25 – Castletown, the Print Room

26 – Print room, early design for the layout of prints

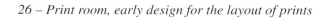

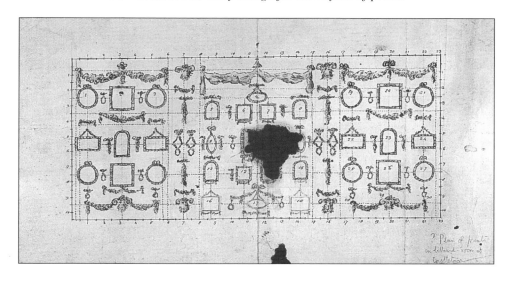

27 – Ground-floor library
(former bedroom)

28 – Lady Louisa's boudoir, detail of painted ceiling

29a – First-floor sketch plan, ideal date 1759
(reconstruction by David J. Griffin, 1998)

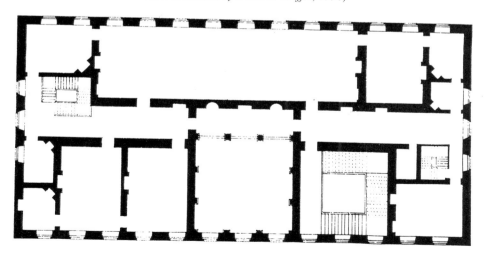

paintings (Plate 6). They were fitted with 'very large fine pinch beck mounted moving grates' and 'very fine open work bow'd fenders' supplied by Richard Wilson, whose bill dated 23 December 1774 survives.[38] Above these chimney-pieces hung Joshua Reynolds' portrait of Lady Louisa (now in the Fogg Art Museum, Harvard), and Tom Conolly by Raphael Mengs, painted in Rome in 1758 (now in the National Gallery of Ireland). The lunette of Aurora is based on a painting by Guido Reni (1575-1642). It should be mentioned that the picture gallery at Leinster House, designed by James Wyatt (1746-1813) for William Robert, Second Duke of Leinster (1749-1804), was completed in 1775. The decorative, painted ceiling, dado and shutters in Lady Louisa's boudoir (Plate 28), though undocumented, are probably contemporary with those in the gallery.

At about the same time, the west staircase, which was open to the corridor, was replaced by one of Portland stone and enclosed. The east staircase, though not replaced, was also enclosed. Most of the remaining first-floor panelled rooms were covered with canvas and paper in order to modernise them. The front door was also replaced, and ten of the ground-floor front windows were lowered – as on the east front at Wentwood Castle, Yorkshire – towards the end of the century and not in 1759 as has been suggested. Two small rooms were created in the first bays of the colonnade, where steps from the ground floor formerly gave access to the exterior. The roof of the main block was replaced to a different profile with a higher ridge.

29b – First-floor sketch plan, ideal date c 1780
(reconstruction by David J. Griffin, 1998)

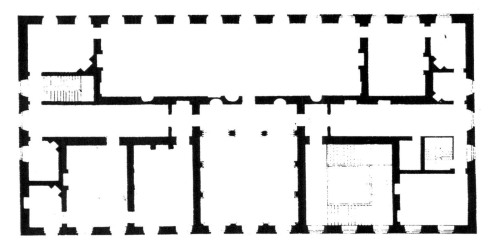

I have tried in this article to show how work at Castletown progressed during Lady Louisa Conolly's long tenure there. She was, without doubt, the principal driving force behind the various phases of activity, and her influence in this respect cannot be under estimated. However, it is clear from both the documentary evidence and from a close examination of the physical structure of the house, that Lady Louisa was not the 'architect' of these alterations. We must look elsewhere to find the guiding hand behind the design decisions, and the figure that emerges is that of James, Earl of Kildare and First Duke of Leinster. Through him, the designs executed by Isaac Ware for Leinster House ten years earlier were filtered, directed and reformed in the Castletown of Lady Louisa.

————

DAVID GRIFFIN is Director of the Irish Architectural Archive, Dublin, and an authority on Irish architecture, particularly Georgian.

ACKNOWLEDGEMENTS

Lena Boylan, John Cahill, Joanna Cramsie, David H. Davison, Hugh Doran, Desmond FitzGerald, Knight of Glin, Hon Desmond Guinness, Anne Henderson, Mary McGrath, Dr Anthony Malcolmson, Colum O'Riordan, the Irish Georgian Foundation, the Castletown Foundation.

Photographs: copyright Irish Architectural Archive; except plates 6 and 10, David H. Davison; plate 27, Hugh Doran.

ENDNOTES

In 1994 the author was commissioned by the Office of Public Works to carry out a detailed report on Castletown. A copy of this seven-volume report is available in the Irish Architectural Archive (ref. D.CAS.6.0).

[1] Christopher Moore, 'Lady Louisa Conolly mistress of Castletown 1759-1821' in J. Fenlon, N. Figgis and C. Marshall, eds., *New Perspectives: Studies in art history in honour of Anne Crookshank* (Dublin 1987).

[2] Public Record Office of Northern Ireland. Strutt papers T3092/1/4.

[3] For a full account of Isaac Ware's work at Leinster House see David J. Griffin 'Leinster House and Isaac Ware' in Agnes Bernelle, ed., *Decantations: A Tribute to Maurice Craig*

(Dublin 1992). Ware's designs are now in the collection of the Irish Architectural Archive (ref. 98/68).

[4] Private collection, Co Kildare.

[5] Ware's designs for Carton are in the collection of the Irish Architectural Archive. (ref. 98/68).

[6] Elton Hall album. Collection Victoria & Albert Museum, London.

[7] Collection Hon Desmond Guinness.

[8] Leinster Letters. Collection National Library of Ireland.

[9] Castletown MS. Property Castletown Foundation on deposit Irish Architectural Archive, Dublin (ref. 97/84).

[10] Sir John Gilbert, *A History of the City of Dublin 1854-8*, iii, 52.

[11] For a full account of Wentworth House see *Survey of London*, xxix and xxx (1960) and John Martin Robinson, 'Wentworth House: St James Square', *Country Life*, 3 November 1988.

[12] Castletown MS.

[13] John Harris, 'C.R. Cockrell's 'Ichnographica Domestica', *Architectural History*, 14 (1971).

[14] For a full account of Wentworth Castle see John Cornforth, *English Country Houses Baroque 1685-1715* (London 1970).

[15] Bunbury Letters. Collection Irish Architectural Archive (ref. 94/136).

[16] Leinster Letters.

[17] Leinster Letters.

[18] Castletown MS.

[19] Castletown MS.

[20] Bunbury Letters.

[21] Castletown MS.

[22] Castletown MS.

[23] John Harris, 'Sir William Chambers friend of Lord Charlemont', *Quarterly Bulletin of the Irish Georgian Society*, iii, no. 3 (1965) and John Harris, *Sir William Chambers, Knight of the Polar Star* (London 1970).

[24] Bunbury Letters.

[25] See note 3 above.

[26] See Brian FitzGerald, 'Carton', *Country Life*, 7, 14 November 1936.

[27] Bunbury Letters.

[28] Photograph Collection Irish Architectural Archive.

[29] Manuscript of Lady Shelbourne. Collection Bowood House, Wiltshire.

[30] Castletown MS.

[31] Castletown MS.

[32] For a full account see Ann Margaret Keller, 'The Long Gallery of Castletown House', *Bulletin of the Irish Georgian Society*, xxii (1979).

[33] Castletown MS.

[34] Illustrated in *Country Life*, 22 August 1936, 198.

[35] Leinster Letters.

[36] Bunbury Letters.

[37] Castletown MS.

[38] Castletown MS.

1 – Inlaid marble chimney-piece, Charlemont House (Hugh Lane Gallery), Dublin
(photo: the author)

In search of Bossi

CONOR O'NEILL

WHILE THERE HAS BEEN EXTENSIVE RESEARCH IN THE AREA OF EIGHTEENTH-century interior decoration in Ireland, with a particular emphasis on plasterwork and painting, chimney-pieces have, by and large, avoided the spotlight of academic interest. As a result little is known about the marble chimney surrounds that were often the focal points adorning many a grand room.

Many difficulties are encountered when researching eighteenth-century chimney-pieces, which may explain the reluctance to pursue this subject. The factors which affect this study become more extreme when an attempt is made to isolate or identify the work of a single craftsman of the period. A further complication is the proliferation of modern reproductions by firms – most notably Sharpe and Emery – which flourished during the early part of this century.

The most important consideration is that these objects are easily installed, taken down or removed, and broken up. Furthermore, many changes have taken place within the boundaries of the Georgian city of Dublin and country houses throughout Ireland, with the result that the chimney-pieces have long since been removed from their original locations. While some chimney-pieces have remained in situ, others have found their way further afield, and often only resurface in house sales or auctions.

The removal and sale of chimney-pieces is not a new phenomenon. In their day they were valuable assets, the value of which could be realised in sales separate to those of the main house or estate. An example of this can be seen in the advertised sale of the Kilruddery estate held on Saturday 28 April 1711 at Dick's Coffee House in Skinners Row, Dublin:

> Memorandum. There are 7 Chimney Pieces, Pillars and Hearths, 17 window plates, and a large Side-board Table, all of pure marble of different Colours, these with the Fish and 120 Brace of Deer, and Pigeons are to be Sold, Separate to the House and the Land, or together...[1]

By contrast, it is also noteworthy that chimney-pieces have been mentioned as fixtures and points of note inclusive in the sale of a property:

> To be sold by Auction by Robert Crowe, Upholder and Auctioneer on Thursday the 10th February 1780, by order of the Assignees of Stephen Moore Esq., at his Dwelling-house, the North Side of St Stephen's-green. The Interest in the Lease said House, and also the Household Furniture, highly finished and fashionable Plate, plated Ware, etc. of the said Stephen Moore; the Lease is a Term of 3 lives (all the Lives in Being) at the small Rent of 100l per annum, and a Pepper Corn Fine on each Removal. The House is no longer built than 3 Years, by the late Lord de Montalt; it is capitally finished, and has every necessary inside and outside Office. The Purchaser will not have one Shilling to Lay out for many Years either on the House or Offices. Its Situation for Air cannot be equalled, having to its front the Beaux Walk. Mr Moore paid a fine of 1200l and expended 300l in putting up superb and elegant variegated Chimneypieces and other necessary Improvements.[2]

SCAGLIOLA

The term scagliola is derived from the manner in which small chips of marble, or scaglia, were employed in its production. This was a substance which was used to imitate marble and ornamental hard stones. The composition of different recipes for scagliola appear to have varied considerably. In this respect, it is important to bear in mind the great versatility and many applications of scagliola; it is interesting to note that craftsmen in the eighteenth century often combined the trades of marble-worker, stucco-worker and scagliolist.

Scagliola exists in two forms: architecturally in columns, wall and floor veneers imitating marble; and pictorially recreating scenes on marble or scagliola slabs, or inlaid designs applied in a decorative manner to various grounds. A legacy of Pietro Bossi's great renown was the designation of the terms 'Bossi-work' or 'Bossi-inlay' to describe the technique of inlaying marble.

The process was first developed by the Romans and was used to veneer walls and floors. It was brought to such a high standard then and later during the eighteenth century that it was often difficult to distinguish between the real stone and the imitation. According to tradition, the art was revived by a native of Lombardy, Guido del Conte, a master mason born at Carpi in the mid-sixteenth century. The technique was already known in the area, and in southern Germany, but Guido del Conte, also known as Fassi or Sassi, is generally accredited with its perfection.[3] The art of scagliola thrived at Carpi and the surrounding area until the middle of the eighteenth century, during which time the tradition was passed on through families, most notably the Griffoni and the Gavignani.

The decorative technique of scagliola reached its most celebrated period during the eighteenth century at the Tuscan monasteries of Vallombrosano, and S Reparata at Marradi. This was largely due to the work of the Friar Don Enrico Hugford, and his assistants Don Petro Belloni and Don Torello Mannini.[4] Along with them, there was the only known lay apprentice to Don Enrico Hugford, Lamberto Christiano Gori, from Leghorn. Gori provided our only contemporary description of the scagliola techniques practised by the monks. An extract from it reveals not only the method and uses, but also offers an explanation for the great delays endured by patrons:

> This material called scagliola or specchio d'asino is calcinated or reduced to a friable condition by heat, ground into a very fine powder and then made into a paste which can be rolled out into various shapes and sizes. When the slab of paste hardens the surface is indented according to the design or pattern to be depicted, and then inlaid with fresh paste mixed with whatever colours are needed for the picture. Only with extreme application and patience can such painstaking work be brought to completion and perfection. The Object of the technique is to emulate the art of painting (in oils or fresco) by representing in coloured scagliola and with equal naturalism, landscapes, seascapes, flowers, fruits, animals etc. and even the human figure itself. When completed the surface of the scagliola can be polished and all trace of the inlaying technique is thus concealed. Indeed, scagliola pictures have often been mistaken for paintings under glass. Scagliola is so hard it can be used for floors and so durable it is often used instead of marble for tombs and church monuments.[5]

PIETRO BOSSI: THE EVIDENCE

There is a generally recognised belief that during the late eighteenth century, an Italian craftsman came to Ireland and was involved in the manufacture of inlaid marble chimney-pieces and table-tops. Over the decades and centuries which have passed since Pietro Bossi appears to have suddenly ceased production, a large body of colourful myth has been built up around his character. It is now the case that his local reputation has influenced the attribution of many chimney-pieces in Dublin, Ireland, and further afield. This is largely perpetuated by dealers and auctioneers who are all too aware of the financial implications that follow from attributing a chimney-piece to Bossi.

With such a reputation it would be reasonable to expect that a great deal of information existed surrounding this craftsman's work. This is certainly the case for a number of contemporary craftsmen working in England, performing well documented contracts for illustrious and clients. However, no similar records have, as yet, come to light regarding any work carried out by Bossi. It is important to note that there is no single documented chimney-piece that can be linked to Bossi. No contemporary diaries, journals or correspondence dealing directly with the subject have been found. Furthermore, no advertisements have been found in newspapers, where Bossi would have proposed to introduce himself and his skills to the public. The task of attributing any one chimney-piece to his hand is not only difficult, but probably impossible in the circumstances. The only evidence that exists linking Pietro Bossi to Dublin, or indeed Ireland, is the registration of his name in *Wilson's Dublin Directory* from 1785 until 1798. The directory was, to quote the compiler, 'An alphabetical list of the Names, Occupations, and places of Abode (numbered) of the Merchants and Traders of the City of Dublin'.[6]

Bossi arrived in Ireland prior to 1785. In order to appear in the 1785 edition it would have been necessary to register with the compilers of the directory in 1784. In the 1785 edition, a certain 'P. Bossi' appeared, registered as an 'Inlayer in Marble and Stucco-worker', with an address at no. 22 Fleet Street. The same advertisement was published in 1786. However, in the 1787 edition, the registered 'place of abode' was changed to no. 38 Fleet Street, and remained as such until 1798. The only other alteration to the registration in the directory was the inclusion of the Christian name Peter in the 1790 edition. It was often the practice for foreigners who were working in Dublin to anglicise their Christian names in the directory during this period.

No reference to no. 22 Fleet Street can be found in the Registry of Deeds during this period. However, no. 38 was referred to in a deed registered on 9 October 1787.[7] It recorded a mortgage of a leasehold interest in no. 37 held by Micheal Dalton, an apothecary, to Alice Chaigneau of Aungier Street. In the mortgage, no. 38 was said to be on the north side of Fleet Street and in the possession of Mr Salkeld esq.

Prior to 1775, properties or sites were not numbered and were often identified by description, which included the side of the street they were situated and the length of frontage. The Registry of Deeds only records two properties on Fleet Street with workshops during this period, both belonging to cabinet-makers.[8] No. 38 Fleet Street was probably where Bossi had lodgings. The marble panels for a chimney-piece or table-top would not have been inlaid in the house where it was commissioned, and it is unlikely that he had a workshop at that address because there would not have been the space to store and work large quantities of marble. In addition, no. 38 Fleet Street was let to more than one person. In *Wilson's Dublin Directory*, Jacob Pemberton was registered as a 'Harpsicord maker' at the same address from 1793 until 1797.

There are very few clues as to where Pietro Bossi originated or where he may have worked before arriving in Ireland. Thieme Becker may offer some assistance. The lexicon records the existence of an eighteenth-century family of stuccodores called Bossi from the area of Porto d'Arcisate, near Como in northern Italy. These itinerant craftsmen worked mainly in the affluent cities of southern Germany and Czechoslovakia. Towards the end of the entry on the Bossi family, there is an interesting aside where a family member is recorded combining the trades of stuccoworker and marbleworker: 'The stuccowork of the columns and the other stuccowork in the Catholic Hofkirche in Dresden was completed in 1765 by a marbleworker called Bossi.' [9]

It is more than likely that Pietro Bossi was one of a great number of itinerant craftsman working throughout England, Germany and Italy. It is quite believable that en route to Ireland Bossi passed through England, where his inlaying techniques were much in practice, but there is no record of him working there. Similar research in England points to the fact that the one thing all these people have in common is that they do not appear in the normal documents or records concerned with residents.[10] Perhaps if there was no free directory in Dublin during the eighteenth century we would have little or no idea who may have been responsible for a great number of inlaid marble chimney-pieces.

While Pietro himself has not yet been found recorded in any receipt or account book, a possible kinsman of his, George Bossi, was receiving payments for work as a 'Stucco-man' at Mountainstown, County Meath, from 11 April 1813 until 13 August 1814.[11]

SCAGLIOLA IN ENGLAND

Furniture decorated with scagliola inlays had been introduced into Britain as early as the 1670s. An example of this early work, attributed to Dutch craftsmen, can still be seen in the Queen's drawing room at Ham House in Middlesex. It was not until the 1760s and 1770s that scagliola became fully accepted as a fashionable technique of decoration. By the 1780s it was being exploited by the some of most prominent designers of the day, such as Robert Adam, James Wyatt, John Carr, Thomas Leverton, George Steuart and George Richardson, for columns, pilasters, pedestals, table-tops, and for the richly decorated chimney-pieces: 'We frequently see friezes and pilasters inlaid with various coloured marbles, but they always appear flat and dull: on the contrary, those done in scagliola in various colours, look lively and brilliant.'[12]

The names of the craftsmen who worked in England are recorded, and include the most celebrated Domenico and Guiseppe Bartoli, a father and son from Leghorn. John Augustus Richter resided in Dresden until the early 1760s before coming to England where he took out a patent protecting his technique (1770 no. 978): 'an Art or Method of inlaying Scagliola or plaister in and upon Marble and Metals to imitate flowers, trees, fruits, birds ... and all sorts of ornaments'.[13] He later exhibited his decorative scagliola work in the Free Society of Artists in 1782 and 1783.[14] Richter was operated in successful partnership with the Bartolis, and they shared a premises in Great Newport Street from 1767 until 1797.[15]

Another craftsman, called Vassalli, was recorded working in the Temple of the Winds at Castle Howard in 1739.[16] Charles Clerici worked in France before collaborating with John Carr at Thoresby in Nottinghamshire, and later worked for Lord Rockingham at Wentworth.[17] Native craftsman such as Vincent Bellman and Joseph Alcott were eventually deemed to be competent in the production of scagliola, and were being commissioned in the 1790s.

Many of the English inlaid marble chimney-pieces were highly decorated. Picturesque scagliola panels and inlaid scagliola motifs were often combined with encaustic and painted images and ormolu. The Irish inlaid chimney-pieces and table-tops are not comparable to those produced in England. The inlaid decoration found on the Irish examples is more restrained the and colours stronger in tone, allowing the elegant white marble and decorative inlays to complement each other.

SCAGLIOLA IN IRELAND

A taste for furniture decorated with scagliola had developed quite early in Ireland. In the early 1750s, Joseph Leeson and Ralph Howard travelled to Italy on their grand tour. There was another reason for the trip as both had commissioned scagliola table-tops for their respective houses: Russborough House and Shelton Abbey in Co Wicklow. In a letter dated 11 July 1747 from Sir Horace Mann, British Ambassador in Florence, to Horace Walpole, reference is made to Joseph Leeson's commission:

> You bid me get two scagliola tables, but don't mention the size or any other particulars. The Man [Don Enrico Hugford] who made yours is no longer in Florence. Here is a scholar of his [Don Petro Belloni], but vastly inferior to him, and so slow in working that he has been almost three years about a pair for a Mr Leeson, and requires still six months more.[18]

In a letter, signed 'Hippocrates' sent from Florence and dated 20 July 1753, reference is also made to Howard's table and another for Henry Theophilis Clements.[19]

> Dear Sir [Ralph Howard]
> Give me leave to return you many sincere thanks for your kind favour of the 18th of June, and for the Ale which is now I hope not far from Leghorn; Mr Montgomery desires his compliment to you, and so do's Mr Clements, son to our Irish Treasurer [Nathaniel] for Whom Don Belloni is hard at work, I am heartily glad that his Scagliola Tables please you so much, and don't doubt but Mr Clements will like his also...[20]

A later example – and possibly contemporary with Pietro Bossi's registration entry in *Wilson's Dublin Directory* – of Irish interest in scagliola can be found in an advertisement placed in *Faulkner's Dublin Journal*:

> W. Barber, I beg Leave to acquaint the Nobility and the Gentry of Ireland, that he has at very great Expense and Labour, compleated an Apparatus for finishing Glasses of the largest Dimensions (ten Feet or upwards) equal to those done in England or elsewhere and has now some very fine plates for Inspection, being the first-of-the-Kind ever finished in this Kingdom. He also has Pier Tables, beautifully painted on Satinwood, Scijolia ditto, in Statuary Marble, with Gerandoles, Trypods, and Carving and Gilding in different Articles to accompany his large Glasses ... He is just returned from London, where he has collected the newest Taste and Improvements ... great Georges-street.[21]

Notable craftsmen operating in England also received commissions to work in Ireland. During the early 1790s Domenico Bartoli was employed by Lord Belmore at Castlecoole, Co Fermanagh, to produce scagliola columns and pilasters.[22] Links between England and Ireland were strong in the eighteenth century, and contemporary tastes travelled relatively quickly from London to Dublin.

THE CHIMNEY-PIECE INDUSTRY IN DUBLIN

A number of stories have arisen in relation to Bossi. Most notably they deal with the need to protect the inlaying technique and the secrecy Bossi required to go about his work. There is a tale which Rev C. Scantlebury SJ recounted:

> A legend relates that while he was engaged at work in Belvedere House, Lady Belvedere, with the curiosity of Eve, Looked through the keyhole to try and see what was going on. Bossi, however sensed her presence and blew

some powder through the keyhole which caused the lady a certain amount of physical discomfort.[23]

It is likely that there is a certain element of truth to these stories; they are consistent with those of craftsmen working elsewhere attempting to protect what they may have considered a monopoly. In reality, the monopoly on the technique probably did not exist. Techniques may have differed but the end products cannot have been too dissimilar, and as a result Bossi had to compete with the great range of wares offered by the local Dublin chimney-piece makers and stone-cutters. The contemporary newspaper advertisements testify to the range of styles and services offered by the Dublin makers:

> To be sold by Auction by Charles Shiel on Monday the 14th of June 1779, at No. 38, Mecklenburgh-street, a curious and extensive Variety of Foreign Marbles, consisting of the finest Jasper, Brocatella, Sienna, Black and Gold, Statuary, Purple Dove and Black Marble being the Stock of the late Mr Thomas Oldham, deceased, also a grand Collection of whole Column and three-quarter Chimney Pieces, solid and curiously inlaid; the Enrichments on the Cornices, Mouldings and Sculpture in Tablets were finished by the best Artists in this City, and a Variety of Term, Pliaster and Console Chimney Pieces all of the best Statuary Marble; some plain Chimney Pieces for Bed Chambers or Attic Stories, these highly finished as Mr Oldham spared neither Pains nor Expense to have them executed in the most exquisite Taste...[24]

In 1786 James Lynam submitted this notice to the *Faulkner's Dublin Journal*:

> Elegant Marble Chimney Pieces, Carved, Inlaid and Plain, James Lynam, Stone Cutter, Successor to the late Charles Lynam, deceased, begs Leave to acquaint the Nobility, Gentry, his Friends, & os that he carries on that Business in all its Branches, Marlborough-street, near the Green. N.B. He is determined that his Work shall be executed in the best Manner and the highest Taste, and at the most reduced Terms.[25]

In addition to the above, reports and advertisements reveal the identities of other scagliolists working in Dublin. The Dublin Evening Post carried an advertisement for Artificial Marble in 1782:

> ARTIFICIAL MARBLE, At No. 2, KING's-STREET, Stephen's Green. Joseph Butcher, from Frankfort, in Germany, imitates all kinds of MARBLE, viz, Colomns, Half Columns, Pilastres, & c. in the same manner as on the Pantheon on London;- also Chimney Pieces; Side-Boards, & c. all which he engages to be equal in colour and polish to any kind of Marble.[26]

An item of news in 1786 reported:

> A gentleman on the Ranelagh Road, Already eminently distinguished for his abilities in painting, sculpture and the most masterly and elegant designs, has, after an intense application of several years, found out a composition, which when laid on even common stone, bears a polish equal to the finest marble. It can be diversified like the most beautiful granite or porphyry, and has an equal degree of hardness with those precious preductions of nature; and perceives moreover its first appearence, which never wears or falls off, though not placed above half an inch in thickness over the surface of the stone or flag. Chimney pieces, tables, vases, urns, (most highly decorated) are already to be seen, which would no doubt be a considerable saving to the nobility and gentry, when it is considered what vast sums are sent annually to Italy and other foreign parts for articles of this nature, such an invention must be a great advantage to the kingdom in general. When execution is in every respect equal to the most elegant that modern times can possibly produce, and that symmetry and ornament cannot be surpassed, the skilful artist must meet the countenance of every person of true and refined taste.[27]

Within two years John Baptiste Cuvillie, 'the gentleman on the Ranelagh Road', had died. Several notices were to be found in the newspapers advertising his stock in trade. The following notice appeared in the *Dublin Evening Post* in late 1788:

> Pictures
>
> The celebrated Collection of the late John Baptist Cuvillié, will be sold by Auction some time in January next.- Catalogues may be had before that time, at No. 25, Ranelagh Road. There are several of the most beautiful of his Composition Chimney-pieces, Tables, Urns & c. yet to be sold. These are well worth the attention of Builders.[28]

At the risk of conjecture, contemporary notices would appear to suggest the possibility that Bossi may have limited himself entirely to the inlaying of the marble panels of the chimney-piece. The chimney-pieces themselves would have been produced to order, and manufactured, when required, by one of the Dublin makers. The auction notice of Charles Shiel, selling the stock of Thomas Oldham, suggests that many craftsmen were employed in the production of a chimney-piece – stone-cutters to produce the body of the chimney-piece, carvers to supply bas-reliefs and inlayers the decoration.

Another notice in the *Dublin Newsletter* from 1754 testifies not only to this system of finishing chimney-pieces, but also announces to patrons the great skill of the Dublin chimney-piece makers:

A most magnificent and superb chimney piece of white Italian marble, is now finished, for the most excellent young nobleman, Lord Kenmare, to be erected at his seat in the county of Kerry, the whole taken from the design of Indigo Jones [sic]; the stone work was executed by the ingenious Mr Shehan, stone cutter, in Marlborough St, and the carvings by the great Mr Houghton, of Golden lane. This fine piece is compleated with so masterly a hand, as to render both stonecutter and carver an honour to their country, and is a demonstration, that works of this kind, as well as monumental performances, need not be purchased abroad, to the destruction of the trade, and to the prejudice of the natives of this country, who, if properly encouraged, as they are by that worthy patron of the Arts and Sciences, would bring our arts and manufacturers to infinite perfection.[29]

It is possible many of the craftsman who were involved in the finishing of chimney-pieces did not advertise or announce their services to the public in the newspapers. It is also reasonable to assume their names would not have appeared on receipts. If we are to associate Pietro Bossi with any one identifiable group of inlaid marble panels, the fact that he may have worked for a number of stone-cutters may explain the variety of chimney-pieces with comparable inlaid panels. Furthermore, he may not have been involved in the installation of the chimney-piece, as 'L's have been found carved on the backs of left blockings to act as a guide for another craftsman.

IDENTIFIABLE GROUPS OF INLAID CHIMNEY-PIECES

Continuing studies by the author have shown that there are identifiable groups of chimney-pieces with scagliola inlaid panels. A number of groups can be attributed to the same hand because of the constant repetition of motifs and designs. Of these, the 'Etruscan' group is the most prominent and striking. The elegant decoration of this group includes the repeated use of a limited number of medallions depicting reclining figures, profiles of antique busts, and various standing figures, including dancing muses. The inlaid busts and figures are nearly always distinctively depicted in red or orange silhouette against a dark brown or black ground. Eleven chimney-pieces and a pair of table-tops belong to this group, the most recent addition being a chimney-piece auctioned by Christies in New York on 12 October 1996. The most famous member of this group can be found in the Bossi room at Charlemont House (now the Hugh Lane Municipal Gallery of Modern Art), Dublin (Plate 1).

The excavations at Pompeii and Herculaneum from the mid-eighteenth century inspired an elaborate antique style known as the 'Etruscan style', and deeply influenced the decorative arts for many years. The style manifested itself in all areas of the furnished interior, from plasterwork and wall coverings to chimney-pieces. The dancing figures which appear upon the chimney-piece in Charlemont House (Plates 2, 3) and on a chimney-piece at Castletownshend are derived from wall paintings discovered in excavations near Pompeii.

The profiled heads and figures inlaid on the chimney-pieces have been inspired by antique gems, cameos and intaglios. These were highly prized, and during the eighteenth century many copies were produced to satisfy the eager demand for them. Many contemporary influences for the various inlaid scenes depicted on the marble panels can be referred to. The same deliberate preference for these subjects can also be found in many other contemporary fashionable modes of decoration. Like many of the ceramic producers of their day, Wedgwood and Bentley relied heavily for inspiration upon the classical discoveries and collections. Their 1774 catalogue advertised the sale of 'Bas-Reliefs, Medallions, Cameo Medallions, Tablets, & c. chiefly classical subjects':

> The pieces in this class are of various Sizes, from two or three inches in diameter, to sixteen or eighteen. The subjects are either made in the Black Basaltes, which in large pieces, has the Appearance of Antique Bronze; or in the polished biscuit with encaustic Grounds, and have the Effect of Large

2-3 – Charlemont House, Dublin, details of inlay work on left and right jambs
(*photos: the author*)

Cameos. In this class is included a set of Herculaneum Figures finely Modelled, and highly finished, made both in the Black Basaltes with Etruscan red burnt in Grounds; fit either for inlaying, as Medallions, in the pannels of Rooms, as tablets for Chimney-Pieces or for Hanging up as Ornaments, in Libraries & c...Tablets for Chimneypieces made in this Way, are capable of the highest Finishing, and most perfect Sharpness...[30]

Another prominent group is easily recognised by its highly realistic portrayal of vine leaves. The subtle and colourful rendering of the broad vine leaves and ribbons are a distinctive characteristic of this group. Examples are to be found in Russborough, Co Wicklow, [31] and in the director's office of the Victoria and Albert Museum in London.[32] There are important comparisons to be made between these two groups, in particular, the excellence of their execution and composition, but moreover the elegant rendering of the foliage and the repetition of motifs confirms that the same craftsman was responsible for both groups.[33]

CONCLUSIONS

I have chosen to highlight some of the most important topics and considerations which affect and guide this research. These are constantly reviewed as new information emerges. Obviously the salient point from this study is that there is a lack of contemporary information dealing with Pietro Bossi's activities in Dublin, consistent with itinerant craftsmen of the time. This lack of information is disappointing but important, and when considered, has led to the deduction that Bossi may not have produced his own chimney-pieces or had his own workshop. Instead he may have worked for the various stone-cutters' yards around Dublin, inlaying chimney-pieces and table-tops. No reference can be found to his other advertised, and much forgotten, trade as a stucco-worker. Again, he may have been working with a group of established stuccodores.

There was only one 'Inlayer in Marble' advertising in Dublin during the last quarter of the eighteenth century. With this fact in mind, there is an urge to link Bossi with groups of elegantly inlaid chimney-pieces and table-tops found in Ireland and further afield. The eighteenth-century Dublin chimney-piece makers were highly skilled craftsmen, supplying a large market, and in light of the evidence, it cannot be denied that they produced some fine inlaid marble chimney-pieces. Until such time documentation is found, no attribution to Pietro Bossi can be said to be conclusive.

———

4 – Inlaid marble chimney-piece, Castletownshend, Co Cork
(photo: the author)

APPENDIX

Provisional list of scagliola-inlaid chimney-pieces and table-tops

This is a provisional summary list of scagliola-inlaid marble chimney-pieces and table-tops in Ireland, and examples related to those in Ireland found elsewhere. This catalogue is far from being complete as many more examples exist in public and private hands. The chimney-pieces and table-tops are listed by reference to their last known location; further provenance details, where known, are also described.

The list has been divided into various groups of chimney-pieces and table-tops, some of which share similar decorative characteristics. These characteristics may be confined to inlaid medallions, such as in the 'Etruscan' Group, chimney-pieces and table-tops that are almost identical in execution, or chimney-pieces with similar decoration on the pilasters or frieze. The chimney-pieces in group B are most notable for the exquisite rendering of vine leaves on the pilasters and frieze. Groups C and D contain chimney-pieces almost identical in their decoration. Group E is a miscellaneous collection of chimney-pieces and table-tops, some of which share common decorative elements. Instances of similar inlay or decoration are referred to in the entries. An asterisk (*) indicates a table-top.

GROUP A   THE 'ETRUSCAN' GROUP

1   **Bray, Co Wicklow** (private collection)
Provenance: Powerscourt, Co Wicklow
Illustration: author's collection

2   **Carrickmines, Co Dublin**
Illustration: *Georgian Society Records*, i, pl. lxxxvii

3   **Castletownshend, Co Cork** (Plate 4)
External dimensions: height 144.7 cm, width 196 cm
Internal dimensions: height 113 cm, width 130.8 cm

4, 5   **Christie's auction,** 7 July 1988*
Provenance: Carton House, Co Kildare
Comment: a pair of inlaid marble table-tops
Illustration: auction catalogue
Dimensions: width 145 cm; depth 54cm

6   **Christie's auction,** 12 October 1996 (Lot 69)
Provenance: property of a Lady; previously with Messrs Pratt & Sons, London, bought from H. Blairman & Sons Ltd, London, in 1952
Illustration: auction catalogue
External dimensions: height 144 cm, width 192 cm; depth of shelf: 17 cm
Internal dimensions: height 119 cm, width 126 cm

7   **Charlemont House (Hugh Lane Municipal Gallery of Modern Art), Dublin**
(cover illustrations; Plates 1-3)
External dimensions: height 155 cm, width 197 cm
Internal dimensions: height 122.5 cm, width 131.7 cm

8   **Mayfair, London** (private collection)
Illustration: author's collection

9   **39 Mountjoy Square, Dublin** (Plate 6)
Comment: The inlaid marble panels were stolen from this chimney-piece in 1991. A design for a chimney-piece without inlay decoration, very similar to this chimney-piece, is to be found in the Darley collection of drawings housed in the Royal Irish Academy (ref. 3C34).
External dimensions: height 135.9 cm, width 182.9 cm
Internal dimensions: height 106.7 cm, width 121.9 cm

10   **Partridges, London**, 1990
Provenance: unknown
Illustration: author's collection
External dimensions: height 135.2 cm, width 185.5 cm

11   **Office of An Taoiseach, Government Buildings, Dublin**
Provenance: 45 Merrion Square
Illustration: *Georgian Society Records*, i, pl. lxxxix

12   **1 Upper Mount Street, Dublin** (Plate 5)

13   **Unknown provenance**
Illustration: Howard Cescinsky, *English furniture of the eighteenth century*, 3 vols (London 1909-11) iii, 65, pl. 60
External dimensions: height 137.1 cm, width 175.2 cm
Internal dimensions: height 111.7 cm, width 118.1 cm

GROUP B   14   **Russborough House, Co Wicklow** (Plate 7)

15   **Victoria & Albert Museum, London**, A1-1909
Provenance: This chimney-piece originated in Dublin and became the property of Cecil Goodrich Dolmage esq, LLD, DCLRP, of 33 Warwick Road, London. It was donated to the Victoria and Albert Museum by J.A. Dolmage, on behalf of his late father, in 1909.
Illustration: *Georgian Society Records*, i, pl. vc
External Dimensions: height 141.6 cm, width 187.3 cm

5 – Inlaid marble chimney-piece, 1 Upper Mount Street, Dublin
(Irish Georgian Society Records)

6 – Inlaid marble chimney-piece, 39 Mountjoy Square, Dublin
(courtesy Irish Architectural Archive)

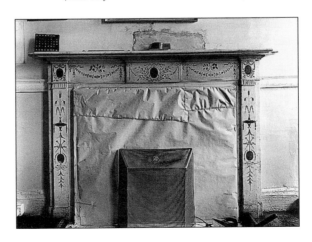

7 – Inlaid marble chimney-piece and table-top, Russborough House, Co Wicklow
(photo: Thomas Gunn, collection Irish Architectural Archive)

8 – Inlaid marble chimney-piece, Avondale House, Co Wicklow
(courtesy Irish Architectural Archive)

GROUP C   16   National Museum of Ireland, Kildare Street, Dublin
Provenance: from one of three houses demolished in 1886 to make way for the National Library
Illustration: author's collection
External dimensions: height 147 cm, width 186 cm; depth of shelf: 21.2 cm
Internal dimensions: height 120 cm, width 122 cm

17   6 Randolph's Cliff, Edinburgh
Provenance: 20 North Great George's Street
Illustration: *Georgian Society Records*, i, pl. lxxxvii

GROUP D   18   T. Crowther & Son, London
Provenance: bought from a house sale at Oak Park, Co Carlow, in 1957, and subsequently sold by T. Crowther & Son in 1959
Illustration: author's collection
External dimensions: height 157.5 cm, width 198 cm
Internal dimensions: height 122 cm, width 132 cm

19   Vizcaya Museum and Gardens, South Miami, Florida
Provenance: Pratt & Son, London; previously from a house in Merrion Sq.
Illustration: F. Lewis Hinckley, *A directory of antique furniture; the authentic classification of European and American designs for professionals and connoisseurs* (New York 1953) pl. 878A

20   Unknown provenance
Illustration: author's collection

GROUP E   21   Áras an Uachtaráin (Vice Regal Lodge), Dublin
Similar or identical inlay: nos 31, 51, 55
Illustration: Irish Architectural Archive

22   Avondale House, Co Wicklow (Plate 8)
Similar or identical inlay: no. 52

23   Baltracy House, Co Kildare
Similar or identical inlay: nos 2, 30, 44, 45, 54, 50
Comment: now removed
Illustration: author's collection

24   Belvedere House (Belvedere College SJ), Dublin
Comment: the inlaid marble plaques above the pilasters were stolen in 1996
Illustration: author's collection
External dimensions: height 137.7 cm, width 186 cm
Internal dimensions: height 114 cm, width 118.7 cm

25 **Belvedere House (Belvedere College SJ), Dublin**
Comment: The style and colouring of the inlay in this chimney-piece is
very similar to that found in England.
Illustration: authors collection
External dimensions: height 138.5 cm, width 186 cm
Internal dimensions: height 103.5 cm, width 113 cm

26 **Castle Blunden, Co Kilkenny**
Comment: very simple inlay decoration upon the plaque in the frieze
Illustration: Irish Architectural Archive

27 **Christie's auction**, 1 October 1991 (Lot 92)
Provenance: property of a nobleman
Similar or identical inlay: no. 19
Illustration: auction catalogue
External dimensions: height 138 cm, width 152 cm

28 **Cooke Antiques**
Provenance: unknown
Comment: inlay-work restored
Illustration: *Apollo*, cxxxii, no. 353, July 1991, 8

29 **Leinster House (Dáil Éireann), Dublin**
Provenance: 6 Upper Merrion Street
Similar or identical inlay: no. 43
Illustration: *Georgian Society Records*, i, pl. lxix

30 **Drum's auction, Co Dublin**, 15 February 1997
Provenance: unknown
Similar or identical inlay: nos 2, 23, 30, 44, 45, 71
Illustration: author's collection
External dimensions: height 137 cm, width 178cm
Internal dimensions: height 110 cm, width 109 cm

31 **Dublin**
Similar or identical inlay: no. 21
Comment: Carved plaques on this chimney-piece are similar to those in
the Darley drawings in the Royal Irish Academy (ref. 3C34).
Illustration: *Georgian Society Records*, iii, pl. c

32 **Duleek House, Co Meath**
Illustration: author's collection
External dimensions: height 142.2 cm, width 167.6 cm;
depth of shelf: 11.4 cm
Internal dimensions: height 114.3 cm, width 110.5 cm

33   **Dunsany Castle, Co Meath** *

Similar or identical inlay: pair of marble table-tops with similar border decoration to the table-top at no. 59

Illustration: Irish Architectural Archive

34   **Glenaulin House, Chapelizod, Dublin**

Provenance: Mountjoy Square

Comment: simple inlaid plaque with foliate spray

Illustration: Irish Architectural Archive

External dimensions: height 134.6cm, width 172.7cm

35   **Glin Castle, Co Limerick** (Plate 9)

Comment: simple foliate inlays

36   **Headfort House, Co Meath**

Comment: This Chimney-piece was possibly imported from England during the 1770s when work was carried out on the house to the designs of Robert Adam.

Illustration: Irish Architectural Archive

37   **Headfort House, Co Meath** *

Comment: see note above

Illustration: Irish Architectural Archive

9 – Inlaid marble chimney-piece, Glin Castle
Co Limerick (photo: author)

38   43 Kildare Street, Dublin
      Similar or identical inlay: no. 72
      Comment: two chimney-pieces photographed in this house with the same
      simple naive inlaid decoration
      Illustration: *Georgian Society Records*, iv, pl. c

39   Lucan House, Co Dublin
      Comment: simple inlay on frieze
      Illustration: Irish Architectural Archive

40   Malahide Castle, Co Dublin *
      Provenance: Russborough House, Co Wicklow; sold as lot 11 in a sale of
      the contents of Newtown Park House, Co Dublin, 20 September 1976
      Similar or identical inlay: nos 55 and 76
      Illustration: auction catalogue
      Dimensions: width: 182 cm, depth: 52 cm

41   Mallett, London, 1994
      Provenance: stated to be from Rossmore Park, Co Monaghan, and adver-
      tised by T. Crowther & Son in 1965
      Illustration: Mallett Catalogue, 1994; *Connoisseur*, 160, no. 645,
      November 1965, lxix
      External dimensions: height 145 cm, width 201 cm
      Internal dimensions: height 121.9 cm, width 127 cm

42   Mallett, London
      Provenance: auctioned by Sotheby's, 18 November 1994 (lot 43)
      Illustrated: Mallett Catalogue, 1995
      External dimensions: height 149 cm, width 174 cm
      Internal dimensions: height 122 cm, width 117 cm

43   Marlay Park, Co Dublin
      Similar or identical inlay: no. 29
      Illustration: Irish Architectural Archive

44   Mount Ievers, Co Clare (Plate 12)
      Similar or identical inlay: nos 2, 23, 30, 45, 54, 71

45   Mountjoy Square, Dublin
      Similar or identical inlay: nos 2, 23, 30, 44, 54, 71, 77
      Illustration: *Georgian Society Records*, i, pl. xc

46   Mount Kennedy, Co Wicklow
      Illustration: Irish Architectural Archive

Inlaid marble chimney-pieces
10 – Newlands House, Co Dublin (Irish Georgian Society Records)
11 – 39 North Great Georges Street, Dublin (Irish Architectural Archive)
opposite *12 – Mount Ievers, Co Clare (photo: Hugh Doran, collection IAA)*

47   Antrim House
       (National Maternity Hospital), Dublin
       Comment: three chimney-pieces incorporating panels inlaid with simple
       foliate sprays
       Illustration: Irish Architectural Archive

48   Newlands Golf Club, Co Dublin (Plate 10)
       Provenance: Newlands House (demolished)
       Similar or identical inlay: no. 53

49   Newtown Park House, Co Dublin
       Comments: chimney-piece may not be eighteenth century; auctioned as lot
       23 in a sale of the contents of Newtown Park House, 20 September 1976
       Illustration: auction catalogue
       External dimensions; height 144.8 cm, width 188 cm

50   39 North Great George's Street, Dublin (Plate 11)
       Similar or identical inlay: nos 18, 19, 20, 74

51   Powerscourt House, Co Wicklow
       Similar or identical inlay: no. 55
       Comment: Christie's sale of the contents of Powerscourt House, 24 & 25
       September 1984 (lot 504)
       Illustration: auction catalogue
       External dimensions: height 148.6 cm, width 174 cm
       Internal dimensions: height 120 cm, width 121.3 cm

52   Pratt & Burgess, London
       Similar or identical inlay: very similar decoration to the chimney-piece at
       Avondale House (no. 22)
       Illustration: author's collection

53   Russborough House, Co Wicklow (Plate 7) *
       Similar or identical inlay: The table-top in this illustration is maybe one of
       a pair, its possible twin being in Malahide Castle.

54   Schull, Co Cork (private collection)
       Similar or identical inlay: nos 2, 23, 30, 44, 45, 71
       Comment: The plaque in the frieze is upside down.
       Illustration: author's Collection

55   Shanganagh Castle, Co Dublin
       Similar or identical inlay: nos 21, 51
       Illustrated: Irish Architectural Archive

56   **Sotheby's auction, New York,** 15 April 1994 (lot 291)
Provenance: property of a private collector
Comment: This elegant chimney-piece, described as being 'probably Irish', has a number of characteristics in common with both English and Irish inlaid marble chimney-pieces.
Illustration: auction catalogue
External dimensions: height 147 cm, width 2.08 cm; depth of shelf: 21 cm

57   **Stackallen House, Co Meath**
Provenance: 6 Merrion Square
Comment: It is possible that this chimney-piece was produced by the same maker that made the chimney-piece in Charlemont House.
Illustration: *Georgian Society Records*, i, pl. lxxxix

58   **8 St Stephens Green, Dublin**
External dimensions: height 137.1 cm, width 167.6 cm (excluding shelf)
Internal dimensions: height 101.6 cm, width 129.5 cm

59   **Strokestown Park House, Co Roscommon** *
Similar or identical inlay: no. 33
Comment: This inlaid marble table-top was sold and is no longer in the house.
Illustration: Irish Architectural Archive

60   **Sullivan Antiques, Dublin**
Similar or identical inlay: nos 64, 70
Comments: inlay heavily restored
Illustration: author's collection

61   **Summerhill, Co Meath**
Comment: very simple inlay decoration
Illustration: *Georgian Society Records*, v, pl. xl

62   **T. Crowther & Son, London**
Provenance: unknown
Illustration: *Apollo*, lxxx, no. 32, October 1964, xlvii
External dimensions: height 139.7 cm, width 173.9 cm
Internal dimensions: height 108.6 cm, width 113 cm

63   **T. Crowther & Son, London**
Provenance: unknown
Comment: simple foliate sprays
Illustration: *Apollo*, lxxxi, no. 40, June 1965, xxxviii
External dimensions: height 130.8 cm, width 158.7 cm
Internal dimensions: height 104.1 cm, width 99 cm

64 T. Crowther & Son, London
Provenance: unknown
Similar or identical inlay: nos 60, 70
Illustration: *Connoisseur*, 171, no. 689, July 1969, xvii
External dimensions: height 146 cm, width 180.3 cm
Internal dimensions: height 120.6 cm, width 120.6 cm

65 T. Crowther & Son, London
Provenance: unknown
Comment: simple foliate sprays
Illustration: *Connoisseur*, 172, no. 691, September 1969, xvii
External dimensions: height 140.3 cm, width 170.2 cm
Internal dimensions: height 104.1 cm, width 113 cm

66 T. Crowther & Son, London, 1972
Provenance: unknown
Illustration: *Connoisseur*, 180, no. 724, June 1972, 2
External dimensions: height 144.8 cm, width 185.5 cm
Internal dimensions: height 116.8 cm; width 120.6 cm

67 T. Crowther & Son, London
Provenance: unknown
Illustration: *Connoisseur*, 183, no. 738, August 1973, 2
External dimensions: height 146.7 cm, width 185.4 cm
Internal dimensions: height 119.4 cm, width 121.9 cm

68 T. Crowther & Son, London
Provenance: unknown
Illustration: *Burlington* magazine, cxxvii, no. 990, September 1985, 47
External dimensions: height 144.7 cm, width 187.9 cm

69 T. Crowther & Son, London
Provenance: unknown
Illustration: Apollo, cxxvi, no. 307, September 1987, 95
External dimensions: height 146. cm, width 187.9 cm
Internal dimensions: height 115.6 cm, width 124.4 cm

70 T. Crowther & Son, London
Provenance: Fitzwilliam Square, Dublin
Similar or identical inlay: nos 60, 64
Illustration: author's collection
External dimensions: height 155 cm, width 183 cm
Internal dimensions: height 124.5 cm, width 123.2 cm

71   T. Crowther & Son, London
Provenance: unknown
Similar or identical inlay: nos 45, 77
Illustration: author's collection
External dimensions: height 138.4 cm, width 182.9 cm
Internal dimensions: height 109.2 cm, width 121.9 cm

72   Temple Street Hospital, Dublin
Similar or identical inlay: no. 38
Illustration: author's collection

73   Tulfarris House, Co Wicklow
Illustration: Irish Architectural Archive

74   Tyrone House (Department of Education), Dublin
Similar or identical inlay: no. 50
Comment: The pilasters have been replaced upside down.
Illustrated: *Georgian Society Records*, iii, pl. xxxvii

75   Victoria and Albert Museum (GD-1042)
Provenance: Stanley Pratt Ltd, 1961
Illustration: *Connoisseur*, 147, no. 592, March 1961 (back cover)
External dimensions: height 157.5 cm, width 226 cm
Internal dimensions: height 106.7 cm, width 142.2 cm

76   Unknown provenance *
Similar or identical inlay: nos 40, 55
Illustration: Margaret Jourdain, *English decoration and furniture of the
18th century* (London 1923) fig. 82 (photo: National Museum of Ireland)

77   Unknown provenance
Similar or identical inlay: nos 45, 71
Illustration: author's collection

78   Unknown provenance
Similar or identical inlay: nos 6, 14
Comment: The central plaque from this chimney-piece, depicting
Summer, is to be found elsewhere on chimney-pieces in Belvedere
College, Blarney Castle, and on a chimney-piece from 20 Parnell Square.
Illustration: author's collection

79   Co Wicklow (private collection)
Illustration: author's collection
External dimensions: height 134.6 cm, width 160 cm; depth of shelf: 15.2 cm
Internal dimensions: height 109.2 cm, width 106.7 cm

CONOR O'NEILL graduated from Trinity College in 1991. As an under-graduate he developed a continuing interest in the work of Pietro Bossi. He now works as an apprentice solicitor in Dublin.

ACKNOWLEDGEMENTS

I am very grateful for the helpful and enthusiastic support shown by Dr Edward McParland throughout the course of this research. My thanks are also extended to Donald Cameron for his assistance.

NOTES

[1]   *Dublin Intelligence*, 14 April 1711, 2.

[2]   *Faulkner's Dublin Journal*, 29 January – 1 February 1780, 3.

[3]   Erwin Neumann, *Materialien Zur Geschichte Der Scagliola, Jahrbuch Der Kunsthistorichen Sammlungen in Wien*, 55 (Vienna 1959) 75-134. Blausius Fistulator and his family worked as scaglolists in Munich as early as 1585.

[4]   John Fleming, 'The Hugfords of Florence', *Connoisseur*, 136 (1955) 106-110, 106.

[5]   *ibid.*, 106.

[6]   *Wilson's Dublin Directory* (Dublin 1784).

[7]   Registry of Deeds, Book 392, no. 258644, 213.

[8]   Registry of Deeds, Book 376, 8, no. 247548. This refers to the last will and testament of Jacob Moss, a cabinet-maker from Mary Street, which was registered on 10 August 1785. His interest in this property was a twenty-three year lease at the yearly rent of thirty pounds. Registry of Deeds, Dublin Street Index, Book 90, F168, records a memorial of Jas Dillon, also a cabinet-maker, and his interest in a property in Fleet Street with a workshop.

[9]   Thieme Becker, *Allgemeines lexikon der bildenden Kunstler*, 37 vols (Leipzig 1912) iv, 405.

[10] Author's correspondence with Dr Geoffrey Beard.

[11] I am very grateful to Diana and John Pollock for bringing this information to my attention.

[12] George Richardson, *A New Collection of Chimney Pieces, Ornamented in the Style of The Etruscan, Greek, and Roman Architecture; containing thirty six designs...* (London 1781) 7.

[13] Geoffrey Beard, 'Robert Adam and his craftsmen', *Connoisseur*, 198 (1978), 181-193, 193.

[14] A. Graves, *The Society of Artists of Great Britain 1761-1791, The Free Society of Artists 1761-1783* (London 1907) 121. John Augustus Richter collaborated with Edward Hodgson, a painter from Dublin, producing floral and landscape scenes in scagliola.

[15] Robert Brian Wragg, 'The history of scagliola', *Country Life*, cxxii (1957) 718-721, 719.

[16] Robert Brian Wragg, 'The use of scagliola', *Country Life*, cxxii (1957) 988-891. Stucco-work at Ditchley Park, Sutton Scarsdale, Towneley Hall and Hagley has also been linked to Vassalli.

[17] Rupert Gunnis, *Dictionary of British Sculptors 1660-1851* (London 1953) 104.

[18] Anthony Coleridge, 'Don Petro's table-tops: scagliola and grand tour clients', *Apollo*, 83 (1966) 184-187, 185.

[19] John Ingamells, *A dictionary of British and Irish travellers in Italy 1701-1800, compiled from the Brinsley Ford Archive* (London 1997) 960-961. This letter is attributed to Dr James

Tyrrell, a physician of a Co Westmeath family who settled in Florence (1737-69) and acted as agent to Irish grand tourists.

[20] National Library of Ireland, Howard Papers (unsorted) packing case 2255. I am very grateful to Dr Edward Mc Parland for directing my attention to this quotation.

[21] *Faulkner's Dublin Journal*, 18-20 May 1784, 2.

[22] PRONI, Abstract of Sundry expenditures for Lord Belmore's building at Castlecoole, commencing May 2d, 1788 and ending April 18th, 1795. Amot. £49269-8-3-1/4. Scagliola work – paid Dominick Bartoli for workmanship etc. & Travelling charges for his men.

[23] Rev C. Scantlebury SJ, Belvedere House, *Dublin Historical Record*, xiii, nos 3 & 4 (1953) 129-132, 131.

[24] *Faulkner's Dublin Journal*, 1-3 June 1779, 3.

[25] *Faulkner's Dublin Journal*, 28-31 October 1786, 1.

[26] *Dublin Evening Post*, 2 July 1782, 2. Joseph Butcher was obviously another travelling craftsman who had decided to make his way to Dublin to carry on his trade. It is more than likely that his surname was anglicised from Metzger or Fleischer. Also noteworthy is the fact that he did not chose to advertise in *Wilson's Dublin Directory*.

[27] *Faulkner's Dublin Journal*, 31 August – 2 September 1786, 4. The 'gentleman on the Ranelagh Road' was John Baptiste Cuvillie of 22 Charlemont Street. He died in 1788. Advertisements appeared in the *Faulkner's Dublin Journal* from 20-23, 23-25 and 25-27 September 1788 for the sale of his stock in trade.

[28] *Dublin Evening Post*, 27 November 1788.

[29] *Dublin Newsletter*, 19-22 January, 1754.

[30] Wedgwood and Bentley, *A Catalogue of Cameos, Intaglios, Medals, Busts, Small Statues, and Bas-reliefs, with a general account of vases and other ornament after the Antique...* (London 1774) 16.

[31] *Georgian Society Records*, 5 vols (Dublin 1909-13; reprinted Shannon 1969) v, pl. lxvii.

[32] *ibid.*, i, pl. xc. This chimney-piece was described as being 'from a house in Dublin, not identified; now in England'. It was donated to the Victoria and Albert Museum by J.A. Dolmage esq., on behalf of his late father Cecil Goodrich Dolmage esq, LLD, DCLRP, of 33 Warwick Road, London.

[33] A garland of vine leaves similar to those from the chimney-pieces at Russborough House and the Victoria and Albert Museum can be found in the centre tablet in the frieze of lot 69 auctioned in New York by Christie's, 12 October 1996.

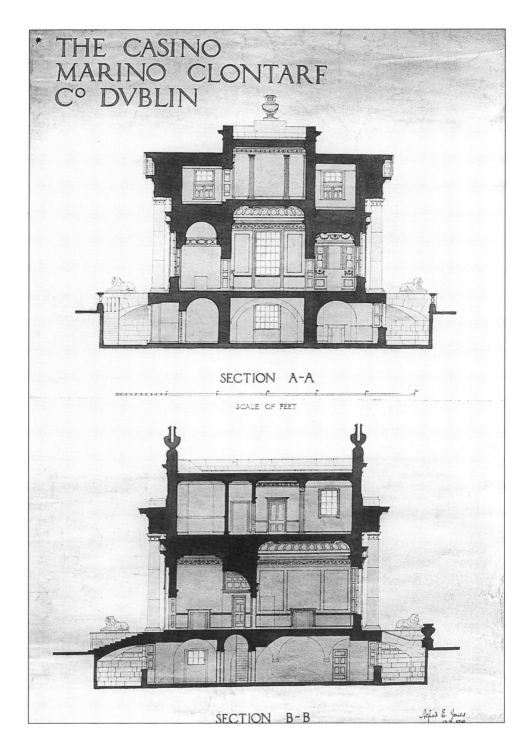

THE CASINO
MARINO CLONTARF
Cº DVBLIN

SECTION A-A

SCALE OF FEET

SECTION B-B

A database of
Irish architects 1720-1940: C

IRISH ARCHITECTURAL ARCHIVE

AT THE IRISH ARCHITECTURAL ARCHIVE IN DUBLIN, A DATABASE OF IRISH architects and their works is being compiled. The project was described in the *Bulletin of the Irish Georgian Society*, xxxvi (1994) 75-77. Since that article was written, inputting has reached the letter H. There has also been a slight contraction of the date range. The rather arbitrary range of 1700-1950 has been changed to 1720-1940. 1720 has been preferred as being the date at which Rolf Loeber's *A biographical dictionary of architects in Ireland 1600-1720* (1981) ends, and 1940 as reflecting the natural break in architectural and building activity in Ireland caused by the Second World War.

The following list is of persons included in the database whose names begin with the letter C. It includes some engineers and some builders and craftsmen. The symbol * following the name indicates a builder or craftsman; the symbol # indicates a foreigner – usually English or Scottish – who carried out work in Ireland but was never based in this country. Dates of birth and death are given, when known, followed by the quarter centuries in which the subject is believed to have been active professionally.

ANN MARTHA ROWAN
Irish Architectural Archive

ANN-MARTHA ROWAN is engaged on the compilation of the database of Irish architects for the Irish Architectural Archive.

opposite   *1 – Sir William Chambers, Casino at Marino (1758-)*
survey drawings by Alfred E. Jones

name	born / died	flourished
C., J.		18c4
C., J.J.		19c1
CAFFREY, John	b.1873	20c1
CAFFREY, John J.		20c2, 20c3
CAFFREY, John Patrick		20c2, 20c3
CAHILL, James *	d.1890	19c3, 19c4
CAHILL, Matthew *		19c1
CAHILL, Peter	d.c 1926	19c3, 19c4, 20c1
CAIRNES, F.E.		20c1
CAIRNS, Joseph S.		20c1
CAIRNS, Thomas		20c1
CALDBECK & DUNLOP		20c1
CALDBECK, Francis Curran		19c4, 20c1
CALDBECK, William Francis	c 1824-1872	19c2, 19c3
CALDBECK, William	1733-1803	18c4
CALDWELL, -- #*		19c3
CALDWELL, -- [2]		19c1
CALDWELL, -- [1]		n.a.
CALDWELL, Henry		19c3
CALDWELL, James		19c1, 19c2
CALDWELL, James Edwin Lees		20c2
CALLAGHAN, John		19c1
CALLAGHAN, William C.		20c2
CALLAN, Patrick *	d.1831	19c1, 19c2
CALLENDER, Thomas	d.1949	20c1, 20c2
CALNAN, J. *		19c1, 19c2
CALRY, Joseph		19c3
CALWELL, Robert Inkerman	1854-1927	19c4, 20c1, 20c2
CAMBI, Carlo #*		19c4, 20c1
CAMERON, ANGUS		19c2
CAMPBELL & FAIRHURST #		20c1
CAMPBELL, Charles	d.1850	19c1, 19c2
CAMPBELL, Daniel		19c2
CAMPBELL, James *		19c1
CAMPBELL, John [1]		19c1
CAMPBELL, John [2]		19c3
CAMPBELL, John [3]		19c2, 19c3

CAMPBELL, John C.		19c3, 19c4
CAMPBELL, Thomas #*	1790-1858	19c1, 19c2, 19c3
CAMPBELL, Thomas	1733-1795	18c3, 18c4
CAMPBELL, W. Walpole		19c3, 19c4
CAMPBELL, William [2] *		19c3, 19c4
CAMPBELL, William [3]		19c2
CAMPBELL, William [1]		19c1
CAMPLING, James #	b.c 1741	18c3
CANDY, Joseph Phelan	1895-1960	20c1, 20c2, 20c3
CANEILLE, Rodolph		17c4
CANETTA, Geronimo #		17c4
CANNAN, Peter *		19c1
CANNING, —		19c3
CANNON, John		19c2
CANTRELL, Peter		19c1
CAPON, William #	1757-1827	18c3, 19c1, 19c2
CAPPER, John *		19c2
CAPRONNIER, J.B. #*		19c3
CARBERY, Peter P.		20c1, 20c2
CARDEN, Robert Walter #		20c1
CARDY, Samuel	d.1774	18c2, 18c3
CAREN, Joseph L.		20c1, 20c2
CAREN, Juan		20c1
CAREW, John		18c4
CAREW, Matthew *		19c1
CAREY, John		n.a.
CARLINI, Agostino #*	d.1790	18c3, 18c4
CARMICHAEL & JONES		19c3
CARMICHAEL, Hugh	d.1860	19c2, 19c3
CARMICHAEL, Thomas *		18c4
CAROE, William Douglas #	1857-1938	19c3, 20c1, 20c2
CAROLIN, Charles *	d.1846?	19c2
CAROLIN, Edward *		19c1, 19c2
CAROLIN, George *		19c3
CAROLIN, John *	c 1796-1877	19c1, 19c2, 19c3
CAROLIN, Robinson	c 1793-1878	19c1, 19c2, 19c3
CARPENTER, Richard Herbert #	1841-1893	19c3, 19c4
CARPENTER, Richard Cromwell #	1812-1855	19c2, 19c3
CARPENTER, William *		19c1, 19c2

name	born / died	flourished
CARR, John #	1723-1807	18c3, 18c4
CARROLL & BATCHELOR		19c4, 20c1
CARROLL & PENTLAND		19c4
CARROLL, Charles Owens	d.1859	19c3
CARROLL, Edward	c 1847-1883	19c3, 19c4
CARROLL, Howard		19c2
CARROLL, James		19c2
CARROLL, James Rawson	1830-1911	19c3, 19c4, 20c1
CARROLL, Joseph Stanislaus		20c2, 20c3
CARROLL, Nicholas *		19c2
CARROLL, Robert *		18c4
CARROLL, Thomas Henry *		19c3
CARROLL, William [1] *	1817-1889	19c2, 19c3, 19c4
CARROLL, William [2]	d.c 1912	19c3, 19c4, 20c1
CARROLL, William [3]		19c3, 19c4
CARSON, Edward Henry	1822-1881	19c2, 19c3, 19c4
CARSON, James		19c4
CARTER, John	1748-1817	18c3, 18c4, 19c1
CARTER, Nicholas *		18c1, 18c2
CARTER, Samson	c 1804-1860	19c2, 19c3
CARTWRIGHT, Thomas *	c 1707-1765	18c2, 18c3
CARUTH, S.C.		20c2
CASE, John #		18c3
CASEY, John *		19c2, 19c3
CASEY, William P.		20c1
CASH, John		18c3, 18c4
CASHEN, Martin		19c4
CASTLE, Richard	c 1690-1751	18c1, 18c2, 18c3
CATCHESIDE, Henry *		19c1
CATCHSIDE, John		19c1
CAULFIELD, Patrick *		19c4
CAVANAGH, Jacob		18c4
CAVANAGH, James *		19c4
CAVENAGH, B.		19c1
CAVENAGH, James *		18c4
CECCARINI, Francesco *		19c3
CHACE, George *		19c1

2 – James Rawson Carroll, County Courthouse, Sligo (1880)

Carroll, a Dublin architect, won the competition for the courthouse in 1874.

3 – Richard Castle, Bellinter, Co Meath (1750-)

Built for John Preston MP at the end of Castle's life.

4 – Nathaniel Clements, Phoenix Lodge, Phoenix Park, Dublin (c 1751)
Designed by Clements for his own occupation, it now forms the nucleus of Áras an Uachtaráin.

5 – Sir William Chambers, Charlemont House (c 1762)
Charlemont House is now the Hugh Lane Municipal Gallery of Modern Art.

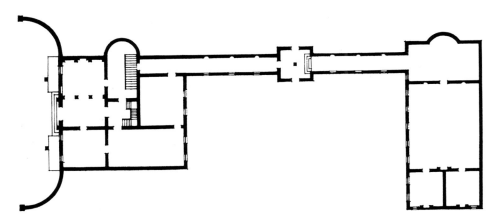

name	born / died	flourished
CHADWICK, William J.	d.1951	20c2, 20c3
CHAIGNEAU, Edward (or Andrew)		18c3
CHAIGNEAU, Henry		18c4, 19c1
CHALMERS, Peter McGregor #	1859-1922	19c4, 20c1
CHAMBERS, D.W.		20c2, 20c3
CHAMBERS, John *		18c3
CHAMBERS, William Isaac #		19c4, 20c1
CHAMBERS, William (Sir) #	1726-1796	18c2, 18c3, 18c4
CHANCE, Norman Albert	1887-c 1964	20c1, 20c2, 20c3
CHANDLER, John *		19c1
CHANDLER, Thomas *		19c2
CHANTREY, Francis Legatt (Sir) #	1781-1841	19c1, 19c2
CHAPMAN, --		19c1
CHAPMAN, Edward #		18c4, 19c1
CHAPMAN, FREDERICK William	d.c 1953	20c2
CHAPMAN, William [1] #	1749-1832	18c4, 19c1, 19c2
CHAPMAN, William [2]		19c2
CHAPPELL, Henry	d.1924	19c3, 19c4, 20c1
CHARLEMONT, James, 1st Earl	1728-1799	18c2, 18c3, 18c4
CHARLES, Henry *		19c2
CHARLES, Richard [1]		18c4
CHARLES, Richard [2] *		19c2
CHARLES, William *		19c2
CHARLEVILLE, Charles William Bury, 1st Earl	1764-1835	18c4, 19c1, 19c2
CHARLTON, James W. (Capt.)		20c2
CHATTERTON, George	1853-1910	19c4, 20c1
CHATTERTON, Thomas *		18c1
CHEAL & SONS #		20c1
CHEARNLEY, Anthony	d.c 1786	18c2, 18c3, 18c4
CHEARNLEY, Samuel	c 1717-1746	18c2
CHEERE, Henry #*	1703-1781	18c2, 18c3, 18c4
CHERRY, Frederick		19c4
CHERRY, John Joseph	d.1867	19c3
CHERRY, Richard *		19c3
CHESNEY, John		19c1, 19c2
CHEVERS, Charles V.		19c4

name	born / died	flourished
CHILD, Alfred Ernest *	1875-1939	20c1, 20c2
CHILLINGWORTH & LEVIE		20c1, 20c2, 20c3
CHILLINGWORTH, Robert Boyle	c 1878-c 1917	19c4, 20c1
CHRISTOPHER, John Thomas #	c 1829-1910	19c3, 19c4, 20c1
CIPRIANI, Giovanni Battista #	1727-1785	18c3, 18c4
CLANCY, Thomas *		19c2
CLANCY, William *		19c2
CLAPHAM, Frederick Dare #	1873-1914	19c4, 20c1
CLARE & ROSS #		20c1
CLARENDON, Frederick Villiers	c 1820-1904	19c2, 19c3, 19c4
CLARKE, Albert J.		20c1, 20c2
CLARKE, Archibald		19c2, 19c3
CLARKE, Charles *		18c4
CLARKE, Esmond		19c4
CLARKE, Eugene O'Neill		19c3, 20c1, 20c2
CLARKE, Frederick *		19c2
CLARKE, Harold S.		20c1
CLARKE, Harry *	1889-1931	20c1, 20c2
CLARKE, James [1]	d.c 1838	19c2
CLARKE, James [2] *		19c1
CLARKE, John [1] *		19c1, 19c2
CLARKE, John [2] #	1852-1936	19c3, 20c1
CLARKE, Joshua *	c 1868-1921	19c4, 20c1
CLARKE, M.		19c4
CLARKE, MAXIMILIAN #	1851-1938	20c1
CLARKE, Michael *	d.1900	19c4
CLARKE, Richard		19c1
CLARKE, Robert Edmund Lear		20c1, 20c2
CLARKE, S.C.		19c4
CLARKE, Samuel		18c4
CLARKE, Thomas [2] *		19c2
CLARKE, Thomas [3]		19c2
CLARKE, Thomas [1] *		18c3, 18c4
CLARKE, William		19c1
CLAYTON & BELL #*		19c4
CLAYTON, -- #		19c3
CLAYTON, George		18c3

CLAYTON, Robert #		19c3
CLAYTON, William Geraty		19c4, 20c1
CLEARY, William		18c4
CLEERE, Henry		19c3
CLEMENTS, Henry		19c2, 19c3
CLEMENTS, Nathaniel	1705-1777	18c2, 18c3, 18c4
CLERKE, William John Bird	1838-1896	19c3, 19c4
CLINCH, Brendan Joseph		20c2
CLINCH, Bryan J.	d.1906	20c1
CLINCH, John *		19c1, 19c2
CLOSE, Richard Mills	d.1949	20c1, 20c2
CLOSE, Samuel Patrick	1842-1925	19c3, 19c4, 20c1
COAKLEY, Daniel J.		20c1, 20c2
COAKLEY, Dominick J.	d.1914	19c4, 20c1
COATES, George *		19c1
COBDEN, Thomas Alfred #		19c2
COCHRANE, Robert	1846-1916	19c3, 19c4, 20c1
COCHRANE, William	c 1823-1907	19c3, 19c4, 20c1
COCKBURN, Gilbert [1] *	c 1789-1862	19c1, 19c2, 19c3
COCKBURN, Gilbert [2] *	d.1900	19c3, 19c4
COCKBURN, John	d.1829?	19c3
COCKBURN, Samuel		19c4, 20c1
COCKBURN, Thomas Baker *	d.1899	19c2, 19c3, 19c4
COCKBURNE, Peter		19c1
COCKERELL, Charles Robert #	1788-1863	19c1, 19c2, 19c3
COCKERELL, Frederick Pepys #	1833-1878	19c3, 19c4
COE & GOODWIN #		19c2, 19c3
COFFEE, James		19c1
COFFEY, Andrew [1]		18c4, 19c1, 19c2
COFFEY, Andrew [2] *		19c2
COFFEY, Denis	c 1896-1955	20c2
COFFEY, Michael		19c1
COGAN, J.		19c1
COGAN, John		19c3
COGHLAN, David		19c2
COGHLAN, John *		19c2
COLBORN, Ed		19c1
COLBOURNE, Thomas		19c1
COLBY, Thomas Frederick #	1784-1852	19c1, 19c2, 19c3

name	born / died	flourished
COLCLOUGH, Noble C.		19c4
COLE-BAKER, George Hannyngton	1866-1894	19c4
COLEBERT, John *		19c1, 19c2
COLEBROOK, William		19c2
COLEMAN, George Drumgold	c 1795-1844	19c1, 19c2
COLEMAN, J. [1]		20c1
COLEMAN, J. [2]		20c2
COLEMAN, John		18c4
COLEMAN, Thomas Aloysius	1865-1950	19c4, 20c1, 20c2
COLGAN, --		20c2
COLHOUN, Joseph		19c4
COLLEN BROS. *		19c4, 20c1, 20c2
COLLEN, John *	c 1837-1921	19c3, 19c4, 20c1
COLLEN, William	d.1932	19c4, 20c1, 20c2
COLLES, Christopher	1738-1816	18c3, 18c4, 19c1
COLLES, William *	c 1710-770	18c2, 18c3
COLLIE, George *	1904-1975	20c1, 20c2, 20c3
COLLINS, James B.	d.c 1959	20c1, 20c2
COLLINS, James [2]		19c2
COLLINS, James [1] *		19c2
COLLINS, Jeremiah	c 1894-1937	20c1, 20c2
COLLINS, John		19c1
COLLINS, Robert		19c3, 19c4
COLLMANN, Leonard W. #		19c2
COLLOT, Thomas	c 1848-1871	19c3
COLSTON (or COULSTON), John		19c2
COLTSMAN, John		18c1, 18c2
COLUMBANI, Placido #	b.1744	18c4
COLWELL, Matthew		19c2
COMBER, Patrick Forstall	1831-1909	19c3, 19c4, 20c1
COMBS, Hugh *		18c4
COMERFORD, James J.	1899-1950	20c1, 20c2
CONATY, --		19c3
CONEYS, --		19c1
CONNELL, James Christopher		20c2
CONNELL, John		18c4, 19c1
CONNELL, Richard		18c3, 18c4

CONNER, Charles *		19c2
CONNICK, Thomas		19c1
CONNOLLY & McAVOY		20c1
CONNOLLY, Andrew *		19c2
CONNOLLY, James		19c1
CONNOLLY, John J.		20c1, 20c2
CONNOLLY, Joseph S.	1840-1904	19c3, 19c4, 20c1
CONNOLLY, Joseph		20c1, 20c2, 20c3
CONNOLLY, Martin *		19c1
CONNOLLY, Thomas *		19c3
CONNOR, Christopher		18c4
CONNOR, Michael		19c1
CONNOR, Robert		18c4
CONNOR, Thomas [1] *		19c2
CONNOR, Thomas [2]		19c2
CONOLLY, James *	d.1852	19c2, 19c3
CONOLLY, John *		19c3
CONOLLY, Thomas *		18c2, 18c3
CONOLLY, William & Son *		20c1
CONRAN, John		19c1
CONRON, Thomas		19c4
CONROY, Daniel	d.1912	19c4, 20c1
CONROY, John *		19c2
CONROY, Thomas		19c1, 19c2
CONSTABLE, --		19c3
CONVERY, W.J.		20c1, 20c2, 20c3
CONWAY & CONWAY		20c2
CONWAY, Francis Robert Aloysius		20c2, 20c3
CONWAY, Henry *		19c1
CONWAY, J.		20c2
CONWAY, James		19c1
CONWAY, John		19c1
CONWAY, Michael		20c1, 20c2
CONYBEARE, Henry #		19c2, 19c3
CONYERS, E.F.		20c2
COOK, Robert		18c4
COOKE, Francis *	d.1757	18c3
COOKE, James		19c1, 19c2
COOKE, Theodore	c 1837-c 1911	19c3, 19c4, 20c1

6 – Thomas Cooley, Royal Exchange, Dublin (1769-)
Cooley settled in Ireland after winning the competition for what is now City Hall.

7 – Thomas Cooley, Mount Kennedy, Co Wicklow (1784)
Attributed to Cooley, who modified the original design by James Wyatt.

name	born / died	flourished
COOKE, William Henry Howard	1881-1977	20c1, 20c2, 20c3
COOLEY, Edward *		18c2
COOLEY, Thomas	1740-1784	18c3, 18c4
COOPER, --		18c4
COOPER, David M.		20c1
COOPER, Herbert F.T. #		19c4
COOPER, William *		18c3, 18c4
COPE, Grace		20c1, 20c2
CORBETT, John		19c4
CORBETT, Joseph *		18c4
CORBETT, William Edward	1824-1904	19c2, 19c3
CORE, Fred C.	c 1882-1908	19c4, 20c1
CORKER, John		19c1
CORKRAN, Timothy *		19c1
CORLETT, Henry Lee	1826-1883	19c2, 19c3, 19c4
CORNEILLE, Daniel (Capt.)		18c4, 19c1
CORR, Frank M.		20c2, 20c3
CORRY, George		18c3
CORRY, James *		19c2, 19c3
CORRY, John		19c3
CORRY, Michael		19c1
CORRY, Robert *		19c4, 20c1
CORRY, Stwphen		18c3
COSGROVE, Thomas Mackney		19c1
COSTELLO, Michael Francis		20c2
COSTELLOE, P.		20c1
COTTINGHAM, Lewis Nockalls #	1787-1847	19c1, 19c2
COTTON & FLEMYNG		19c3
COTTON, Charles Philip	1832-1904	19c3, 19c4
COTTRELL, Charles		19c1, 19c2, 19c3
COTTRELL, Francis	d.1819	18c4, 19c1
COUGHLAN, Patrick W.		20c1, 20c2, 20c3
COULSON, --		19c4
COULSON, Richard		20c1
COULTON, Edward		19c1
COULTON, John		19c2
COULTON, Thomas *		19c1

name	born / died	flourished
COUREMENOS, Basile #		20c1
COURTNEY, F.W.		19c3
COURTNEY, STEPHENS & BAILEY *		19c3, 19c4
COURTNEY, Thaddeus C.	1893-1961	20c1, 20c2
COVEY, Thomas		18c3
COWAN, James		19c1
COWAN, John		19c1
COWAN, Peter Chalmers	c 1859-1930	19c4, 20c1, 20c2
COWELL, G.		19c1
COWLISHAW, Alfred		20c1
COWSER & SMYTH		20c2
COWSER, Benjamin	1897-1981	20c2, 20c3
COX & BUCKLEY *		19c4
COX & SON #*		19c3
COX, John		19c4
COX, Lemuel #	1736-1806	18c3, 18c4, 19c1
COX, William		18c4
COX, William Sidney	d.1892	19c3, 19c4
COYLE, Charles		19c4
COYLE, Harold Edgar		20c1, 20c2
COYLE, James H.		19c4
COYLE, Peter		20c1, 20c2
CRACE, John Dibblee #*	1838-1919	19c3, 19c4, 20c1
CRACE, John Gregory #*	1809-1889	19c2, 19c3, 19c4
CRAIG, Francis Brownrigg	1880-1943	20c1, 20c2
CRAIG, R.		19c3
CRAIG, Vincent	1869-1925	19c4, 20c1
CRAIGIE, George W.		19c4, 20c1
CRAMILLION, Barthelemy #*		18c3
CRAMPTON, William		19c3, 19c4
CRANFIELD, Richard *	1731-1809	18c3, 18c4, 19c1
CRAWFORD, Andrew H.	1891	19c2, 19c3, 19c4
CRAWFORD, Oliver		18c3
CRAWFORD, R.		20c1, 20c2
CRAWFORD, Robert	1831-1914	19c3, 19c4, 20c1
CREASER, Thomas *		19c3
CREGAN, Francis George		19c2

8 – Vincent Craig, Belfast Bank, Rathmines, Dublin (1899-)
Craig, who practised in Belfast, designed what is now a branch of AIB.

9 – Thomas Joseph Cullen, County Hospital, Dundalk, Co Louth (1932)
Cullen's proposed design was not executed.

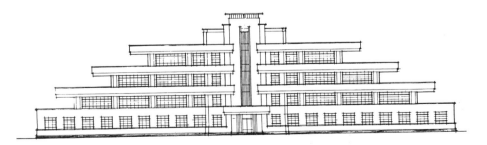

name	born / died	flourished
CREGAN, T.M.		19c4
CREIGHTON, R.W.		20c1
CREWE, Bertie #	d.1937	20c1, 20c2
CRISP, Henry #	1825-1896	19c2, 19c3, 19c4
CROFTS, Freeman Wills	1879-1957	20c1, 20c2, 20c3
CROMIE, John		19c1
CRONIN, William		19c2
CROOM & TOYE		19c4
CROOM, James		19c4
CROSBIE, James *		19c1, 19c2
CROSBY, John		19c2
CROSS, F. #		19c2, 19c3
CROSS, Richard Ernest		20c2, 20c3
CROSSLEY, H.J.		20c1
CROSTHWAIT, P. *		19c1
CROWE BROS.		19c3
CROWE, Daniel *		19c2, 19C3
CROWE, George William		19c4, 20c1, 20c2
CROWE, Michael Frederick		19c3, 19c4, 20c1
CROWLEY, James J.		20c1, 20c2
CROWLEY, John F.	c 1884-1951	20c1, 20c2
CRUISE, BROWNE & FOGERTY		19c4
CRUNDEN, John #	1740-c 1828	18c3, 18c4, 19c1
CUBITT, William (Sir) #	1785-1861	19c1, 19c2, 19c3
CUDMORE, Richard		19c1
CUFFE, Francis		17c4
CUFFE, Luan C.	d.1980	20c2, 20c3, 20C4
CULLEN, Edward		18c1
CULLEN, James		17c4, 18c1
CULLEN, T.J. & CO.		20c2, 20c3, 20c4
CULLEN, Thomas Joseph	1879-1947	19c4, 20c1, 20c2
CULLIMORE, Thomas Lockington	d.1953	19c4, 20c1, 20c2
CULLINAN, John		19c2
CULVERWELL, George P.		19c4, 20c1
CUMING, Richard C.		19c2
CUMMIN, --		19c2
CUMMING, S.		19c4

CUMMINGS, H.		19c4, 20c1
CUNDY, Thomas #	1765-1825	18c4, 19c1
CUNIM, John *		18c1, 18c2
CUNNINGHAM, Robert Alfred	d.c 1936	20c2
CUNNINGHAM, Thomas		18c4
CURLE, John		18c1
CURRAGH, William *		19c4, 20c1
CURRAN, John *		19c1, 19c2
CURRAN, Matthew *		18c4, 19c1, 19c2
CUSACK, James		19c1, 19c2
CUTHBERT, Charles D.	1820?-1892?	19c2, 19c3
CUTLAR, Robert Anthony	d.1964	20c2, 20c3
CUTLER, Henry Albert	1861-1952	19c4, 20c1, 20c2
CUVILLIE, John-Baptist *	d.1788	18c2, 18c3, 18c4

———

All illustrations courtesy of the Irish Architectural Archive, except plates 1 and 5, Gandon Archive, Kinsale; and plate 10, St Andrew's Select Vestry, Dublin.

10 – Thomas Cunningham, St Andrew's Church, Dublin (c 1800)

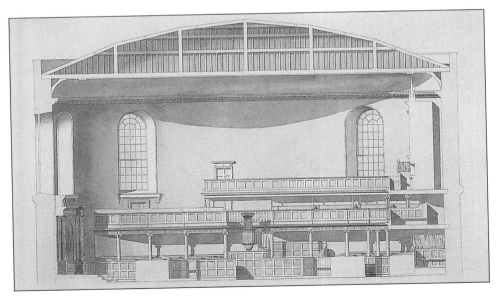

1 – Castletown, Co Kildare – clerestory window in hall
showing the impressionistic effect of crown glass (photo: the author)

Capturing the light: window-glasshouses in Georgian Ireland

NESSA M ROCHE

THE SUBLIME BEAUTY OF GLASS OF ANY SORT ARISES NOT ONLY FROM ITS appearance, but from the extraordinary transformation of sand, kelp and other base ingredients into a transparent liquid, capable of being fashioned into almost any shape and colour, for vessels, optical instruments and, of course, windows. Window-glass, by reason of its shimmering surface, is a marvellous, unintentional art form. Despite the ravages of time, many Georgian houses are still enhanced beyond the ordinary by the character of their windows. Variations in quality and tints of colour personalise old glass panes, imparting a life not found in any other element of a building. The mix of ingredients was guarded by each glassmaker in this fiercely private, closed craft, which resulted in endless variations in the ingredients of sand, soda and lime, ensuring that no two pots of molten glass ever contained the same chemically exact mixture. In window-glass, common 'colours', and sometimes iridescence, result from these variations, denoting surplus amounts of chemicals present. In combination, the look of whole buildings can be enhanced. Castletown, Co Kildare, is a prime example of the individuality given to the building by blown glass (Plate 1). Tints visible in the Castletown windows include green-yellow, caused by excess of iron in the sand, and a purple-blue or a brownish yellow, caused by too much oxide of manganese used in the first instance to counteract protoxide of iron. As well as the ingredients, the methods used and the individual skills give different appearances.

The best recorded eighteenth and early nineteenth-century window-glasshouses are noted here in brief, to illustrate the scope of window-glassmaking in Ireland. The earliest glasshouses in Ireland date back as far as the 1580s, and a number are recorded in the seventeenth century. From 1745, the exemption of Ireland from the glass tax provided a favourable climate for such enterprises. The curb on Irish glass exports was lifted in 1780, and for several decades from this date Irish window-glass competed favourably at home and abroad. However, advances in technology (and a general depression in the late 1830s) overtook this most labour-intensive

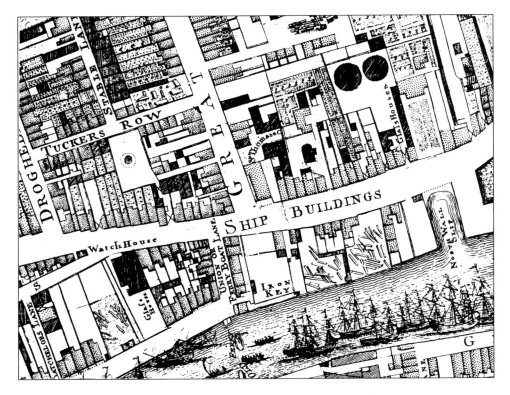

2 – Rocque's map of Dublin, 1756 (detail)
showing the Square Glasshouse, Bachelor's Walk / Abbey Street
and the Williams' Glasshouses, Marlborough Green

3 – Ballycastle, Co Antrim, glasshouse of 1754, pulled down in 1877/1878

industry by the 1850s, in which decade the last mention is found of Irish window-glass.

The earliest crown window-glasshouse known in Dublin was at Bachelor's Quay, set up in 1726. This works, which was sporadically active until the 1740s, also produced bottles. The site of Bachelor's Quay (now Walk) and Abbey Street continued in glassmaking use, with occasional breaks until after 1801 (Plate 2). As part of a larger concern, it produced window-glass from 1760. It is thought that crown glass was made here into the 1790s at least.

Williams and Co, natives of Chester, at Marlborough Green, Dublin, made crown and plate glass from about 1764 until about 1827. While the Williams had been producing flint glass since the 1750s, the earliest mention of window-glass is in two advertisements of 1770 in the *Belfast Newsletter* and *Limerick Chronicle*. In 1777 plate glass for looking glasses, coaches and windows of their own manufacture was advertised; they won premiums from the Dublin Society for both types of glass.

A number of glasshouses were in operation at various dates on North Strand near Ballybough Bridge, Co Dublin, in the 1770s and 1780s, producing plate and flint glass. The information concerning these glasshouses is confusing, and it is not known which one – or perhaps more – produced plate glass. The *Dublin Chronicle*, 18 October 1787, mentioned Chebsey's Venice Glass Works, which produced glass vessels at Ballybough, stating in the same sentence that 'plate glass for coaches etc, is also made and polished near the North Strand. Add to this another glasshouse is erecting on a very extensive scale near the North Wall'. The *Dublin Chronicle* of 10-13 May 1788 included the notice that 'William Williams, proprietor of the new Baths near the point of the North Wall [near the North Strand] first brought to perfection in Dublin the manufacture of flint and plate glass'.

It was proposed to set up a Crown Glass Factory at Ringsend Co Dublin in 1787, especially for export. The *Dublin Journal* noted, in August 1787, that demand from the French market had encouraged an English company to erect a glasshouse at the foot of Ringsend Bridge. The next mention of a Ringsend glasshouse occurs in 1798. The *Dublin Evening Post* of 1 March 1798 stated that 'window glass of a large size and good colour is now ready for sale' from an 'infant manufactory' at this site, the buyers to apply to John Raper's window-glass warehouse in Dublin. No further information is forthcoming.

A barely recorded glasshouse – or series of them, possibly on the same site – was started in Ringsend in the early nineteenth century. This may have been a continuation of that last heard of in 1798. At any rate, in about 1820, a well known flint glassmaker, Charles Mulvany, set up a crown glass factory, which appeared to be short-lived. A whole series of window-glasshouse lease holders follow in unspecified Ringsend locations, the last mentioned being Samuel Davis, window-glass maker, who had a glasshouse for several years until the early 1850s. Davis is listed as a glass manufacturer in the *Irish Industrial Exhibition Catalogue* (1853) selling glass shades, tables of crown glass and bent glass.

At Gurteens, Co Waterford, one glasshouse after another operated from early in the eighteenth century. In 1711 an advertisement was put in the *British Mercury* for jobs in the 'glasswork for making crown glass and plate carrying on in Waterford', which was then producing crown and plate glass. A later work, which more than likely used the same premises – as glasshouse chimneys or 'cones' were notoriously difficult to erect safely and properly – also made crown glass. This is known from a notice of sale in 1740: 'a large parcel of ingredients for crown glass, kelp, etc' was for sale along with the glasshouse itself. These works have no known connection with the later flint glass business of the Penrose's, started in 1783.

At Ballycastle, Co Antrim, Hugh Boyd, the local landlord and industrialist, set up a glasshouse in 1754 (Plate 3). It produced bottle and crown glass, employing six blowers. The *Dublin Journal* of 14 October 1755 noted that bottles were ready for sale, with window and plate glass to follow. The only evidence that crown glass was made here comes from archaeological investigations carried out in the 1970s; it had been thought previously that only bottles were made. The works petered out after the death of Boyd, the last notice being that of a cargo of bottles to Belfast, recorded in 1782.

The glassworks of Smylie and Co, at the Long Bridge, Belfast, which operated from about 1784 until about 1797, produced crown glass of a very good quality. Several advertisements in the *Belfast Newsletter* in 1788 noted that crown was now ready for sale. In March 1789, Smylie advertised his prices as being at least fourteen percent cheaper than Bristol and the quality as superior, going on to note that when cut into squares, it was at least fifty per cent cheaper. Smylie went into this business determined to produce on a grand scale, as he erected the largest glass cone in Ireland, standing 150 feet high and 180 feet in circumference. Again, the death of the proprietor caused the enterprise to wind down. Increased industrialisation and the imposition of the glass tax in 1825 forced small Irish entrepreneurs to look elsewhere. Since the 1850s, while bottles have been produced continuously at Ringsend, no window-glass has been made in Ireland.

———

NESSA ROCHE has recently completed a doctoral thesis on the window in Irish classical architecture. She has worked for the National Inventory, and is currently self-employed in the conservation field. She is writing a book on Irish windows.

4 – A table of crown glass attached to the punty
(*photo from Raymond McGrath*, Glass in Architecture, *London 1937*)

*1 – Cover, George Edmund Street and Edward Seymour,
'The Cathedral of the Holy Trinity...' (London, 1882)*

A philosophy of restoration: George Edmund Street at Dublin's Christ Church

SEÁN O'REILLY

... as long as the restorer is able to confine himself to restoring such work as that which was originally done by numerous obedient workmen from the designs and orders of one man, he is not only doing a pious and laudable act, but one which would be wrong to omit and one as to the practicality of which there is neither doubt nor difficulty. The difference between restoring – i.e. repairing exactly on its old lines – a decayed buttress whose fall threatened to bring something else more precious with it, and restoring all the buttresses and windows, is only one of degree.[1]

WITH THESE WORDS, GEORGE EDMUND STREET SUMMARISED HIS APPROACH to restoration in the lengthy and complete ...*Account of the Restoration of the Fabric of Christ Church Cathedral*, published alongside its history in 1882 (Plate 1). The volume was the last in a series of published notices on Christ Church by Street, the first of which had been appeared in 1868 as his R*eport ... on the Restoration*.[2] This preliminary review, accompanying his designs for the restoration of the nave and west front, was developed in 1871 with the publication of a *Report of the rebuilding of the choir...*, in which he elaborated on his proposed reconstruction of the cathedral's eastern end.[3]

This sequence of publications – extending from 1868 to 1882 – provides a unique insight into the methodology, principles and philosophy on which the Victorian Revival's retrieval of the medieval past is founded. It is especially significant as it shows how the issue of the medieval revival in the High Victorian period revolves around and is encompassed by the question of restoration.

Chris Miele has emphasised the extent of the professional response to the matter of restoration in the mid-Victorian era.[4] The integrity of that response was defended at length by the *bête noir* of the newly founded Society for the Protection of Ancient Buildings (SPAB), George Gilbert Scott. In his *Recollections*, Scott went so far as to quote at length relevant texts, publicly reasserting his confidence in the position taken by himself and his professional fellows.[5] Scott, of course, pleaded guilty to SPAB's accusations of destruction but, steadfastly defending the professional establishment, sought mitigation in blaming the patron. Yet he made this guilty plea without realising the real issues under discussion.

For all the espousal of restoration principles by the architectural profession, and SPAB's corresponding criticisms, it was not recognised that the two actually expounded on quite different concepts. Even a cursory reading of Scott's responses to SPAB's accusations shows that although he and SPAB shared the use of the term restoration, they were too far apart in their understanding of that word even to realise that they did not share its meaning. Simply if summarily put, for SPAB restoration was preservation of that which remained, while for the professional establishment it was, as often as not, the reconstruction of what had existed. This semantic disparity has a history too complex to explore in detail here, but Scott's own paper on restoration in 1850 is a key text in that confusion.[6] That history is aggravated too by Street's own presentation on the topic in 1861, and the confusion reaches its zenith during the early years of SPAB's existence.[7]

Street, distinguishing no more between the different meanings of restoration than Scott or SPAB, could never have accepted the accusations brought by SPAB against the profession. Rather he tried to explain the issue of restoration as it related to his own work, with the restoration of Christ Church as his example. Throughout the almost fifteen years of his reports on the cathedral, we may see a carefully considered philosophy of restoration that, while voicing sympathy with that which Scott would have classed as conservative restoration, remained far from SPAB's principles.

RESTORATION

As the capital's first cathedral, and having survived the ravages of restoration that had recently caused such controversy at St Patrick's cathedral a few streets away, the issue of the restoration of Christ Church was particularly sensitive (Plate 2). Certainly the financier of the restoration, the distiller Henry Roe, proclaimed from the start a restorationist – more specifically a preservationist – approach. In a letter of 31 March 1871 to the Archbishop of Dublin, in which he offered to 'restore the fabric', he pointed out that he was 'desirous that the restoration should be satisfactorily carried out, and the architectural beauties of the Cathedral scrupulously preserved', consequently proposing 'to leave the restoration exclusively under the control of George Edmund Street, Esq., in whom the public will repose the fullest confidence that all justice will be done it'.[8] Yet for all this expression of preservationist ideals by the sponsor, the removal of the choir, intimated by Street as early as 1868,

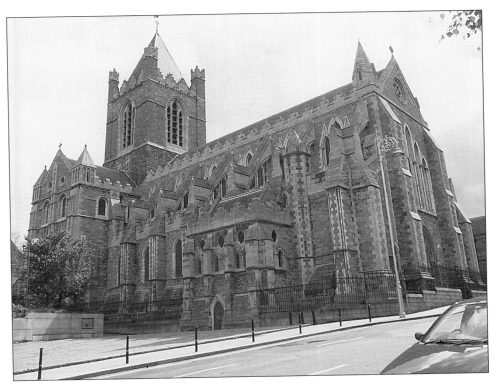

2 – View from the steeply sloping ground to the north-west and showing the exterior of the baptistery (photo: the author)

3 – G.E. Street, survey plan combining ground plan with crypt, 1868
(published in Edward Seymour, Christ Church Cathedral, Dublin *(Dublin 1869))*

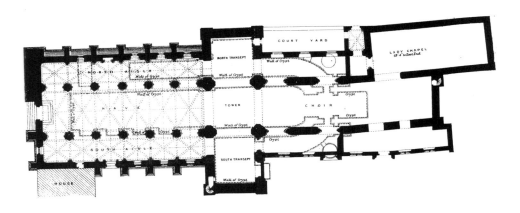

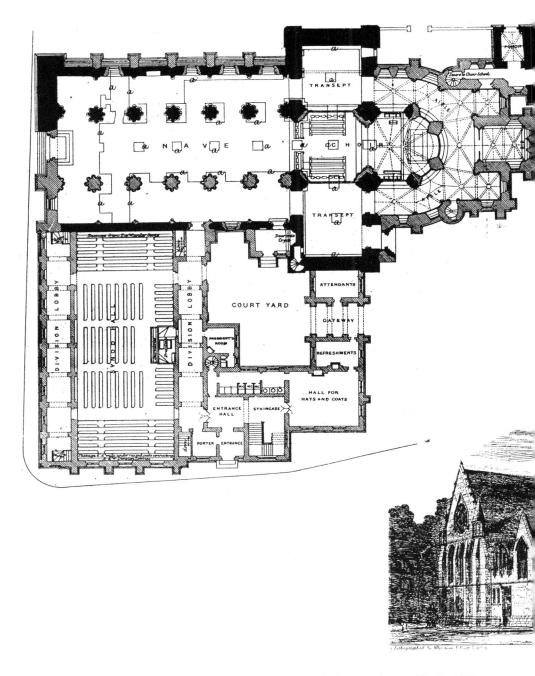

4 – G.E. Street, plan of cathedral showing proposed choir and synod hall, 1871
(published in Street, Report on the rebuilding *, 1871)*

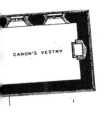

DESIGN FOR RESTORATION OF CATHEDRAL, AND FOR SYNOD HOUSE, CHRIST CHURCH, DUBLIN. *George Edmund Street, ARA Ab*

5 – View of cathedral showing Street's first proposal for an apsidal chevet
(published in Street, Report on the rebuilding *, 1871)*

would have been an obvious consequence of citing him as the architect.

Yet the professionalism of Street's approach was exemplary for its day. The consistency of Street's methodology ensured the coherence of his interpretation, the astuteness of his writings and, ultimately, his own confidence in the restoration. As recorded in his first report of 1868, Street's initial approach combined comparatively scholarly historical research alongside the preliminary study of the building fabric in a procedure inspired by Pugin.[9] Any conclusions might then properly be based on this essential preliminary work. Indeed Street was careful to determine the documentary history – thereby securing the appropriate historical authority – before making any qualitative assessment concerning the cathedral's 'existing remains, so far as they have any historical or architectural value'.[10] This sequence of documentary history, building study and qualitative assessment provides the basis for showing 'the propriety of the work' to be proposed (Plate 3).[11]

In Street's report of 1871, again following what might be considered proper procedure, he registered a further level of response to fabric undergoing restoration. He retained the option to modify proposals based upon evidence that might be uncovered, particularly with regard to determining the arrangement of the original eastern end. At this point, and before the commencement of any significant work, he noted that there were 'many questions of detail in the planning of the apse ... to leave for final decision until I can take up the pavement of the choir ... and trace ... the plan of the choir above the crypt'.[12] He reiterated the need to be able to respond to changing circumstances when he pointed out that there were 'points in the arrangement which [were] hypothetical, and in which some alterations may hereafter be required'. Here at least some of these questions would 'be settled by remains ... pretty sure to be found in the course of the removal of the modern choir'. In addition, he would 'make a point of looking carefully for whatever evidence of this kind ... whenever ... the opportunity' arose.[13] The intention was that restoration might manifest itself in its most appealing form, as a dialectic between design and discovery. The success of this procedure, and the efficiency of its execution, supported the impressive intellectual continuity evident throughout Street's concern for the phenomenon of the structure: historical, liturgical, architectural and aesthetic.

Despite such clearly defined interests, Street's philosophy did not encompass or encourage a blanket respect for old architecture. The restorationist procedure adopted at Christ Church was used to recreate an early history of the cathedral that might be restored in place of a significant part of the surviving fabric. When viewing the crypt, as part of his building study, Street 'discovered ... the whole history of the fabric written in a very clear and un-mistakable way'.[14] With the eastern end of the crypt suggesting in the choir above an arrangement consisting of a chevet terminating in square chapels beyond the ambulatory, he was to promote the reconstruction of what he saw to be the original layout.

Yet in 1868 Street cited no evidence that a choir actually had been built following this outline. All he did say was that he could 'see no reason whatever to doubt it'.[15] Furthermore, he did voice an ominous dissatisfaction with the surviving choir, though at first he dismissed 'consideration altogether, of the possibility of restoring the Choir' because of limited finances and the structural integrity of the fabric.[16] Its 'present state and its present arrangements are most unsatisfactory', he reported, and regretted 'beyond measure that we have not still in existence the short thirteenth century Choir, with its Apse – its Eastern Chapels, and its Turrets'. Already the urge to reconstruct was barely resistible.

Though aware of the need for alterations Street had, relatively early in the process, decided on the designs for the restoration of the original choir. Largely this was based on a preliminary survey and stripping back around the choir, and was worked out in some detail by 1871 (Plate 4). Within the fabric then extant, he identified the first two arches east of the crossing as original, being part of what he described as 'the circular face of the apse wall' of the original chevet.[17] This, 'upon careful examination' he noted somewhat ambitiously, would 'be found to be planned on lines radiating from the centre'. Consequently, he first proposed an apsidal termination to the new chevet, the standard treatment for the day (Plate 5). However, based upon the recovery of further evidence, the scheme was to be revised in execution to form the polygonal termination finally executed.[18]

More imaginative inference was adopted in the layout of the choir east of the two surviving arches adjacent to the crossing. The survival in the long choir of an arch identified by Street as the eastern-most arch of the original chevet – which he interpreted as having been relocated northerly from and perpendicular to its original position, to form the northern arch at the entrance to the later choir – suggested the unique arrangement of alternating large and small arches in the choir as presented in his own reconstruction. Despite its curiosity, this arrangement appealed to Street, and was retained on the grounds of historical authenticity. The subordinate arches in the choir were less fortunate. Found to be semicircular, Street thought these 'a peculiarity ... unwise to follow' as the 'choir will be seen fully from, and in connection with the nave'.[19] In effect, given the pointed character of the nave's restored fabric, for aesthetic reasons these arches acquired from their new architect a pointed profile.

The significant degree of inference represented by this conjectural reconstruction of the choir, and the architect's daring willingness to reinvent as part of his restoration, indicates the remarkable extent of presumption about the past. Such presumption is reflected also in Street's removal of the existing choir, in this case on the basis of its architectural failings. It is epitomised, however, in his confidence in the reconstructed scheme. This exceptional presumption, effected within a methodology comparatively refined within the wider context of restoration in Ireland and England, suggests a different approach to the past than that expressed by preservationists.

Street preferred a rather more radical restoration, in fact a restoration of the past. The principle upon which he worked may be summarised quite easily, with the continuity between the thirteenth and nineteenth centuries – the fact of these two worlds being in effect the same – permitting the true restoration of the original layout, provided it be based on inference from adequate surviving fabric. For Street, rejecting the social imperatives invoked since Pugin, the fundamentals of architecture and building were no different in the thirteenth century than in the nineteenth, or than they had been at any other time. Consequently, responses in the form of architectural design and construction might be exactly similar. Issues such as poor construction, the quality of worker, architectural responsibility, creative design and even church layout – and all the attendant variables – persisted through all ages, linking them together rather than separating them. Naturally specific high points of architecture might be identified, such as the thirteenth century and – implicitly – Street's own, and these achieved especial importance and shared a special sympathy.

For a consummate professional such as Street, the initial proof of continuity between the ages lay in his observation of the persistent failings of the builder or workman:

> The truth is that unwise constructors and dishonest builders have not been confined to any one period. At some times good and honest construction has been very generally the rule; at other times it has been sadly neglected.[20]

For Street,

> the mere workman of the thirteenth century was in no respect whatever superior to the mere workman of the nineteenth century. He confined himself to doing explicitly what he was told, implicitly following the directions of his master.[21]

Certainly, as throughout the history of architecture, given the failure of the master, in Street's eyes the worker would never come to the rescue. He cited the original piers at Christ Church as an example, these being 'all but in the worst possible way'. He then went on to observe that it

> is a fair assumption that some thirty masons at the least were at work on these columns, and can it be supposed that not one of these men was aware that that the work he was doing was bad, and could not be safely done? The supposition would be absurd, and it is clear that what happened was the

workmen absolved themselves of all responsibility, worked the stones they were ordered to work, and ate their meals between times with the same *sang froid* that marks their successors at the present day.[22]

For Street, the principle of the architect as the creative force in building design also persists throughout the ages, including the medieval period. Although a building may be 'the work of a number of men', they 'work from instructions given to them probably by one man', the true artist in the design.[23] Thus, for example, in medieval architecture, 'no feature ... is more important, or more affects the general effect of a building, than the great moulded plinth', and though 'its execution may have occupied a gang of workmen for weeks or months ... this base must have been designed by one man'.[24]

The controlling supervisor – architect or master-mason – in addition held the position of final responsibility in whichever era one considered. In the thirteenth century, for example, the architect 'balanced and counterpoised his walls and thrusts with extraordinary dexterity', and when these failed, as at Beauvais, he took responsibility: 'It was not bad workmanship, but too great daring.'[25] Similarly the designer of the later long choir at Christ Church might be castigated for his failings, notably its misalignment. On this matter, Street observed that, after its demolition, the 'architect who was content to make the bend in the length of the choir in so rude and unsightly a fashion, was not a man of great parts; and it is hardly a subject of regret, therefore, that none of his handiwork remains'.[26]

As the architect accepted responsibility for failure, so too he received credit for triumph. It was always the artistry of the architect that could allow for the quality of the whole. Reluctantly admitting that the 'workman ... impressed himself at most on the carved works of the capitals' ('at Christ Church these have been religiously retained', Street reminds us),

> the rest of the design was the work of an able master-mason or architect who decided all ... One hand is evident ... and the master's ideas have been carried out with exact skill by the multitude of workmen under him.[27]

Within this aesthetic, 'the design ... in a piece of architecture is the really precious thing', not the actual fabric. In restoration, consequently, despite the loss of the original material, given sufficient evidence the building might be returned to 'exactly' the state the original architect had 'left it'.[28] To this Street added one proviso, that proper procedures should be followed.

Street illustrated the possibility of correctly copying original details by following that which he took to be the original practice, where craftsmen worked 'from models made by the architect himself'.[29] The medieval precedent for this method was suggested to Street by 'the regular and repeated foliage of the cornices of the aisles of York Minster', and he boasted also of following it in the Courts of Justice in London, where

> the carving and sculpture has first been sketched, and then modelled, or altered and corrected in the clay, by [the architect's] own hands, and then executed from casts by a number of skilled and excellent carvers.[30]

Consequently by simply repeating the procedures of the past in the present day, secure in the knowledge that for his own workmen 'there was no more to invent than ... [the original architect's] workmen invented', Street could guarantee the essential authenticity of his new work.

Clearly, while continuity was of the essence, certain eras naturally possessed a greater degree of inherent sympathy, and the special links between thirteenth and nineteenth century promoted Street's confidence in the rightness of reconstructing the original choir (Plate 6). Ecclesiologically, the issues raised by the original arrangement were especially appealing to Street for, considering

> our reduced Cathedral establishments, and our desire to see our Cathedral naves made thoroughly useful, it is probable that any architect who had to build a new Cathedral would now revert to some such plan as that which ... was originally seen in the Choir.[31]

Street reasons that

> such a choir would not only be more effective than the present Choir ever can be, but it would at the same time have been admirably adapted for our modern use and for the reduced staff of Clergy and Choir who serve the Cathedral.[32]

He developed this theme more fully in his report on the finished work in 1882, again emphasising the special harmony between the two centuries.

In both thirteenth and nineteenth centuries 'the constructional choir' was 'a very small and very unimportant part of the whole edifice' as the clergy were 'comparatively few in number'.[33] Choirs which had been originally small, after the thirteenth century increased in scale due to the specific needs of monasteries 'which had to provide ... for the large number of regular inmates, all of them bound to be in their places for daily worship', thereby requiring that churches be 'built with longer choirs'.[34] In the nineteenth century, the needs paralleled the earlier rather than the later pattern, and

> Beautiful as are the enlarged choirs of our cathedrals ... the architect who thinks of the services of the Church of the present day ... finds himself most at ease when the choir ... is ... only of moderate size.[35]

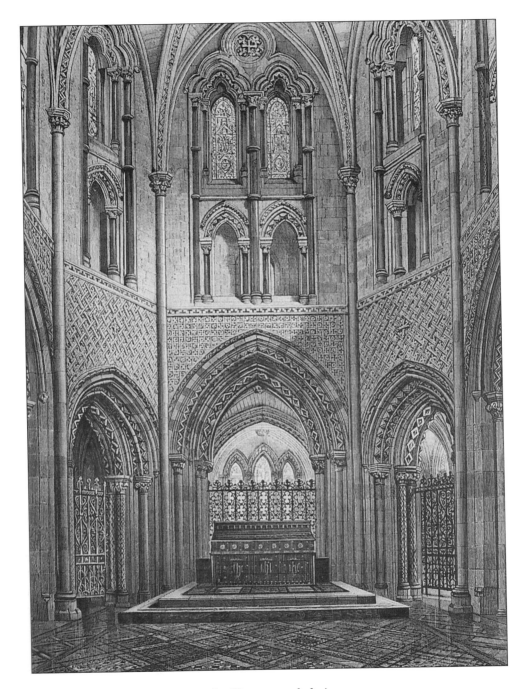

6 – The restored choir
(*published in Street and Seymour,* Christ Church Cathedral, *1882)*

Thereby he provided final confirmation of the reasonableness of restoring the original arrangement. Consequently, even liturgically the thirteenth and nineteenth centuries possessed a special affinity. Furthermore, the ideology of ecclesiology may be seen to be an acceptable consideration within restoration objectives.

Given such a need to reinstate, on those occasions where little or no evidence survived to indicate details or even features, the invention of the good modern architect could be at least as successful as that of the original designer, provided appropriate finance was available. Indeed the new work should be so effective as to allow the original work to be reinvented despite the lack of clear evidence. For Street, proof positive of that sympathetic continuity occurred in his reinstatement of the west front. This had been 'entirely modernised', with 'nothing to respect and nothing that the most zealous stickler for the conservation of old work could have desired to remain unaltered' (Plate 7).[36] Realising that originally a fine front would have existed, he 'designed a large double-doorway'. During its construction 'a large jamb-stone [was] discovered in the wall'. Fortunately this 'exactly agreed with my full-size section'. As the stone was 'discovered in time to be used', it was 'built into the new doorway'(Plate 8).[37] No finer confirmation of the unity and continuity of original and restoration could be desired. Indeed the contrast between these two designs, each in their day presented under the title of 'restoration', emphasises the distances that might be covered under the one term.

It is at this point that we see justification for the architect taking on the role of inventor, ostensibly sympathetic and improving, but requiring no authority from on-site precedent. Street's internal remodelling of the crossing tower could be effected without any immediate historic authority, but simply on the basis of aesthetic judgement and ecclesiological function. Inside the cathedral, the tower's arches remained 'several feet lower than the arches of the vaulting ... and an intolerable obstruction to the whole effect of the internal perspective'.[38] The sound construction of the tower required that Street retain it, despite its detrimental effect on the internal space, and so, with no other justification than aesthetics and liturgical practicality, Street proposed to raise the arches of the tower in line with the vault (Plate 9).

Sensitive to the degree of intervention required of his proposed improvement through modernisation, the tower suffered proportionately greater architectural criticism by Street. It was

> carried on very rude pointed arches ... their piers were rude and unsightly, plain, roughly dressed and, in short, their existence was a complete eye-sore ... they had no kind of merit, artistic, historic or antiquarian. They were hideous in themselves; they were comparatively modern, and no one knew exactly who built them ... also the tower had been altered in so wretched a

7 – G.E. Street,
west elevation, 1868
(published in Street, Report
... on the Restoration*)*

8 – Restored west front
(published in Street and
Seymour, Christ Church
Cathedral, *1882)*

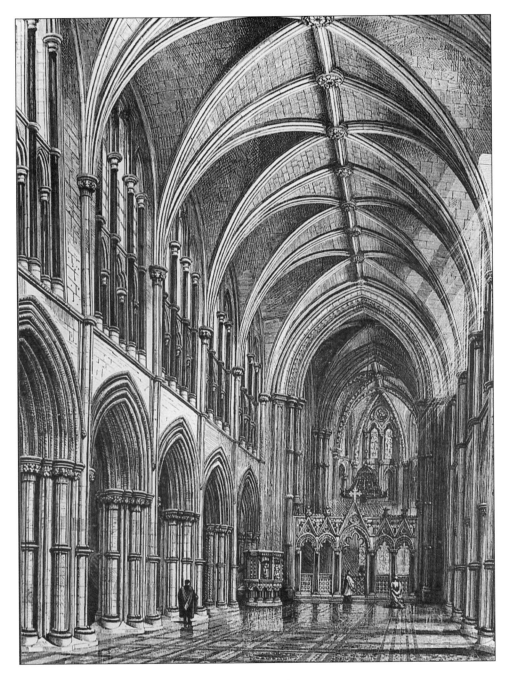

9 – The restored nave
(published in Street and Seymour, Christ Church Cathedral, *1882)*

style that not a vestige remained of any work so good as the rude pointed arches which carried it.[39]

Street found some comfort in his raising of the arches through executing the alteration 'in the old fashion, rather than in the new', that is, 'by leaving the old work, and cutting out by degrees, and inserting bit by bit, and stone by stone, new arches above the old'.[40]

With less historic fabric extant on the exterior, Street could take more license. As early as 1868, when finance was still limited, he decided 'to take the opportunity afforded by these works to make some alterations', among which were to be included 'the characteristic Irish battlements', double-stepped crenellations later much criticised for their incongruity.[41] Similarly, with the foundations of a single circular tower recovered on the south-east of the choir, and thinking 'it very probable' that there had been a respond on the north side, as 'we usually find two such turrets if there is one', Street proposed to 'restore' this northern tower too.[42] The flying buttresses were equally personal innovations. Flying buttresses were first introduced by Street on the cathedral as an expedient when in 1868 they were placed on the north wall to stop it toppling.[43] When, through Roe's generosity, additional funds became available, Street repeated the buttresses throughout. Evidently, pragmatic expediency founded on necessity was developed into more complete expression.

Street's will to invent manifested itself with equal imagination, if more subtlety, in his designs based on existing features. Nowhere were more demands made on his invention than in the development of the choir above the main arches, an area for which no significant evidence survived. Here he 'decided to introduce freely the same kind of enriched mouldings throughout as those of the five arches of the lower stages',[44] admitting to indulging his admiration for the early style,[45] but remaining scrupulous in originating his designs in existing details (Plate 6). Despite such improvisation, Street firmly believed in the historical validity of the choir that he rebuilt, and considered it first as a restoration. Of the design, he wrote: 'I know of few works of restoration which might be undertaken with more certainty that a really ancient feature is being recovered',[46] it being 'recovered, as it were, almost from the grave, before our eyes and under our hands'.[47]

The design of the baptistery has been described as 'the most stupendous example of Street's architectural detailing at Christ Church', with its exterior possessing 'the stunning force of a waterfall' (Plates 10, 11).[48] The scheme was developed after the discovery beside the north-western aisle bay of 'a chamber which had evidently been vaulted in three narrow bays, the spaces under the vaulting being panelled with two pointed arches and a vescia above'.[49] This Street transformed into highly sophisticated architectural creation. However, he could retain no

*10-11 – The exterior
and interior of the
restored baptistery*
(published in Street and
Seymour, Christ Church
Cathedral, *1882).*

original fabric, as 'every portion, not only of this chapel, but also of the aisle wall, had for safety's sake to be re-built'.[50] Furthermore, due to the narrowness of the adjacent lane, he was required to move the site one bay east of its original location. Street, notably and not surprisingly, persists in describing the new baptistery as a restoration.[51] However it is equally evident that, following this procedure, the actual fabric of the 'restored' structure bears no more necessary relation to its antecedent at Christ Church than any design bears to its artistic source. Yet for Street the new design, for all its physical and formal distance from the original, is still a restoration.

This clarifies the central issue concerning the question of reviving the Gothic. One may observe at Christ Church a methodology based on the overlapping procedures of reinstatement, using inference from surviving medieval work; of re-creation, presuming continuity between medieval and modern to justify extrapolation; and pure artistic invention, based on the privilege of the creative artist to design in sympathy with historic precedent, as required – indeed as demanded – of any revivalist.

Throughout this work in Dublin, no less in the revival's last flowering in 1868 than in 1882, after the arrival of SPAB, we find these distinct approaches encompassed under the single heading of restoration. Yet here restoration is conservative in intention, eclectic in inspiration and destructive on occasion, even if always ostensibly justified by a confident sense of continuity between past and present. However, despite the vociferous aspiration to restoration, there in no more demand for a specific precedent than there is in any other works in the style of the medieval revival, or indeed of any other revived style of architecture.

Ecclesiastical architecture, as a type, possessed further justification for more radical intervention. Street's restoration of Christ Church to the original state intended by its first designer, was allied with the reinstatement of an arrangement presented as liturgically appropriate to modern requirements as it had been to such needs originally, and could easily justify the sacrifice of a poorly built choir. Street's sympathy with Scott's perception of the peculiar needs of ecclesiastical architecture is clear. Street asserted, as did Scott, the need for considering ecclesiastical function within the concept of restoration, and both Street and his patron might be included among those 'seriously thinking people' described by Scott who could never be convinced that 'it is wrong "to restore churches from motives of religion"', all agreeing that the churches 'were built from such motives, and must ever be treated with like aim'.[52]

Street differed from Scott in seeing practical demands as being encompassed within the philosophy of restoration, not as justifying exceptions to its procedures. While Street agreed at the most fundamental level with Scott's demand to recognise that 'any attempt to banish religious motives from the treatment of churches is suicidal',[53] he saw the need for intervention as a wider issue both within restoration and revival. As Scott enthusiastically demanded, so too Street reasoned, and founded on his own assertion of continuity between past and present a philosophy restoration that was equally one of revival.

Following Pugin, for Street, alongside the establishment Goths of his generation, the revival of the Gothic was a real possibility, and restoration simultaneously proof of and a synonym for that revival. For members of SPAB, the possibilities of the medieval revival were more problematic, but the texture wrought by time certainly unique. Their restoration, a synonym for preservation, was defined by its antithesis, destruction. It remains a long way from Street's understanding, represented by the quotation presented at the start of this paper. For George Edmund Street, the Gothic revival and the Gothic were one.

————

Dr Seán O'Reilly is Director of the Architectural Heritage Society of Scotland; editor of *Irish Architectural and Decorative Studies*, the journal of The Irish Georgian Society; and author of *Irish Country Houses and Gardens – From the archives of 'Country Life'* (1988).

ENDNOTES

This essay is developed from a paper presented at the annual symposium of the Society of Architectural Historians of Great Britain held in February 1997 and entitled 'Gothic and the Gothic Revival'. The author is grateful to the organisers of the symposium for permission to advance here the arguments discussed there; to Professor Roger Stalley, who in the preparation of his complementary paper on the history of the medieval Christ Church, provided this author with essential background; to Professor Alistair Rowan for his suggestions, and to Dr Deborah Mays for her refinement of both text and structure.

[1]   George Edmund Street and Edward Seymour, *The Cathedral of the Holy Trinity commonly called Christ Church Cathedral, Dublin...* (London 1882) 78.

[2]   George Edmund Street, *Report to the Dean and Chapter of Christ Church Cathedral, Dublin, on the Restoration of the Cathedral* (Dublin 1868).

[3]   George Edmund Street, *Report on the rebuilding of the choir of Christ Church Cathedral Dublin, and on the erection of a Synod Hall for the Church of Ireland* (Dublin 1871).

[4]   Chris Miele, 'Their interest and habit': professionalism and the restoration of medieval

churches, 1837-77', in Chris Brooks and Andrew Saint, eds, *The Victorian Church, Architecture and Society* (Manchester and New York 1995) 151-72.

5   George Gilbert Scott, *Personal and Professional Recollections* (Stamford, 1995 (1879)).

6   George Gilbert Scott, *A plea for the faithful restoration of our ancient churches* (1850).

7   (George Street), 'On the restoration of Ancient Buildings – Architectural Exhibition', *Builder*, 8 June 1861, 388-90; and Miele, loc. cit.

8   Street and Seymour, *Christ Church Cathedral*, 54.

9   Street, *Report ... on the Restoration*, 3-8. Among numerous sources relating to the background to Street's procedure of restoration at Christ Church, the reader is directed to the following, in addition to those listed separately in the notes: 'Observations on the proposed restoration of the cathedral and suggestions as to new site for new Synod hall...', *Irish Builder*, 1 June 1871, 137-39; William Butler, 'Christ Church Cathedral...', *Irish Builder*, 1 March 1871, 60-63; 15 March 1871, 70-71; William Butler, *The Cathedral Church of the Holy Trinity Dublin (Christ Church)...* (London 1901); Thomas Drew, 'Christchurch or the Cathedral of the Holy Trinity, Dublin', *Builder*, 5 May 1894, 349-52; Robert B. M'Vittie, *Details of the restoration of Christ Church Cathedral, Dublin....* (Dublin 1878); Edward Seymour, *Christ Church Cathedral, Dublin* (Dublin 1869).

10   *ibid.*, 3.

11   *ibid.*

12   Street, *Report on the rebuilding*, 8-9.

13   *ibid.*, 12.

14   Street, *Report ... on the Restoration*, 9.

15   *ibid.*, 11.

16   *ibid.*, 15. The recent re-evaluation of this part of the building by Prof Roger Stalley, presented as part of the conference for which this paper was prepared and is in press, considers in detail what was actually sacrificed by Street here in more detail. As may be observed in the discussion below, with regard to any reinstatement Street makes only limited distinction between the sacrifice of medieval and of Georgian Gothic.

17   Street, *Report on the rebuilding*, 6.

18   For which see the scheme illustrated in 'Christ Church Cathedral, Dublin', *The Architect*, 3 October 1874.

19   Street, *Report on the rebuilding*, 7.

20   Street and Seymour, *Christ Church Cathedral*, 111.

21   *ibid.*, 74.

22   *ibid.*, 75.

23   *ibid.*, 74.

24   *ibid.*

25   *ibid.*, 111.

26   *ibid.*, 92.

27   *ibid.*, 118.

28   *ibid.*, 117.

29   *ibid.*, 76.

30   *ibid.*

31   Street, *Report ... on the Restoration*, 12.

32   *ibid.*, 15.

33 Street and Seymour, *Christ Church Cathedral*, 81.
34 *ibid.*
35 *ibid.*, 85.
36 *ibid.*, 117.
37 *ibid.*
38 *ibid.*, 128.
39 *ibid.*
40 *ibid.*
41 Street, *Report ... on the Restoration*, 18. It is interesting to note that he had this in mind as early as 1868.
42 Street, *Report on the rebuilding*, 7.
43 Street, *Report ... on the Restoration*, 17.
44 Street and Seymour, *Christ Church Cathedral*, 94.
45 *ibid.*, 95.
46 Street, *Report on the rebuilding*, 8.
47 Street and Seymour, *Christ Church Cathedral*, 150.
48 Douglas Scott Richardson, *Gothic Revival Architecture in Ireland*, 2 vols (Yale PhD, 1970 (annotated hard copy in the collection of the Irish Architectural Archive, Dublin)) ii, 620.
49 Street and Seymour, *Christ Church Cathedral*, 122. The feature is discussed in further detail by Prof Stalley in the paper cited in note 16 above.
50 *ibid.*, 123
51 *ibid.*
52 Scott, *Recollections*, 420.
53 Street and Seymour, *Christ Church Cathedral*, 421.

Shorter Notices

Desmond Guinness Scholarship

The Desmond Guinness Scholarship will be awarded annually by the Irish Georgian Foundation to an applicant or applicants resident in Ireland engaged in research on the visual arts in Ireland, or on the work of Irish architects, artists and craftsmen at home and abroad from 1600 to 1900. Special emphasis will be placed on work based on original documentary research. The total value of the scholarship fund available for distribution in any year is in the region of one thousand pounds.

Forms are available from:

Irish Georgian Society
74 Merrion Square
Dublin 2

tel: 01-6767073
fax: 01-6620290
e-mail: igs@iol.ie

Irish Georgian Society

CONSERVING IRELAND'S ARCHITECTURAL HERITAGE

The Society aims to encourage an interest in and to promote the preservation of distinguished examples of architecture and the allied arts in Ireland. These aims are achieved by:

- MEMBERSHIP – The Society has 3,000 members worldwide. Its headquarters are in Dublin, and there is a thriving and long-established London Chapter and two local Irish chapters in Birr and Limerick. The headquarters of the US membership, IGS Inc., is in New York, and there are local chapters in Boston, Chicago, Cleveland, Columbus, Washington, Minneapolis and Atlanta. The benefits of membership include: (i) a twice-yearly newsletter which includes the events programme; (ii) the annual journal; (iii) free entry to selected historic houses in Ireland.
- FUNDRAISING – The Society runs an events programme which includes: (i) lectures, (ii) private theatre evenings, (iii) architectural walking tours, (iv) conferences and seminars, (v) day tours, including visits to houses not normally open to the public, and (vi) tours abroad.
- EDUCATION – The Society's annual journal, which has been published regularly since 1958, contains articles of original research, and is the only Irish periodical devoted entirely to the architectural history of Ireland. In addition, valuable research in the field of conservation is funded by the Desmond Guinness Scholarship.
- GRANTS – Donations to the Society and funds raised through the events programme enable the Society to make grants towards the restoration of historic properties.
- PLANNING PARTICIPATION – The Society takes an active part in the planning process on a country-wide basis, and opposes planning applications which are not compatible with the principles of good conservation. It also provides general advice on other aspects of conservation.

The Society liaises with government departments in the area of conservation. The Government has accepted that the preservation and conservation of Ireland's historic buildings, precincts, properties and collections should be given high priority.

HISTORY

The Irish Georgian Society was founded in 1958 by the Hon Desmond Guinness and his late wife, Mariga, for the protection of buildings of architectural merit in Ireland. Many fine houses have been saved through their enthusiasm and commitment, and the dedication of members and supporters. The current President is Desmond FitzGerald, Knight of Glin.

The Society's main achievements include, among others, the saving of threatened great buildings such as: Castletown, Co Kildare; Damer House, Co Tipperary; Doneraile Court, Co Cork; Roundwood, Co Laois; Tailors Hall, Dublin, and 13 Henrietta Street, Dublin. Restoration work is being carried out at Ledwithstown, Co Longford, and Mount Ievers Court, Co Clare, and the Society is assisting with the urban restoration at 2 Pery Square, Limerick. The Society has provided grants for many other projects, including the restoration of correct windows in historic urban houses, such as 20 Lr Dominick Street, George Bernard Shaw's house in Synge Street, and 3-4 Fownes Street, Dublin.

These efforts are funded by our members' participation in the events programme, by the fundraising activities of our chapters, by donations, by sales from the Society's book and gift shop, and by generous royalties from Kindel & Co Inc., Scalamandre Inc., Chelsea House, and the Obelisk Collection.

MEMBERSHIP APPLICATION

Membership application forms are available from:

> Irish Georgian Society, 74 Merrion Square, Dublin 2
> tel: +353 (0)1-676 7053 / fax: +353 (0)1-662 0290 / e-mail: igs@iol.ie

> Arthur Prager, Executive Director, Irish Georgian Society Inc.
> 7 Washington Square North (21A), New York, NY 10003 6647
> tel: (212) 254 4862 / fax: (212) 777 6754

If you are an Irish taxpayer, why not become a Contributing (£101) or Life Member (£1,000) of the Irish Georgian Society. You may be eligible for up to 48% tax refund on your contribution. The Irish Georgian Foundation is an approved Artistic Body under Section 32, Finance Act, 1984.

Donations to the Irish Georgian Society Inc., including membership fees, are tax deductible in the US, subject to the tenets of US tax code 1986.

———